BECOMING A RESPONSIVE SCIENCE TEACHER

Focusing on Student Thinking in Secondary Science

BECOMING A ®ESPONSIVE SCIENCE TEACHER

Focusing on Student Thinking in Secondary Science

Daniel Levin, David Hammer,
Andrew Elby, and Janet Coffey

National Science Teachers Association

Arlington, Virginia

National Science Teachers Association

Claire Reinburg, Director
Jennifer Horak, Managing Editor
Andrew Cooke, Senior Editor
Wendy Rubin, Associate Editor
Agnes Bannigan, Associate Editor
Amy America, Book Acquisitions Coordinator

ART AND DESIGN
Will Thomas Jr., Director
Lucio Bracamontes, cover and interior design

PRINTING AND PRODUCTION
Catherine Lorrain, Director

NATIONAL SCIENCE TEACHERS ASSOCIATION
Gerald F. Wheeler, Interim Executive Director
David Beacom, Publisher
1840 Wilson Blvd., Arlington, VA 22201
www.nsta.org/store
For customer service inquiries, please call 800-277-5300.

Library of Congress Cataloging-in-Publication Data

Becoming a responsive science teacher: focusing on student thinking in secondary science/by Daniel Levin ... [et al.].
      p. cm.
   Includes bibliographical references.
   ISBN 978-1-936959-05-1
   1. Biology—Vocational guidance—United States—Juvenile literature. 2. Science teachers—United States—Juvenile literature. 3. Thought and thinking—Study and teaching—United States—Juvenile literature. I. Levin, Daniel T.
   QH314.B43 2013
   570.23—dc23
                              2012028094
eISBN 978-1-936959-55-6

Contents

Contents

Online Materials: *www.nsta.org/publications/press/extras/responsive.aspx*

Figures
> Chapter 4: Figure 1: Handout on the Owls and Snakes
> Chapter 7: Figure 1: The Free-Falling Bodies Question Set

Transcripts
> Chapter 4: The Owls and the Snakes (1)
> Chapter 5: The Owls and the Snakes (2)
> Chapter 6: The Rime of the Ancient Mariner
> Chapter 8: Free-Falling Bodies (2)

Student Work
> Chapter 7: Free-Falling Bodies (1)

Class Discussion Videos
> Chapter 4: The Owls and the Snakes (1)
> Chapter 5: The Owls and the Snakes (2)
> Chapter 6: The Rime of the Ancient Mariner
> Chapter 8: Free-Falling Bodies (2)

Acknowledgments

This book of case studies came from the final year of a three-year research collaboration among a team of teachers and project staff entitled *What Influences Teachers' Modifications of Curriculum*? (National Science Foundation ESI 0455711). As a regular part of the project, research team members visited teachers' classes to video record, observe, and talk. In the third year of the project, the teachers recorded classes themselves (or had an assistant or student do the recording) and wrote case studies. It wasn't our original plan to develop these materials; that idea came from a conversation with David Campbell, our wonderful program officer at NSF, and Miriam Sherin, a member of our advisory board. They helped us see an opportunity in these cases for professional development materials.

We selected from those case studies to present a broad spectrum of topics and to highlight opportunities for attending to students' thinking. We're very grateful to the project teachers who contributed the case studies included in this book: Sarah Henson, Janet "Izzy" Kovach, Jenny Tanner, Matt Reese and David Hovan, as well as to Terry Grant, whose class we describe in Chapter 1.

The comments presented in the facilitators' notes come from preservice teachers in the Masters' Certification (MCERT) program at the University of Maryland, College Park, Maryland, and from inservice teachers participating in seminars. There are too many of these people to name. Jennifer Richards helped with recording and transcribing the discussions in the MCERT classes.

We'd also like to thank all the teachers who allowed us into their classrooms over the three years of the project. The teachers participated in three different cohorts: a biology cohort and a physics cohort from Montgomery County Public Schools (MCPS), and an environmental science cohort from Baltimore County and Baltimore City. The following teachers were part of the physics cohort for at least one year, and some were in it for three years: Joseph Boettcher, John Haigh, Ken Halperin, Raymond Hodges, Joanna Mysen Cunningham, Cyril Prusko, James Schafer, Caitlin Sullivan, and Lissa Vincent. Natasha Ezerski and Leslie Van started out in the MCPS biology cohort and then switched to the physics cohort as their class schedules changed. The following teachers were in the MCPS biology cohort for at least one year: Shayda Eskandary, Nicole Hopkins, Steven Karig, Jennifer Kempf, Jennifer Kerns, Anne Merrell, Laura Pomerance, Stephen Shifflett. The following teachers were part of the Baltimore environmental science cohort: Kim Bickerstaff, Jacqueline Bilberry, Bradley Harrison, Sharon McClain, and Renee Watson. Alan Berkowitz, Director of Education at the Carey Institute of Ecosystem Studies, served

Acknowledgments

as co-PI on the project, and along with his assistant, Janie Gordon, helped to lead the Baltimore cohort.

Anita Sanyal, Paul Hutchison, Matty Lau, and Xiaowei "Kitty" Tang worked on the project as graduate student research assistants, often taking the lead with video-recording classes and coordinating and talking with teachers. Sandy Honda, a research associate, helped out as well. Luke Conlin and Kitty Tang did most of the processing of the video that appears in this collection, adding captions and blurring or blocking out segments that include students from whom we didn't have consent.

We thank Elaine Henry for her help throughout the project, making sure staff and teachers were paid, rooms were scheduled, and parking and travel were arranged. We'd also like to thank the people at NSTA Press who helped to guide us through the publication process: Andrew Cooke, Jennifer Horak, Claire Reinburg, and Amy America, and three anonymous reviewers, who provided useful feedback on a draft of the manuscript.

Last but not least, we thank the students (and their parents) who gave us permission to include them in these materials.

CHAPTER 1
The Need for Responsive Teaching

Terry's ninth grade high school biology class is about to begin a unit on the chemistry of life. Terry thought it would be a good idea to review concepts of matter and atomic structure before starting on new material, a review he expected to take about 15 minutes. First, they discuss "What is matter?" and the students say matter "takes up space" and "has mass." Terry asks them to say a little more about what that means and students explain: Having mass means "something could be weighed" and occupying space means "something could be seen and touched."

"Seen and touched"? Terry wonders about that and probes a little further. He asks, "Is air matter?" and the class is split on the answer. One student, Barb, argues that air is matter, and she suggests putting air into a balloon and weighing it, predicting that would show air has mass. Terry doesn't have a scale, but he does have balloons, and they blow one up. Terry asks if there's a difference in the amount of matter or "stuff" in the two balloons, and the students aren't sure. Barb jumps in to claim, "You can't put something inside that balloon with air in it—like water." Again, Terry follows up on the reasoning, and here is a snippet of the conversation that follows.

1. Terry: OK. What would happen to the air in the balloon, if I put water in it too?

2. Barb: There wouldn't be as MUCH air.

3. Terry: Because?

4. India: The water's taking up space.

5. Terry: OK, so ...

6. Laura: The air is the space.

7. Terry: Say it again.

8. Laura: The air IS the space.

9. Terry: So air IS the space. Are you saying it takes up space? Is that the idea?

10. Ari: The air is the space that gets taken up.

For science teachers, this is an all-too-familiar situation. Terry expected a quick review of ideas the students understood, but instead he finds out that half the students do not understand that air is matter, a prerequisite idea for the new unit. Laura and Ari have just said it plainly: Air is not matter; it is *space*.

So what should Terry do? Should he affirm Barb's and India's claim that air is matter, and correct Laura and Ari? It isn't in his lesson plan to spend time debating whether air is matter. This, after all, is a biology class, and there is a great deal of material in the new unit. His plan had been to start in on the chemistry of living things (properties of water, structure and function of macro-molecules, and so on). Maybe it was a mistake to bring up the topic, when there is so much else to do.

That's where discussions about teaching tend to begin: What should the teacher do? Of course it's an important question, but it is not the first question to ask.

Any ideas we have about what the teacher should or shouldn't do (or have done) depend on how we think about students and learning in general and, more importantly, about the particular students in the particular moment. We form opinions about what the students are thinking; we have or form objectives for them and for how we want them to be thinking. And they need discussion, those opinions and objectives, first. Before we talk about what the teacher should do, we need to talk about the students and where they are with respect to the content of the course.

Would it serve the students, in this moment, for Terry to provide the correct information that air is matter? Maybe. A lesson on photosynthesis is of no value to students who do not understand that air is matter. But are they ready to believe and understand that information? They seem to have reasons for believing that air is "the space that gets taken up," and they may need to talk about those reasons before they are willing to accept an alternative.

What do the students need, in this moment? That question comes before "What should the teacher do?" But to understand what the students need in this moment, we have to assess what's happening, and that requires careful, close attention to how they are reasoning now.

In other words, before we think about what the teacher should or could do, we need to think about the students. We need to assess where they are, what they believe, what they understand, how they are reasoning. More to the point, the teacher needs to be making those assessments: What Terry does in this moment should depend on his sense of the students' thinking, of *these* students' thinking in this moment.

What are the students thinking? That is the first question to ask, and the primary question we pose in this book, in case studies of moments like this.

It's often a difficult question to answer, even when students seem to speak clearly. Terry wasn't sure what the students meant when they said that matter "has mass" and "takes up space"—that's how this conversation got started, and once it did he learned more about what they were thinking that he wouldn't have guessed. In other moments, as we'll see, students have trouble articulating what they mean. Consider, Brian, in the discussion described in Chapter 6, trying to explain why wood boards on a boat in the ocean would shrink, as described in the poem, "The Rime of the Ancient Mariner."

> Brian: Okay, so if the water is the universal solvent and, like, there's always so like so much, like, water inside the boards then, like, salt water goes into the boards as well the water is dissolving—is dissolving the salt—and as it does that then there's no more water—let, just let somebody else go!

It's hard to tell what he's thinking! Brian's exclamation, "Just let somebody else go!"—asking the teacher to call on another student—signals his difficulty in expressing what he had been thinking. Part of what we'd hope for Brian, and for all our students, is that they become able to communicate ideas with clarity. Of course, there is little chance they will learn to do that if they don't get practice at it, but it places the challenge on the teacher to interpret what they are saying.

Why might they be thinking that? In the "Is air matter?" discussion, Laura and Ari say quite clearly that air is space. Why would they think that? Do they not know that scuba divers carry air (lots of air!) in tanks they carry on their backs? Do they not know what suffocation is, or do they somehow think it is a matter of running out of *space*? Or do they know those things but aren't thinking of them in this moment?

And there's much more to wonder about what and how the students are reasoning. What do they think could settle this question of whether air is matter? Do they expect it is a matter of personal opinion? A matter of the teacher's or scientists' authority? Do they expect it is something they can reason about based on what they know, or that it is something they could investigate? Do they expect that science should fit with what they experience, or do they expect it is information to memorize?

How we answer these questions about what, how, and why the students are thinking will help us form a sense of what they need, to the end of making progress as scientists, and that will help us think about the possibly productive ways the teacher might respond. These are difficult questions that teachers face everyday, but that get little explicit attention in teacher preparation and professional development, which almost always focus on methods and curriculum, rather than on the challenges of hearing and interpreting student reasoning.

Our purpose with this book is to address that lack, paying explicit attention to student thinking, interpreting it, assessing it, and making judgments about how possibly to respond. The case studies presented here provide richly documented examples, with transcripts and the video on the NSTA website. As you read and watch them, we hope you begin with a focus on the substance of the students' reasoning: What are they doing? What are they thinking? Why might they be doing and thinking those things? And then, having discussed those questions for a while, move on to consider what might help the students' progress toward the knowledge and practices of science: What might the teacher do in this moment to help?

The Need for Responsive Teaching, Part 1

"Responsive" teaching genuinely attends and responds to the substance of student thinking. It's different from what most people expect should happen in a science class, which is usually the teacher presenting information, hopefully clearly, for students to hear and, hopefully, understand and retain. In reformed science classes, there's a similar objective, but the methods shift from teacher presentation to students learning the concepts "by inquiry." So, rather than presenting information, the teacher arranges some situation that will guide students to construct the concept for themselves.

By "responsive teaching" we mean something that goes beyond these images of teachers presenting information or crafting experiences, to teachers really focusing attention on student thinking. We mean something closely connected to *assessment*, not just in the sense of exams and scores but in the sense of teachers' ongoing awareness of what and how the students are doing. Research on "everyday assessment" highlights this: teachers' awareness of student thinking leads to better student learning.

Responsive teaching is part of what expert teachers do *regardless of the curriculum*. Teachers pay attention to what students say, catching fleeting clues of their reasoning (like "something that could be seen and touched") and take the opportunities to hear more. If the lesson is about presenting information, they pause in the presentation in various ways to hear from students what sense they are making of that information; if the lesson is a guided inquiry, they monitor students' reasoning along the way. What they find out, hearing and watching in these ways, informs how they proceed, and it's the nature of the profession that they often discover student ideas they hadn't expected (like "air is the space that gets taken up.")

Terry's plan for the day called for a quick review and then starting the new unit, but what he noticed suggested that the students didn't really understand that air is matter. Here is an example of why we need responsive teaching: If the goal is for students really to understand the concepts in science—and it turns out they haven't yet for a prerequisite idea—we need teachers to notice and address the need. When he discovered that half the class did not think air is matter, Terry shifted his agenda in response.

To be clear, we aren't holding up Terry as an expert responsive practitioner. In fact, he's an experienced teacher who, at the time of this snippet, is working on becoming more responsive in his instruction. As he told us, ordinarily he would not even have noticed the clues about student understanding—matter is "something that could be seen and touched"—or thought to follow up with his question about air. And if he did notice, he'd have given a quick explanation that air is matter and moved on to the new material. This year, he is trying to reinvent himself as a teacher, and this lesson, he tells us, reflects some of that reinvention. He's paying attention to his student thinking and responding to it in real time.

"There's Something in There"

Let's get back to the class. We pick up the conversation where we left off.

10. Ari: The air is the space that gets taken up.

11. Terry: So it's an empty space until I put water in it? I'm trying, I'm trying to work your way…I'm not trying to say you're right or wrong, I'm asking. This is not a graded assignment or anything.

12. Ari: Yes.

13. Terry: Yes? How many people agree with that? Air is empty space that the water is taking up.

14. Brianna and Laura (simultaneously): There's something in there.

15. Terry: Okay, what's the something?

16. Students: Air! Air!

17. Terry: So, does it take up space?

18. Students: Yes!

Now it looks as though the students agree air takes up space, including Laura, who says with Brianna, that "there's something in there," in the empty space before you put water in, and that something is air. We don't know what Ari is thinking, but Laura seems to have changed her mind. India captures the gist of the conversation at this point.

24. India: Or like it IS matter I guess, but...'cause if you were to put something in there, the same amount of air wouldn't still be in there because something else would have taken up the space.

With apparent consensus on the question of whether air takes up space, Terry brings the students back to the question of weight: Can you weigh air?

30. Brianna: I don't know ... um ... you can't weigh it ... you can weigh the balloon with the air in it.

31. Terry: Ok, weigh the balloon ... Ok go ahead Ashley.

32. Ashley: Air is not meant to be weighed.

33. Terry: Not meant to be weighed? Tell me what you're thinking.

34 Ashley: Like you can weigh the balloon with the air IN there.

35. Terry: I can weigh this? (holds up the blown-up balloon)

36. Brianna: Yeah.

37. India: But first you would have to weigh the balloon without the air, and then subtract it.

38. Terry: If I subtracted it?

39. India: It would be the same. Because it doesn't have a ...

40. Laura: Confused!

When we show snippets of student inquiry like this for prospective teachers in our credential courses, or for inservice teachers in professional development seminars, we stop at a moment like this to ask what there is to see: *What are the students doing? What are they thinking?*

While the students have agreed, at least for the moment, that air takes up space, they seem torn over whether it will weigh anything. Brianna suggests that air can't be weighed by itself, but it could be weighed inside the balloon. Ashley's statement is odd. What does she mean by, "Air is not meant to be weighed" in line 32? Apparently, Terry isn't sure what she means either, because he repeats what she says and asks her to "Tell me what you're thinking." When she clarifies, it sounds as though she is thinking something like Brianna, that they can't weigh air by itself.

India fills out the idea a little further, explaining that they would have to "weigh the balloon without the air, and then subtract it." Her response to Terry's question "If I subtracted it?" is ambiguous. Is she saying, "It would be the same," meaning that the blown-up balloon and the empty balloon would be the same, so she doesn't think air weighs anything? Or is she saying that the balloon's weight would be the same, so you could measure the air's weight? Either way, she seems uncertain what she means, leaving her last sentence unfinished. Laura says the word that it seems others in the class are feeling: "Confused!"

Why might they be confused? Maybe it's that on the one hand they believe—they can *see*—that air takes up space. After all, if you blow up a balloon, the balloon inflates. But on the other hand, air doesn't *feel* like it weighs anything. A blown-up balloon doesn't feel heavier than an empty one, does it? It might even seem lighter: drop an empty balloon and it just falls; drop an inflated balloon and it sort of floats down. They haven't said any of this, of course, but we can imagine why they might feel torn over whether air really is *matter* that takes up space and has mass.

They might also feel confused because they're not quite sure what they're supposed to be doing. Most of their experience in science class has had the teacher giving them information. Terry isn't doing that; he's throwing the questions back at them. At one point (line 11) he seems to think that might be happening, that the students are getting confused over what is going on, so he says something to try to put the students at ease: "This is not a graded assignment or anything."

The Need for Responsive Teaching, Part 2

Everyone in science education cares about the goal that students genuinely understand the concepts scientists have formed—what we sometimes call the "canon" of current scientific understanding. Sometimes educators lose sight of that goal. It can get displaced by goals of curricular coverage and test scores. Getting through the curriculum on schedule, which for Terry in this moment would mean starting the new unit, can be at odds with students really learning the ideas. Maybe worse, high test scores do not necessarily mean good understanding. It is clear and often discussed how strategies for learning to get high scores are not necessarily the same strategies for learning to have a deep understanding.

That's all part of our first reason for responsive practice, that it serves the objective of students coming to genuine understanding of the concepts in the canon. We don't want students simply having memorized the idea that air is matter, when they secretly don't understand or believe it, even if they get that multiple choice question right. We want them to be able to explain *why* air is matter; we want them to be able to answer the questions someone who doesn't believe air takes up space or has mass might have.

But there's another reason we argue for responsive practice, another goal for science education that should have priority, especially in early science education: Students should *learn how to learn science*. Today, many if not most high school and college students come to their science classes expecting to memorize information they secretly (or not so secretly) don't really understand or believe. They learn to plug into formulas or repeat key phrases or follow protocols they have rehearsed and *retained* without making sense of it all, without connecting and reconciling it with their intuitions and experience. That, of course, affects the quality of their understanding. They learn science as disconnected from their genuine sense of how the world works, which often has them giving silly, nonsensical answers, not because they believe them but because they're trying to use an idea they memorized.

It's important to acknowledge that this goal is not the same as the first. Consider what India has to say in this last segment. Assessing her thinking with respect to the goal of correct understanding, the teacher should notice and respond to the possibility that she has a wrong idea—a misconception, perhaps—that air doesn't have mass. But in several important ways she's behaving like a novice scientist. She's being open and honest about what she thinks, and she's considering ideas other than her own. She's also trying to figure out how to get experimental evidence, helping to design a controlled experiment to find out if air weighs anything. With respect to this second goal of her learning how to learn, the teacher should recognize and support the beginnings of good inquiry.

We're not only concerned with students coming out of science class understanding some target concepts. We're also concerned with their coming out of class able to participate in the formation, assessment, and elaboration of concepts. Science, after all, is not only a body of knowledge but also the pursuit of that knowledge. A professional scientist is, fundamentally, a professional *learner;* what scientists do for a living is learn about the natural world. In this fundamental, essential sense, learning how to learn is itself learning science.

We define *science* as a pursuit and its results. The pursuit is of coherent, mechanistic accounts of the natural world—*coherent,* meaning that evidence and ideas fit together and support each other, and *mechanistic,* meaning scientists look for explanations of phenomena in terms of familiar, established causes and effects. And the results of that pursuit include the canon of accepted knowledge as well as the gaps in that knowledge and the questions it raises.

Almost all science education focuses on the results, and in particular on the canon of accepted knowledge. We argue that the pursuit itself needs priority, because for students, as for scientists, it is through participating in the pursuit that they can achieve understanding.

It is popular among science educators to advocate "inquiry-based approaches to teaching science" or "inquiry-based science," *as if there's another kind*. Science *is* inquiry; inquiry meaning the pursuit of coherent, mechanistic accounts of the natural world. And scientific knowledge is the result of that pursuit—inquiry is what scientists and students do to learn about the natural world. Watching and listening to students, we want to notice whether and how students engage in that pursuit, along with where that pursuit takes them.

Watching and listening to the students, we see the beginnings of that pursuit. Like India, Brianna and Ashley are working on articulating their ideas clearly, and they are thinking about what it would mean to get information from the world—how is it possible to weigh air? The students seem to be wrestling with conflicting ideas, struggling to articulate those ideas, and thinking about how they could get answers from experiments. The students have ideas, about air, about how to study whether air is matter. Instead of looking to Terry to provide the definitive information, they are trying to think it through for themselves. For his part, Terry is paying attention to what they are doing, and he is trying to support it.

"Can You Weigh Them?"

With students stalled on how to explain what confuses them or why they think air has no mass, Terry stops the conversation and asks them to write down a prediction: If they weigh the empty balloon and the balloon with air in it, would the balloon with air in it weigh more?

The room is quiet for a few minutes as the students write. Caitlyn interrupts the silence to suggest that they actually weigh the balloons: "Can you weigh them?" When Terry answers that he doesn't have a scale, Barb offers to get one from the chemistry lab. While she is doing that, Terry asks the students to "hypothesize."

57. Terry: So hypothesize, oh yes ma'am?

58. India: But doesn't it, shouldn't it weigh something because like if you put helium in it then it's lighter than the air and so it like rises.

59. Terry: Ooh. Ok, yes ma'am?

60. Brianna: If you were like to like let both of them go, the first balloon, like the empty balloon would probably hit the ground first, and that one would go slower.

They try it, and Brianna is correct. Terry asks if that means the blown-up balloon is lighter than the empty balloon, and the students aren't sure. India says that the air outside was "bigger" and was "holding (the balloon) up."

At this point Barb walks in with the scale and the class weighs both balloons. To their surprise, the balloons weigh the same whether they were blown up or not.

84. Caitlyn: Oooh. What? Not fair! How can that happen? What? Air is everywhere ... If I put air in my mouth like ... [laughter] I'd weigh more.

85. Terry: Thank you, so-

86. Ashley: Well then there would be a difference. Like if I stuck my hand on there then ...[inaudible]

87. Terry: So you're saying that they're not heavy? Oh go ahead.

88. Laura: Air is like surrounding everything. So like the un-blown balloon would also have air.

89. Terry: Around it?

90. Laura: Yes, around it.

91. Terry: OK.

92. Laura: And a little inside so …

93. Terry: Ok. So the experiment showed that they're the same. Are you happy with that?

Many students are not happy. They claim it was not a "fair" test, citing several concerns. Someone argues that the filled-up balloon was "held up" by the air, because Terry had dropped the balloons onto the scale from a small height ("That one fell first, and that one was dragging along"), and so the full balloon, slowed by the air, recorded less weight than it should have. Another student suggests that the weight should be measured by a person holding a full balloon, and then holding an empty balloon. Another suggests the scale isn't sensitive enough to measure the difference.

The episode presented in this chapter represents about 20 minutes of class time. The conversation continues for another 5 minutes, with students continuing to talk about how to determine the mass, if any, of air. The question of whether air has mass is never fully resolved. Terry says he thinks he has a more sensitive scale, and he promises to bring it to the next class. He also promises that the students will continue this discussion, and then the class moves on to another topic, discussing what students think are the different states of matter.

Educating the Responsive Teacher

Terry, at the time of this episode, is new to this idea of responsive teaching. He has always been a *reflective* practitioner, thinking about his experiences as a teacher, revising and adapting his practices. What was new this year was the extent to which he focused attention on the substance of his students' thinking in that reflection, and this attention came about as a result of his collaboration with us on a project titled *What Influences Teachers' Modifications of Curriculum?*[1]

The title expressed our original purpose. Teachers, we know, make small and large changes to curricula all the time. That they do might be to the dismay of curriculum developers, but we believed—and continue to believe—that is it unavoidable and important. Students vary considerably, even within a single classroom, more within a school, and more from one community to another. No one should expect that the same methods that are effective for some students, even for a majority of students, will be effective for *all* students. If there is any hope of achieving the goal of "leaving no child behind," then it is simply essential that teachers adjust for their particular students with their particular needs.

And so we set out to study what influences teachers making those adjustments. The project included three groups of teachers from major metropolitan suburban areas with diverse groups of students: two biological science groups and a physical science group. We expected to find that some modifications arise out of teachers' informal theories about learning and students, others out of practical contingencies, and others out of general experience. We also expected that some would arise out of teachers' noticing student reasoning—such as happened in this episode, where Terry changed his lesson plan when he heard students' ambivalence on the question of whether air is matter. We called these "responsive modifications," and we conjectured that they would correlate well with student learning.

The surprise for us was that responsive modifications hardly ever happened, among any of the three groups of teachers. More to the point, we found it was rare to have evidence that teachers *noticed*, let alone paid attention or responded to, the substance of student thinking, other than for its alignment with the conceptual objectives of the lesson. If a student had an idea, such as that air has no mass, we had evidence teachers would notice whether it was correct, but not that they would consider the evidence and reasoning that led the student to that idea. Our focus shifted to cultivating practices of attending and responding to student thinking.

---

1. This project was funded by a grant from the National Science Foundation (ESI 0455711).

The Need for Responsive Teaching

We have found that to cultivate those practices, it is important (and effective) to focus extensive attention on what students are saying and doing: *What are the students thinking? Why might they be thinking that?* So that will be the primary focus in the chapters that follow. As teachers shift their attention to the substance of student thinking, they are in a better position to assess that thinking and respond to it—not only at the level of alignment with the concepts of the canon, science as a body of knowledge, but also with respect to the students' participation and facility in science as a pursuit.

So talking about this case, we'd focus first and extensively on all that we can see and infer about the students' thinking. In this last bit, we see their initiative to go try the experiment—it's striking that they have an idea for how, and they want to start *now*! India is now clearly arguing that air must have mass, because of what she knows about helium. Is she thinking that people wouldn't say "lighter than air" if air doesn't have weight? Or is she thinking that the mass of air in a balloon would hold it down, in contrast to the helium?

Brianna is connecting the question of weight to the evidence of how quickly things fall, which draws out other ideas about the effects of the air surrounding the balloon. We see the students' surprise at the results, which many of them had earlier been predicting, that the weights are the same for the inflated and empty balloons, and we see them working to reconcile that result with their now apparently convincing sense that air must have weight. And so on—there is plenty to discuss and consider, and again both with respect to science as a pursuit and as the knowledge resulting from that pursuit.

But just for now consider Terry, who is redesigning his teaching to be more responsive. He had clearly not planned to weigh the balloons—if he even planned to use the balloons, which was Barb's idea—but the class was anxious to try the experiment, so he let Barb go get a scale. We see him asking students to say more about what they are thinking, trying to understand their ideas, such as in lines 87 and 89, asking Ashley and Laura to elaborate. He didn't do that with India; maybe he didn't notice her idea? Or maybe he wanted to balance participation among students, and other students like Brianna had things to say? Important and likely provocative, he did not close the discussion by providing the "right" answer. Instead, he listened to students' arguments about the validity of the experiment and promised to continue the investigation in the next class.

This is an example of what we mean by responsive practice. Terry was attending to the substance of the students' thinking, with respect to both their ideas and to how the students were taking up the pursuit.

The Book's Purpose and Organization

We aim this book at teacher educators, and the teachers and student teachers they work with, to help develop practices of attending to the substance of students' thinking, a necessary first step in developing responsive practices that take students' thinking into account. We hope that teacher educators will use the book as we have used it, in preservice teacher education courses and in seminars with practicing teachers, and we provide facilitators' notes capturing our experiences using the case studies to draw attention to student thinking.

The book itself includes the teachers' case studies, the facilitators' notes, and supporting chapters. The videos and transcripts for each of the case studies (and student work from Chapter 7) are on the NSTA Press website at *www. nsta.org/publications/press/extras/responsive.aspx*. You'll notice that the videos accompanying Chapters 4, 6, and 7 are blurry. This is intentional: While most students (and their parents/guardians) in each of these classes gave us their consent for their images to appear on video, a few in each class did not. In our experience, people get used to it quickly.

We continue, in Chapter 2, with a framework for thinking about the beginnings of scientific thinking in secondary students. What might we see in what students say and do that can be a starting point for their participation in science as a way of knowing? What are the productive resources that we can see and hear in students' ideas and reasoning?

We then turn to the case studies. Chapter 3 provides an overview of the cases and some general suggestions for how to use them productively. Chapters 4–8 present the case studies, which come from teachers in our project during the third and final year. In Chapter 9, we'll discuss how to move forward from here, including suggestions on how to build on this beginning by supporting teachers in collecting data and studying students' inquiry in their own classes. We'll also discuss issues of systematic impediments to a focus on student thinking, in common practices of teacher assessment and supervision that focus on teacher behaviors independent of student thinking, as well as on the influence of local, state, and national standards. We'll offer recommendations for maintaining a focus on student thinking as part of teacher supervision. We'll continue with a discussion of the prospects for inquiry-oriented science education, toward a new framework for understanding progress in secondary schools.

Finally, we'll close with some additional comments and references to other materials in the Notes section at the end of the book. These notes are organized by chapter and page number, with phrases from the text used to identify what they concern. (We decided not to include most of these in the text based on feedback from teachers in an earlier project who noted that they were distracting.)

C HAPTER 2

The Refinement of Everyday Thinking

Part A: Everyday Knowledge and Everyday Reasoning

The whole of science is nothing more than a refinement of everyday thinking.

—Albert Einstein

Our motivation to write this book is our sense that there can and should be much more science going on in science classes. Typically there's very little, and that's unfortunate for all sorts of reasons, including and maybe especially that more students would be interested and excited in science if they could experience it. So it seemed in Terry's class: As the discussion became more scientific, that is, as it became more about the students genuinely trying to make sense of air—of what kind of thing it is, if it's a kind of thing—the students became more animated and involved.

We have two interwoven purposes in this chapter. The first is to talk more about science and science learning, to elaborate and support a view of science as "a refinement of everyday thinking," as Einstein put it. The second is to discuss the rich beginnings of science in students' "everyday thinking." In that we'll challenge the prevalent views of students as either lacking abilities or possessed of "misconceptions" that interfere with their learning. By these views, science is "counterintuitive," discontinuous from common sense and experience—and no wonder students have such difficulties! We'll argue instead for views of students as simply *abounding* in productive intellectual resources for science.

This chapter is in two parts. In the first we focus on everyday thinking, dividing our discussion into two sections: "Everyday Knowledge" and "Everyday Reasoning." In the second part of the chapter, we delve into what happens in science class and how everyday thinking can progress toward scientific expertise.

Everyday Knowledge

Einstein's claim about science is one way to express the idea of *constructivism*: that people construct new knowledge out of the knowledge they already

CHAPTER 2

The Refinement of Everyday Thinking

have. In fact, when he wrote it he had met and discussed the idea with Piaget and other psychologists. That science is a refinement of everyday thinking is, Einstein went on to say, a reason for scientists to take on "the problem of analyzing the nature of everyday thinking."

That is where we begin, with a discussion about the nature of everyday thinking. In this section, we'll focus on the nature of everyday knowledge as the beginnings for more refined ideas; in the next section we'll focus on everyday reasoning, such as informal experimentation and logic. Any of this is what you might call "common sense."

Everyday Knowledge Is Vast

The first thing to appreciate about everyday knowledge is that it is vast, in particular, knowledge about natural phenomena and causes and effects. By the time children reach kindergarten, they know an enormous amount about the physical and biological world. There are differences among people, of course, for reasons of culture, opportunities, and abilities, but if you think of any particular child and what she or he knows about the world, you'll never finish the list. If she's a typical kid, she knows what it's like to run hard and then "run out of breath," that she can throw a penny farther than she can throw a brick or a piece of tissue paper (but for different reasons), what it feels like to get into a bathtub when the water is hot, and what it feels like in that bathtub moving her hands through the liquid. She knows that people and dogs and squirrels, and every other animal, need to eat; how sounds differ when she hits different sorts of drums; and that somehow clouds hold the water that can come down as rain.

And on and on—we can't list it all either—and that's the thinking of a five-year-old child. By the time students reach high school, they know still more, such as where babies come from, and that children of all species look a lot like their biological parents, but not exactly; they have a sense of the speed of human reflexes; they can calculate how much time it takes to drive 100 miles going 50 mph; they know that some ailments are contagious, and in different ways, and others are not. And on and on.

With all of their knowledge and experience, there are few questions you could ask about the natural world that would be entirely new to students. There's almost always going to be *something* they know that connects to the topic, whatever it may be.

Everyday Knowledge Is Flexible and Multifaceted

Something else to notice is that everyday knowledge is flexible and multifaceted. People don't have a theory of motion or if they do, it's made up of many different and often inconsistent "mini-theories," rather than a single coherent framework, and that's important for how we think of its "refinement."

In particular, common sense about one situation doesn't necessarily apply in another. Take, for example, the question of whether air takes up space, which Terry's students considered as part of thinking about whether air is matter. In most situations you experience, common sense says no, of course not. (At one point in their conversation, Terry's students even made fun of the idea, as if you have to "leave room for the air" when you move about.) But in the particular situation of inflating a balloon, common sense says yes, of course it does—that's the whole point of blowing up a balloon. What happened for Terry's students was that they thought of the question with both of these situations in mind at once, which means connecting and reconciling these different parts of their everyday knowledge.

For another example, it's common sense that matter can't just come from nowhere. If you want to make something—a cake, a house, pottery, clothing— you need raw material. If it's big, you need a lot of material. Obviously! But it's also common sense that a little seed can grow into a giant tree—and common sense doesn't typically ask where all that material comes from. Ask most adults, "Where does that matter come from that makes a tree?" and their reaction is often puzzled, as if that is a strange question to be asking. Trees grow, obviously, but it's never occurred to them to wonder where all that stuff comes from. Posing them the question has them connecting and trying to reconcile different parts of common sense, which isn't easy to do. Some might say "sunlight," since they know that has something to do with it, although in other situations they'd never think of sunlight as "stuff."

One more example: Think of what it's like to be a passenger in a car, train, ship, or a plane. You know that unless it's noisy or bumpy, it doesn't feel much different from when the vehicle is sitting still. You might even fall asleep in your seat, and when you wake up, if you don't open your eyes, it might be hard to tell how fast you're moving if you don't look out the window. It's something you've experienced so often it's just part of what you know. This bit of everyday knowledge was the beginning of Galileo's and then Einstein's theories of relativity. So when Einstein wrote "a refinement of everyday thinking," he really did mean everyday thinking.

But in many other situations—pushing a cart across the floor, throwing a ball, riding a bike, driving a car—it's common sense that something's got to push on the object to keep it moving. The faster you want it to move, the harder you have to push it. In everyday thinking, nobody notices that the intuitive sense in these situations doesn't quite line up with the intuitive sense in the situation of riding in a plane. (Someone who'd never experienced riding in an airplane could expect it would hurt to be pushed along at 500 mph!) If you call it to their attention, they can try to fit them together somehow—"well, it's the plane that's moving, not you"—but for the moment, the point is that it doesn't typically come to their attention: In different situations, common sense has different things to say.

In fact, if you try to think of other examples of this, you'll probably find it challenging, precisely because we're all so good at compartmentalizing different aspects of our experience. But examples abound: Heating things makes them melt; oh, but heating eggs makes them solidify. Gloves keep hands warm; oh, but oven mitts keep hands from getting hot. Things fall if they aren't supported; but clouds don't, not even "heavy" clouds that are holding water. If you want to reduce the weight of an object, you have to remove material; oh, but exercise will reduce the weight of your body.

Reconciling inconsistencies of understanding such as these, as we'll discuss, is at the heart of scientific thinking. Before we get to that, however, we take a moment to talk about misconceptions.

Misconceptions

The idea of "misconceptions" has been familiar in science education for several decades, and it has had a powerful effect on teaching, assessment, and curriculum development. It originated with research in the late 1970s, including studies that showed similarities between student reasoning and theoretical positions from the history of science: Students seem to have Aristotelian views about motion or Lamarckian ideas about evolution. For this reason, and as part of a general perspective of constructivism, it is a mistake to think of students as "blank slates." They already have "knowledge"—knowledge in the sense of cognitive phenomena and structures—and they will use that knowledge to make sense of what science teachers tell them. Insofar as their knowledge is wrong, it will interfere with their learning.

In other words, students arrive at school with lots of wrong ideas that they need to overcome in order to make progress. Worse, they hang on to those wrong ideas pretty tightly. So science teachers really have to make it a mission to ferret out and fix those ideas. Science educators speak of the need to "overcome," "confront," or "eradicate" students' misconceptions.

Or at least that's been the popular interpretation. In fact, in an important sense, this idea of students' prior knowledge as interfering with learning is the opposite of the original point of misconceptions research, which was to show that these "wrong" ideas reflect sensible, intelligent reasoning. The original argument was that "misconceptions" are part of something that is fundamentally productive and important in student thinking. Students are being *rational* in thinking that force causes motion or that giraffes get longer necks by stretching.

The problem, this research argued, is that science instruction focuses too much on providing students correct information and not enough on supporting rational thinking. The effect is that students learn to separate their everyday thinking from what they see in class. By ignoring the sensible ideas students have already formed, science teaching is making itself irrelevant to how students think about the world. Students learn to give certain answers in class, but that has no effect on how they *really* think. They still have their earlier ways of thinking—the inherently sensible, intelligent, useful ideas.

Unfortunately, most people have misinterpreted the findings, seeing misconceptions as impediments, and in this way misconceptions research has had almost the opposite effect from its original intent. Instead of raising respect for students' prior understandings, it has convinced many educators that students are worse than blank slates: They're slates with wrong ideas written in hard-to-erase chalk!

In 1992, two of the original misconceptions theorists, Ken Strike and George Posner, wrote an update to their original work, in part to challenge how the community had taken it up. For them, the point was to recognize and appreciate students' rationality: "If conceptual change theory suggests anything about instruction, it is that the handles to effective instruction are to be found in persistent attention to the argument and in less attention to right answers."

Conceptual Resources

One reason people came to the "obstacles" interpretation is that the research didn't do a good job explaining what's *good* about misconceptions. Most studies focused on showing that students hold these reasonable but incorrect ideas even after instruction. If all you're thinking about is that the misconception is wrong, then of course you're going to try to get rid of it, not take advantage of it.

Misconceptions research also had the problem that it provided no answers to the key question any constructivist should ask: If students construct new knowledge using knowledge they already have, what do they have that they can use in that construction? Answering that was difficult in misconceptions research, mainly because it treated each misconception as the one way someone had to think about the particular topic.[1]

It will help to focus on an example, so we'll use one made famous by the 1989 film *A Private Universe*. The filmmakers approached Harvard students at their graduation, and asked them to explain, among other things, why it is hotter in the summer than it is in the winter. One gowned student after another explained that it is hotter in the summer because the Earth in its orbit is closer

---

1. Part of Strike's and Posner's 1992 revision was to amend this feature of their original theory, to shift toward a view of a "cognitive ecology."

to the Sun. By the usual interpretation, the students have this misconception firmly engrained in their minds; the point of the film was that this wrong idea had survived throughout all their education.

But there's another interpretation based on an appreciation of common sense as flexible and multifaceted. Students might not have an idea already in mind about why it is hotter in the summer; they might form an idea *in the moment*. Asked why it is hotter in the summer, they do a quick search through their common sense and find the piece of knowledge that "closer means stronger": The closer you are to the source of something (heat, sound, odor), the greater its effect. That's the idea they have firmly engrained in their common sense, *closer means stronger*, and the misconception we hear is a result of their using that idea to answer this question.

With this interpretation, the misconception isn't the single way the graduates have of thinking about seasons; it's what they come up with in the particular moment, in the situation of someone asking them a question. In another moment, they might think up something else instead, starting from a different bit of common sense. The difference in these interpretations is significant: One identifies a wrong idea to confront and eliminate; the other identifies a resource, a bit of knowledge that is useful and valid in many situations. The former interpretation would be part of a program of science instruction to *replace* everyday knowledge; the latter would be part of a program to *refine* everyday knowledge.

It is possible to get evidence to distinguish between these interpretations. In fact, you could try it yourself. You'll need to find volunteers, preferably not scientists, who'd be willing to serve as research subjects. Divide them randomly into two groups, A and B. Ask subjects in group A: "Why is it hotter in the summer than it is in the winter?" The chances are good you'll hear many of them say it's because Earth gets closer to the Sun, replicating the *Private Universe* results. If you give them paper, some of them may draw a sketch of Earth's orbit around the Sun as part of their explanation.

For group B, start out asking this question: "When it's summer in the northern hemisphere, is it summer or winter in the southern hemisphere?" The first interpretation—that people hold a misconception that it gets hotter in the summer because Earth is closer to the Sun—would predict that roughly the same proportion of subjects in group B would say that it is summer in the southern hemisphere—that is what their theory clearly implies. (If Earth is closer to the Sun, *the entire* planet is closer to the Sun, and it should be hotter everywhere.)

We expect most will say that it's winter, something they'll know from their travels or the news, although this could certainly depend on the community, or just because it seems right to them in the moment that the opposite hemisphere would have the opposite season. If that's what happens, you could continue.

You could then ask them that first question, "Why is it hotter in the summer than it is in the winter?" We expect you won't hear as many in group B tell you that the Earth gets closer to the Sun as you do in group A. Instead, you'll hear more about one side of the Earth getting closer. In other words, when they do their quick search through their common sense for an idea, if they find "closer means stronger" they won't be able to use it the same way as the poor Harvard students, because you've made sure they've already found another part of their knowledge. Of course, the people in group A were just as likely to "know" that summer in the north means winter in the south, but that bit of their knowledge might not occur to them at the moment.

You could try other versions of this experiment, too. Spend the first part of the conversation talking about how days are longer in the summer than in the winter. Then when you ask why it's hotter in the summer, it's likely you'll hear some answers about how the Sun has more time to warm things up. When people say that Earth gets closer to the Sun, that's not the only way they have of thinking about seasons. They have other ways, too, which they'd use in other moments depending on the situation. The important point is that common sense—everyday thinking—is flexible, multifaceted, variable, and adaptive to the particular circumstances.

So when you're thinking about common sense, don't picture a mental encyclopedia we consult for answers. Picture instead a rich, varied collection of ideas and experiences and different ways of thinking, knowledge in all sorts of shapes and sizes, many different parts that do many different things.

We call this collection of ideas "resources" or "conceptual resources." Every part is useful in some contexts to some purposes but not others. Different moments "turn on" different resources, which enables us to manage the myriad of circumstances we encounter every day. The collection as a whole doesn't fit together the way an encyclopedia does, with a clear organization and a particular bit of information for each topic. It's much more complicated than that, more idiosyncratic, redundant, and inconsistent. Thinking about any topic at any moment, you might use any of a variety of assorted resources.

An analogy is of an extensive toolbox with lots of different kinds of tools for doing all sorts of things. All the tools are useful, but for any particular job you might grab the wrong one. If you tried to use a can opener on a bottle, you'd find it wouldn't work so well. But you shouldn't throw the can opener away! *Closer means stronger* doesn't work in the way people tend to use it, when they're asked why it's hotter in the summer, but it certainly does work in lots of other situations. It's a resource for thinking that's available in our minds, useful in some moments and not useful in others.

With this view of common sense, thinking involves looking through that collection, grabbing different pieces, and trying them out. Asked why it's hotter in the summer, people look through their common sense, and one of the first things they find in there is *closer means stronger*. They might then stop looking, since they've found something that seems to do the job, and so are less likely to hunt for other pieces in the collection. If they were to keep looking, there are lots of other pieces they could find, such as that winter in the northern hemisphere means summer in the south, that summer days last longer, or that the Sun is more directly overhead in the summer than in the winter. They might also find knowledge about how the Sun doesn't feel as warm early or late in the day when it's low in the sky, that clouds or fog can block the Sun and make it feel cooler, or that when you're outside, the side of your body facing the Sun feels warmer.

Everyday Reasoning

We've been talking about everyday knowledge, and in particular, knowledge about natural phenomena and causes and effects. It's vast and varied; students are rich in conceptual resources for understanding the natural world. But that knowledge is only the beginning of science. It needs refinement. It's fine for everyday thinking, for example, that in some situations air seems to take up space and in others it doesn't, that plants just create matter as they grow, and passengers on a train don't feel anything while in motion. But forming a scientific understanding involves pinning down ideas with clarity and connecting and reconciling disparate parts of common sense. Scientific knowledge is a refinement of everyday knowledge, and the refinement, as we'll discuss, is toward clear, coherent, causal understanding of the natural world.

This is what we mean by *scientific inquiry*: the pursuit of clear, coherent, causal understanding. We need students to take it up if we want them to achieve scientific knowledge. To be sure, that's how scientists achieve scientific knowledge; engaging in that pursuit is what scientists do for a living, which makes them professional learners about the natural world. Scientists have gotten very good at it, having had more practice; they've learned how to learn about the world.

In the previous section we talked about everyday knowledge as the raw material for scientific knowledge. In this section, we'll talk about reasoning, and in particular how everyday reasoning has in it the beginnings of scientific reasoning, much as everyday knowledge has in it the beginnings of scientific knowledge. Here our focus is on cognitive activities, what people do as opposed to what people know, and as before, the first thing to appreciate is the extent of students' raw abilities for thought.

What Students Can Do

The first thing to appreciate is just how much kids are capable of doing. It may not be obvious, if you haven't spent time watching and listening to them think for themselves.

Just to start, though, imagine several children sitting in a room and every time someone comes in they hear a squeak. One says, "The door is squeaking," and another says, "I don't think it's the door." The first one goes to the door and moves it, but there's no sound. "See?" "So what is it?" A third child offers to help. "I'll go out and come in, and everybody listen." They all focus carefully now, and someone thinks it's the floor. "Wait, nobody move!" That child stands at the threshold and bounces. *Squeak, squeak squeak.* "Look, it's bending a little." "Yeah, like a trampoline, kind of."

How old would children need to be, to be able to do that? Five? Maybe four? Of course, if you believe children can do that (you should!), then you believe they have some valuable beginnings of scientific reasoning abilities. They recognized a phenomenon, thought of a plausible hypothesis for the cause (doors often squeak), tested the conjecture, and rejected it. They then shifted into focused observation, came up with another hypothesis, and—controlling variables ("nobody move!")—they confirmed it. Even more, they began to notice aspects of the mechanism (that the floor was bending a little) and considered a connection to another physical context. That isn't to say they're already equipped with all the abilities they need; it's to say they have the beginnings.

There's much more. Spend time watching and listening to children and you find that from very early years they can systematically investigate the natural world, such as to understand how a complex toy works; they can recognize patterns, suppose causes, and use their ideas to make predictions to test. ("If the door is causing the squeak, then if I move the door, I should hear the squeak.") Research on grade-school children shows abilities that surprise adults, maybe especially adults used to working with older children. When fifth-grade students we've watched consider the idea that the Sun causes water to evaporate, they challenge the idea because, they say, that would mean evaporation wouldn't happen indoors or on a cloudy day. A third-grade girl thinking that a heavier object should go faster down a slide than a lighter one comes up with the idea of dropping two paper towels, one soaked with water to make it heavy, to show that weight matters in falling. Fourth graders think that the water on the outside of a glass came from the water inside, oozing through tiny holes in the glass. The teacher adds blue dye and presents the counter-evidence that the water on the outside is clear, and the children rebut that argument by explaining that the tiny pieces of dye are too big to fit through the holes. Again, we could go on and on.

Older students have more abilities still. Consider what Terry's students Laura and Ari accomplished during the discussion we described in Chapter 1. Terry had been asking whether air takes up space, but for Laura that question was supposing air and space are different.

> Laura: The air IS the space.

> Terry: So air IS the space. Are you saying it takes up space? Is that the idea?

> Ari: The air is the space that gets taken up.

In this way, Laura and Ari recognized and challenged a presumption Terry was not even aware he was making, that air and space are distinct ideas. It's hard to imagine a five-year-old having such awareness and control of rhetoric to identify and contest a presumption. In other ways, too, we might expect older students to have more developed abilities and practices of language and representation, such as for recording thoughts in writing, for drawing pictures to illustrate ideas, and for engaging in argumentation.

The important point here is that students are tremendously well equipped with reasoning abilities, along with having all that knowledge about the world we discussed above. They have the beginnings of scientists' technical abilities and practices; in this respect, too, science is a "refinement of everyday thinking."

Different Situations Call for Different Kinds of Reasoning

We're saying students are well equipped with abilities, but that doesn't mean they always use those abilities. Earlier we talked about how common sense varies from one situation to another, and the same applies to reasoning.

Part of what we all learn, in fact, is what kinds of reasoning to use in what kinds of situations. If you're sitting in a job interview, watching an action movie, sitting on a jury, or sitting in a science class, you reason in different ways. The sort of thinking you do planning a meal (deciding what to make, figuring out what you have and what you need) is different from the thinking you do while cooking it (coordinating times, checking for doneness and taste).

The children in the story recognized that they could test the idea that the door caused the squeak; finding out it didn't, they could start a different sort of activity to help them come up with another possibility. They knew they could test that possibility, too, and even start to try to make sense of it. That is, they knew about different sorts of things they could do to generate and assess the validity of claims about the world.

Laura and Ari were able to identify the assumption hidden in the question of whether air takes up space, which didn't make sense to them at first, and they saw it as appropriate to challenge that assumption. In fact, Terry was specifically trying to help them see it as appropriate to speak up, in the ways he emphasized that he wanted to understand their ideas and he was "not trying to say you're right or wrong."

The important thing to realize here is that everyday reasoning, like everyday knowledge, is also flexible and multifaceted. *How* we think varies as much as *what* we think, and in particular with our sense of the situation, our sense of what it is that's taking place.

More of the Beginnings of Science

We can't possibly describe all of the abilities students bring with them that are useful beginnings of science, any more than earlier we could list all the knowledge they bring, but we can give some examples to help show just how much there is. Some of it isn't so obvious, the useful stuff people can do, partly because it's so ordinary, and maybe partly because it's easy to get trapped into thinking of science as a body of established knowledge.

Shopping for Ideas

One bane of science teachers is how students glom onto the first answer that pops into their heads. That's what we suggested happens for a lot of people asked why it's hotter in the summer than it is in the winter: They recall the idea that closer means stronger and go with that. If students and those people would spend a little time poking around in their minds, they could find other relevant ideas and ways of thinking. So why don't they? It's tempting to think that they just can't, that it's beyond them for some reason to locate information in their memories, or maybe they don't have the patience or stamina. But to give in to that temptation would be, well, glomming onto the first explanation that pops into our minds!

Take a moment to poke around in your mind for them, and you'll find lots of examples in which shopping for ideas is just part of common sense: If you can't find your keys, you stop and think of where they could be, and you start a search. You might think through the places you'd been over the day, or the things that you did, to "jog your memory," as they say, to activate different parts of your mind. If you meet someone who seems familiar, but you can't quite place her, you know you can do something similar: Do you see her at the market? Was she at that party last weekend? Or maybe you go through the alphabet, trying to find the letter that starts her name.

Those are examples in which there's a single, simple right answer, and the situation is that you don't have it *yet*, so you know to look. The keys aren't where you thought they were; they are in some other *one* place, and if you find it, you've found them. The search ends when you have the answer or you give up.

In other situations, it's not so clear-cut. If there's an idea you'd like to express, but it's a challenge, you try out different ways of saying it ("I want to say it's *perplexing*, but that's not quite it. More like *disturbing* ..."). If you'd like to go out for dinner, you might spend time tossing around ideas for where: places you've been or places you've heard of that you haven't tried. If you're trying to figure out why your friend was behaving strangely last evening, you think through possibilities—you might poke around in your memory for clues and evidence. In other words, when it seems to you that the situation calls for it, you have ways of shopping around in your mind for ideas. We've used that metaphor in our classes, to help students recognize it as a kind of thing to do. Good shoppers don't buy the first thing they see. Nor do they buy everything that looks good on the rack—they take it out, try it on, and see how it looks. They know that the best stuff might not be in obvious places; they go down aisles other people might miss.

In science, the shopping is for knowledge and experience about the natural world. Studying some question, trying to understand a particular phenomenon, scientists know to browse through their knowledge and experience of other phenomena that might or might not be related. The ideas are very often there, but in a different section of your mind than you first think to look. Part of becoming a scientist is becoming a perseverant and sophisticated idea-shopper.

It is an important kind of creativity, and breakthroughs in science often come from finding new connections to knowledge that already exists. In the study of electricity, for example, key progress came from scientists connecting to their knowledge about liquids, about tension (as in ropes), and even at one point about gears (as in engines). Students learning about electricity need, similarly, to find useful resources in their common sense, resources they use all the time for understanding things that might seem much too ordinary to be relevant—about hallways crowded with people, or cars on roads, or hoses full of water. No one comes to understand electricity without using ideas they originally developed for other purposes.

Shopping for ideas is something to encourage and cultivate in students. For that, it's important to consider how they experience the situation. If students see science class as about knowing right answers, then it wouldn't make sense for them to go shopping in their own minds for ideas; we need them to see science class as about drawing on, considering, and refining their everyday thinking. When, for example, a student ventures an analogy to some other phenomenon (e.g., the topic is metamorphosis and the student thinks of an analogy to human growth), it's important for everyone to appreciate it as a good thing for him to do, to look for connections to other things he knows, try them out, and see if they accomplish something.

Seeking Consistency

Obviously it's not enough to look for ideas; it's essential to assess the *quality* of those ideas, and in particular whether they apply to the question at hand. An important criterion in science is that an idea is consistent, with evidence and with other ideas. This is another bane for science teachers: students' taking no notice of inconsistencies, like the Harvard grads who say, "Earth is closer to the Sun," without checking the answer against other things they know, such as that winter in the United States means summer in South Africa.

Again, our job is to point out how attention to consistency is another variable feature of everyday reasoning. It depends on how you experience the situation you're in, and we've already seen examples.

The reason everyone recognizes the need for thought in the situation of lost keys is that there's something clearly wrong. Terry led his students to notice a mismatch in their intuitions over whether air takes up space, in a balloon (yes) or in the room (no). He also encouraged a sense that it had to be one way or the other: No saying "sometimes it does and sometimes it doesn't," although that's a useful stance in some situations. ("Does pineapple taste good?") The children in the story expected consistency when they tested their ideas about what was causing the squeak. These are beginnings of science, where attention to consistency is paramount, both empirical (such as in evidence of what made the door squeak) and theoretical (such as in different ideas about air).

But everyday thinking isn't consistent about consistency; people don't always notice or care that ideas fit together. And the truth is they shouldn't. Nobody should give you a hard time if some evenings you feel like having a salad for dinner and other evenings you don't. Watching that action movie, reading Lewis Carroll, thinking about tastes in art or music, or talking with Aunt Cecile, it's appropriate to accept inconsistencies. In many situations, too, consistency just takes care of itself—it doesn't need our attention. You didn't check to be sure the chair you're sitting on will still hold you before you sat in it.

It would be impossibly debilitating always to be checking every bit of information in our lives for consistency with every other bit. We have the abilities there available for when we need them, but the truth is that most of the time we don't need them.

At the same time, there are plenty of situations in everyday life that call for attention to consistency. Any six-year-old can think about consistency with respect to fairness, of all the kids getting the same size piece of cake, or starting the race at the same time, or being allowed to stay up to the same hour. Even younger kids, research on learning has shown, notice and care about establishing consistent patterns of causality.

The point here is that students can and will attend to consistency if they experience science class as that kind of situation. If they see science class as about correct information, they could experience it the way you do your chair—the world is what it is, and it doesn't need their attention for it all to work, for it all to fit together. If they see science class as about their shopping for ideas and trying them out, they could learn to pay attention to consistency.

Terry's students hit the question of whether air is matter. They could experience that as a lack of information they have to obtain and go look it up. If that's how they see the question, they don't have to pay attention to consistency; the question is a matter of fact and consistency takes care of itself. If, on the other hand, they experience the question as a problem to think through for themselves, then it makes sense for them to go shopping and checking ideas to see how well they fit together. Suppose air *is* matter; what would that imply, what questions would need answering? Suppose air *isn't* matter. What would that imply, what questions would need answering?

They can do that. It's common sense in many situations when you're not sure what to believe: Try believing something and then see where it gets you. If you're not sure how to arrange the furniture in a room, you might say "let's try putting the couch over there," and then you find out what that would mean for the rest of the furniture.

We call it a *foothold idea*: an idea you choose to assume is true, at least for a moment. Watching and listening to students, we should notice moments when they're behaving this way. It should be part of our assessment of how they're doing. That's especially important when they've picked a foothold idea we know is incorrect, because if we don't recognize the value of their picking a foothold at all, we might not support them in that very scientific behavior.

Attending to Precision and Clarity

One particular kind of consistency that's important in science is the definition and use of terminology, and it's not something that seems to come easily. Ordinary speech doesn't generally work that way. For example:

> "The ball spent a lot of time in the air."

> "We've been angry, and it's time to clear the air."

> "Sshh! We're on the air!"

In each case it seems clear what the speaker probably meant, and none of those meanings was of air as a form of matter.

Everyday language, to continue a theme, is flexible. In almost all situations, that's a very good thing: The context provides lots of information, and communication is much more efficient when it makes use of that information. So if you're sitting at a baseball game, and you hear someone say "the ball spent a lot of time in the air," it would be very strange for you to need clarification of which ball or the precise meaning of "air." If you're in a lab looking at a tarnished bead of copper, you wouldn't need clarification either, but the meanings would be different.

That flexibility of everyday language, to continue another theme, is another bane of science teachers: sometimes students play fast and loose with carefully defined terms, whether *energy, respiration*, or *pressure*. In science, more than in everyday thinking, it's often important to be consistent with terminology, to give particular words precise meanings. Students so often seem incapable of paying close attention to the specific meaning of terminology. But clearly, students have the ability to take words apart and pin them down to precise meaning when they see that as appropriate for the situation. You tell students the homework is due on Friday, but you forget to say "in class," so someone e-mails it to you at 11:45 p.m.—it was still Friday. You assign an eight-page essay, and someone thinks to use 18-point font. Watch teenagers parse the meanings of rules when they're playing board games or negotiating curfews, and it's clear they have the abilities for technical precision.

There are situations in everyday life in which people know to use language with care. Athletes and sports fans have a rich sense of technical precision in their understanding of the rules—what exactly constitutes "carrying" in basketball or volleyball or "offside" in hockey or soccer—and will enter debates over fine points of their interpretation. The same is true for people who take board games seriously. Teenagers with cell phones come to understand technical meanings for *nights* and *minutes* (during nights you can talk for hours without using minutes!); those who join Facebook have to learn specialized meanings for "friend," "like," and "wall." More generally, in any moment of interaction, if you're trying to explain something that's important but might be misunderstood, you take care with language. ("Oh, when I said I was 'perplexed' you thought I was telling you I disagreed, but I actually meant I didn't understand.")

Part of learning science is recognizing the importance of that kind of attention, of distinguishing and specifying within a variety of possible meanings. That's the reason for technical vocabulary, to distinguish and communicate particular ideas. There are rich beginnings of that in everyday thinking, in what students bring with them to class, but students have to experience science class as a situation that calls for careful attention to meaning.

Unfortunately, because of the way science classes often treat vocabulary, it becomes the end in itself, not a means for meaningful communication. If students see science class mainly as a collection of terms—where the point is to say *mass* instead of *weight* and so on—then they won't tap into their very rich abilities for meaningful thought and communication. If they experience it as a place for considering ideas, then they'll experience the need for making distinctions and defining terms. Watching and listening to students, we should notice when they work to articulate an idea carefully. They should learn that that's something to be doing during science class, and they should get practice at it to learn to do it well.

More and More ...

It's important to be clear that we have not even tried to lay out all of the beginnings of science in everyday thinking, for a few reasons. First, that would be an enormous task, and we're just not up to taking it on! Second (and part of why we're not up to it), there's great variation among the sciences, and even among scientists within any branch of science, for what constitutes "scientific reasoning." In fact, it's not hard to find ways in which scientific reasoning itself evolves over time, as new theoretical frameworks and new technologies bring new approaches to research. Nor, certainly, is it hard to find ways that scientific knowledge changes!

Third, and maybe most important here, what constitutes "everyday thinking" varies greatly as well, among individual students, among groups, and among communities. A student who's into dinosaurs or insects, has had a summer job painting houses or flipping burgers or lobstering, spent a lot of time hiking and exploring the woods, and so on, would bring interests and understandings that would be valuable in various moments for learning science. The students on the swim team have more knowledge and experience of water and pressure; the students in the cooking club, the chess club, the debate team, the gymnasts, and so on, all have particular areas in which they've built up knowledge and expertise. The students in any particular teacher's classroom will bring their own particular experiences of the natural world, as well as their own experiences of intellectual activity. Many areas of students' experience are obviously valuable, such as of creatures in nature, or on farms, or around their homes. Other areas aren't so obvious, such as in playing board games or in other forms of friendly intellectual competition. Research on learning has revealed diverse forms of everyday reasoning in students' experience that could be valuable for science.

For this reason, the diversity of "everyday thinking" among students, the challenge ultimately falls on the teacher, to recognize and cultivate the beginnings of science in her or his students' knowledge and experience. That's what this book is about, helping to prepare teachers to meet that challenge.

Part B: Refinement Toward Science

In Part A of this chapter we've given examples of knowledge and reasoning abilities students are likely to have from everyday experience that are productive resources for learning science. Now we think about what happens in science class, starting with "What kind of situation is science class?" From there we proceed to "Progress" and explore how scientific thinking results from the refinement of everyday thinking. Finally, we return to "The Role of Responsive Teaching" in facilitating this progress, revisiting the importance of attending and responding to student thinking in light of the views we've developed of science and science learning.

What Kind of Situation Is Science Class?

Our first purpose with the examples in Part A is to encourage appropriate respect for students and what they bring: They're not a list of aspects to cover; they're examples of what teachers could discover, paying close attention to students' thinking.

Our second purpose is to call attention to this other level of what's always going on: There's the knowledge and abilities, which are typically the main focus of attention in discussions about education, and then there is the students' (and scientists' and our own) sense of what is taking place. How do students and teachers experience the situation?

Research on learning has technical terms for this sort of thing, including *epistemology*, to refer to knowledge about knowledge (a word borrowed and adapted from philosophers), and *metacognition*, to refer to the mental activity of thinking about thinking. These levels of thought and knowledge, of metacognition and epistemology, come into play all the time in everyday thinking, and they're of central importance in the development of scientific reasoning, so we should spend some time on them.

We have already been talking about them; this section is to make them the direct focus of attention. So, we gave the example of how the term *friend* has a particular technical meaning on Facebook that's related to but different from and more precise than its everyday meaning. Someone can be your "friend" who isn't your friend; how you understand the meaning of the word depends critically on your sense of the situation. We gave the example of the word *air*, which has different meanings in different situations, and our understanding of the word is tightly entangled with our understanding of the situation.

Part of what students need to develop is a sense of the situation in science (or more specifically science class, but we hope to see science in science class!) What do they see taking place; what do they see as their role; what are they really trying to accomplish? They might see the situation as one of their following instructions to get points; as trying to find out correct information, without thinking they have a role in assessing correctness; or as trying to make sense of the natural world.

What Kind of Question and What Kind of Answer?

Consider different ways they could expect to decide on an answer. In some situations, the answer is just some matter of fact. If you don't know your friend's middle name, and he says it's Chris, you've gained a piece of information. You might ask "why Chris?" but it would be a little odd to ask why it isn't Michael!

In other situations, the answer is a matter of choice. If you're at a restaurant, and you order the falafel plate, that doesn't mean ordering the macaroni and cheese would have been wrong; it just means that's what you felt like having. If someone asks "why aren't you having mac and cheese?" the answer "I felt like falafel tonight" would be perfectly acceptable.

Sometimes the decision is momentous, say, whether to accept an offer of a teaching position. Then you might list the pros and cons very carefully. On the side in favor, you might have reasons such as "the salary's good" and "the administration is supportive." On the side against, you might have "it's a long commute" and "the class sizes are too large." Then you'd make a decision based on which side "outweighs" the other, and if someone asked why you made that choice, it would be reasonable to expect you'd have reasons. In that situation, once you've decided, it wouldn't be of much value to think any more about the arguments on the other side: Sure, the class sizes are larger than you'd want, but it's worth it to have a supportive principal.

But then there are some situations in which it's not enough to decide on an answer. It's also important really to account for the lines of reasoning that led to other answers. If the usual day you take out the trash is Tuesday, and one week you do that and your spouse tells you "no, the trash doesn't go out today" you might want to know why not. You don't only want to know "what is the answer right now"; you want to tune your mind and understanding so that in the future, you'll be able to produce right answers yourself. If part of your mind says X, but the answer is Y, you want to understand what needs fixing in the reasoning for X.

That's often how people experience the moment, when they find a discrepancy from their common sense in science. Drop a brick and a penny, see that they hit at the same time, and people will often want to understand why: "Why didn't the brick hit first, when it seemed so clear that it would?" Part of students' learning science is their learning to experience more situations in this way, not only to find the answer, but to try to reconcile conflicting lines of reasoning. So we need them to experience science class as this kind of situation, one in which they think it's important to explain—or to ask if they can't explain—why the answer isn't X, even when they're sure the answer is Y.

What's the Math For?

For many students, mathematics is another subject they experience as divorced from everyday thinking, rather than building from it. There are some wonderful things happening in math education, but in most classes students still learn "math" similar to the way most learn "science," memorizing information and procedures. When a mathematical expression comes up, it means a kind of situation that's more about carefully following instructions—algorithms—than about sense-making.

Of course that's not how we want them to experience the situation! Mathematics is the ultimate in precision and consistency: To express an idea mathematically is to make it very precise, and having a mathematical expression (of an idea!) lets you derive its necessary implications. It's not hard to think of everyday examples. Nobody says "Elaine lent me some money, so I've got to give her some money back." People *do* say "I resolve to exercise more this year," and that leaves them all sorts of room for interpretation. Make it precise: "I resolve to run 10 miles every week." Bringing in mathematics lets you derive implications: If you've run 7 miles, you've got 3 to go. (If you've run n miles, you've got $10 - n$ left to go!)

Or take the idea of motion. In everyday use, the word has many meanings. We can describe someone as moving who is fidgeting or spinning or even saying things with powerful feeling. But it's possible to pin down one of those meanings, of "changing location," as in "At noon we were in Des Moines and 30 minutes later we were in Ames." We can quantify that—the change in location was 30 miles, and from that we can say the speed along the highway was 30 miles/30 minutes = 1 mile/minute = 60 mph, heading north. We can write the mathematical expression $x_f - x_i$ of the change in location, from some initial time to some final time. Divide by the amount of time in that interval, and we have a mathematically precise definition of (average) velocity, and that lets us write an expression like "The change in position is the average velocity times the time." Symbols such as Δ (which means "change in") make that quicker: $\Delta x = v\,\Delta t$. From that we can derive implications!

That's what mathematics is all about, deriving and keeping track of the connections and relationships among ideas. It's about necessary connections among ideas; if $\Delta x = 30$ miles, and $\Delta t = 30$ minutes, then $\Delta x/\Delta t$ is necessarily 60 mph. And for that reason it's just wonderful for science, for the pursuit of coherent understanding: If you can express an idea mathematically, then you can figure out what that necessarily implies. That's a big *if,* of course; you can't always express ideas mathematically, but when you can, it's a huge advantage.

It's especially powerful if you want to decide whether to believe the idea is true. You can see what it necessarily implies, and then look to see if that is true.

More and More...

We've provided a couple of examples, but of course there are many more. Why make a graph or chart to record numbers? Why repeat measurements? For students, the situation could be that they're following the instructions they were given, or it could be that they're trying to keep track and make sense of their data.

Our core point here is that much depends on how students understand the situation, the sense they have of what's taking place, in that moment and in the class. That influences, and of course is influenced by, what resources they draw on, from the rich knowledge and abilities we discussed above.

Progress Toward Science

We've been presenting a view of science as a "refinement of everyday thinking." We introduced that idea by citing the authority of Einstein, which isn't a very scientific way to support a claim! But we've also argued for this view by pointing out the rich, relevant resources students have from everyday thinking. We've identified some particular aspects of their everyday thinking that are the beginnings of scientific knowledge and reasoning.

What we haven't done yet is to respond to a conflicting view of science that's fairly widespread: Science is often different from everyday thinking. Many accounts speak of it as counterintuitive, even as unnatural. And it might seem absurd to argue that the esoteric ideas of relativity or quantum mechanics or double helixes or entropy or covalent bonds or glycolysis come out of everyday thinking. We need to reconcile that point of view with ours.

We have discussed how particular ideas can seem counterintuitive in one context but not in another, as we discussed above. The evidence is very strong that intuition does not operate as a single, coherent perspective, and we gave a bunch of examples to illustrate. (Interested readers can consult the endnotes for references to research articles.)

But we haven't yet discussed the refinement, and that's our purpose here. The view that "the whole of science is nothing more than a refinement of everyday thinking" isn't a claim that science is everyday thinking. Your computer is a refinement of natural materials! But really: The silicon in the computer chips started out as silicon in the ground—there's some in the ground right outside your window. It's been refined to the point that it's hard to recognize where it started, but if you were to follow all the steps from the mining to the separation to the purifying to the manufacturing of chips, that's where it came from. Of course, there are other ingredients as well, but they all have natural origins too.

The same is true of ideas. To start, think about the expertise of a chef. Everyone can taste thyme in a recipe, but someone who's lingered and reflected on that taste in many recipes can say, "There's thyme." Chefs can distinguish it from other flavors that are similar but not identical, say, to distinguish thyme from lemon. Almost anyone could do that in a side-by-side comparison, so this is again something that starts with everyday abilities, but chefs have refined those abilities. Similarly, chefs come to recognize flavor combinations that come up often in food, such as to notice or be able to imagine "thyme and rosemary" all at once and recognize it as a theme in Provencal recipes.

So it starts with an everyday sense of flavors, but the chefs have shopped in those sections of their knowledge and experience often, and they know where things are. Of course, they've also tasted more flavors than the rest of us, so they add to their sense in that way too, but it would be a mistake to think that's most of what they've accomplished. (Even then, when they taste something new, they connect it to other flavors they already know—tasting anise for the first time, they compare and contrast it with licorice and fennel.)

Something similar happens in science. As students spend time lingering and reflecting on their sense of various mechanisms, as they gain experience shopping in that part of their common sense, they get to be more familiar with what's there. They refine it in the same ways. They can recognize and imagine particular mechanisms more easily. They can keep track of differences among mechanisms that seem similar to people who haven't given them as much careful thought. They can recognize and imagine combinations all at once that come up in many contexts. And of course, the students have come upon new phenomena and new mechanisms along the way, so they've added to their sense in that way too, but as with the chefs it would be a mistake to think of this as most of what they've accomplished. (Even then, they first understand the new phenomenon by connecting it to others—on first discovering certain new phenomenon in light, scientists compared and contrasted it with what they knew about how waves move on ponds and sound moves through air.)

We're arguing that everyday thinking provides necessary raw materials for science, but those raw materials get refined. Like your computer, the end products can be quite removed from everyday thinking, but that's where it all starts.

Refining Ideas

Here's an example: Think of a large bucket of water with a tiny hole in the bottom. Water drips out, a tiny bit, with each drip. You know that the surface of the water in the bucket is going down, even though you can't see it moving. You know that because each of those tiny drops is taking away a tiny bit of water, a negligible amount on its own, but over time many drops will add up to something noticeable. Now picture an eight-year-old child. Measure his height one day to the next and you won't notice a difference, but you know that over time he gets taller. Thinking of the water and the child at the same time is comparing two parts of common sense most people don't think of at the same time. They share the idea of tiny, unnoticeable changes adding up to something significant over time.

That idea comes up again and again in science and mathematics, and so scientists and mathematicians come to recognize, talk, and think about it easily. They refine that rough idea to greater precision, to the point they can quantify what they're doing. They distinguish different types of the idea: Some kinds of tiny changes stay constant, such as the water droplets from a leaky faucet, coming out at a steady rate. Other kinds of tiny changes don't stay constant: the changes *change*. So the water drips more slowly from the bucket as it runs out of fluid or the child gains height more slowly as he finishes adolescence. Like two similar flavors that a chef distinguishes, these are different types of rates of change that a scientist distinguishes: A constant rate of change and a decreasing (or increasing) rate of change.

Of course the refinement continues. For the faucet, the reason the water drips at a constant rate is that pressure pushing the drops out stays constant. For the bucket, the reason the water is dripping from the bottom is that it's being pushed through the hole by the water above it. The more water in the bucket, the higher the pressure pushing the water out. As the water drains out, the pressure decreases, so the water drips out more slowly. That's a pattern of change that comes up often in science: The amount of stuff determines how quickly the stuff changes. It comes up with rabbits reproducing (the more rabbits there are, the more quickly new rabbits appear); with cooling an oven (the greater the temperature of the oven, the more quickly it cools); with radioactive material (the more you have, the faster it decays), and many more.

Scientists who work with that pattern come to recognize and imagine it all at once, something like the way chefs come to notice flavor combinations. They can describe the pattern precisely with mathematics (the exponential function), which they can then use to derive implications and progress to more elaborate patterns of change. The basic patterns become resources for scientists, the way basic recipes become a resource for chefs, which they can then use to understand still more complicated things. In these ways, what starts as common sense about how small changes can build up to big changes (water dripping, a child growing) refines into the mathematics of calculus.

Of course it doesn't happen quickly, this refinement of ideas; it happens over years of experience—experience, that is, in the pursuit of clear, coherent, causal understandings of natural phenomena.

Refining Approaches to Reasoning

Scientists also refine their strategies for engaging in that pursuit, in their reasoning and their investigations. Earlier we talked about how, in some situations, students feel it is important to respond to counter-arguments they face, to reconcile apparently conflicting lines of reasoning. In those situations, they aren't happy just to find out the answer is Y, they want to know what went wrong with their reasoning for X. As scientists experience these sorts of situations, they learn to expect them and even plan for them. They become more deliberate and systematic in checking their ideas for consistency; they refine their sense of what it takes to have confidence that an idea is true. When they arrive at something that seems right, rather than experience that situation as a moment of conclusion, they learn to experience it as a moment for starting another kind of shopping for ideas: They look for concerns someone could raise to challenge that conclusion.

"Here's my idea," thinks a scientist. "What reasons could there be to disagree with it?" She doesn't just wait for someone else to disagree; she tries to do it herself. She shops for ideas in her own knowledge and experience that might conflict. Like a good lawyer, she anticipates carefully what another side might argue. When she finds something, she tries to figure out how to respond.

Suppose scientists want to find out whether living near high-voltage power lines causes cancer. Someone collects data in some region and finds that the people living near the power lines are more likely to have cancer. A novice might think that answers the question, but scientists know that there must be other arguments they'll need to be able to answer. So they need to start looking: What other explanations might account for the pattern in their data? In this case, maybe it's chance! So they need to figure out the probability of that rate of cancer happening just randomly. And there are other possibilities. If they collected the data with a door-to-door survey, maybe the researcher who canvassed that region was better able to get folks to talk about something so personal as their health? Or maybe people who are willing to live near power lines are more likely to smoke cigarettes, or less likely to have healthy diets?

As in all shopping for ideas, it takes imagination and perseverance to think up possibilities—what else might be causing this? The scientists need to anticipate those arguments and take those other variables into account. When they can, they "control" for those variables—so, for example, they should find out whether the pattern is still there if they only look at people who don't smoke, or people who eat well, and so on.

Similarly when they conduct experiments, scientists need to try things that will test possibilities someone might raise. So if they think that, say, having power lines nearby affects how plants grow, they could design an experiment to grow plants, some near power lines and some not, to see if it makes a difference.

They'd better test enough plants so that if they do find something, they'll be able to say the results weren't likely to happen by chance. They'll need to be sure to treat all of the plants the same way, aside from putting some near power lines. For example, they need to give the plants the same amount of water, otherwise how would they know it wasn't the water that caused the difference?

It's all about argumentation, and it's important to note that it's simply absurd to think of controlling for arbitrary variables! They only need to control for variables someone might argue would matter. Those are the variables for which someone might think there's a mechanism: It's plausible that chemicals or smoking or diet could play causal roles in cancer, so the scientists need to check for those possibilities.

Some science activities have students control for color, for example, in experiments about buoyancy, when nobody has produced any reason to think color might matter. The scientists studying power lines and cancer don't need to control for the names of people who live near power lines, or their astrological signs, or their tastes in music, because no scientist would argue that any of these things could affect whether someone gets cancer. If they're designing an experiment with plants, they don't need to control for what kind of clothing they wear to work, or the language they speak, or what movies they've seen.

Watching and listening to students, it would be good to notice when and how students see it as important to reconcile inconsistencies. When they believe they know the answer is Y, we notice and cultivate their asking why it isn't X. From there, we can try to notice and encourage them to shop for other ways of thinking that aren't immediately apparent, to shop through their minds for counterarguments to their current position, and from there to think about ways of responding. What we absolutely don't want is to teach students it's okay to dismiss ways of thinking without accounting for them, without explaining what exactly is wrong with those ways of thinking.

From Footholds to Principles

For most of our discussion in this chapter we've separated "ideas" and "approaches to reasoning," but for much of what happens in learning and science it's hard to do that, separate "content" and "process." We close with one more example of the refinement of everyday thinking, one in which the ideas and approaches are clearly connected.

We talked earlier about trying foothold ideas, as part of everyday thinking: If you're not sure what to believe, try supposing something and seeing what it implies. We talked about recognizing and supporting that form of everyday thinking as part of the beginnings of science, of students caring about coherence and, as important, willing and unafraid to think about an idea they're not yet positive is correct.

Foothold ideas can last for a moment, or for longer. As students or scientists set footholds and use them, they end up giving some higher priority than others. A foothold idea that's been working well—it fits with other ideas, or even better, it's made some successful predictions—can gain in status as something to believe. When there's a foothold we're pretty committed to accepting, then we'll work hard to reconcile other ideas and even evidence to fit with it.

The idea that the Earth was the stationary center of the universe was a great foothold idea for a long time. It fit with experience, evidence, and reasoning: No one could feel the Earth moving; everyone could see the Sun and the stars and the planets moving. When there was some new evidence and reasoning, from observations that the planets sometimes seem to move backward, it conflicted with the simple model. Scientists tried to reconcile the inconsistencies with ideas about "epicycles" of motion in the planets: The planets don't just move in circles around the Earth, they move in circles around the circles. It got complicated. To scientists today the idea seems silly, but it's critical to realize that it wasn't silly from scientists' perspective at the time.

It was perfectly appropriate for them to try to reconcile other ideas to fit with something that worked so well and made so much sense, that Earth was stationary. In fact, it would have been silly for them to just abandon that idea without a struggle. That remains the case today: Scientists don't abandon ideas easily that have a history of working well for them, and they shouldn't. If an idea makes sense and fits with many aspects of knowledge and experience, we shouldn't be quick to abandon it, even when there's evidence against it. First we should try to explain that evidence, account for it in ways that let us still believe that idea.

In the case of the orbits, explaining the objections got harder and harder, and scientists decided to try a different foothold: Earth orbits the Sun. Then the question was whether they could reconcile all the arguments and evidence that Earth was stationary. If we take it as a foothold that Earth is moving, how do we account for why we don't feel that motion? The answer came from a connection to another part of common sense, the one we mentioned earlier: If you're riding in a ship on smooth seas (or an airplane in smooth air), and you don't look outside, you can't tell you're moving. Galileo made that argument: Earth is moving smoothly through space, and we're all moving along with it, so we can't tell that we're moving. Over time, the idea that Earth orbits the Sun worked; all the other arguments and evidence either fit easily or could be adjusted to fit. Its implications led to new reasons to continue using it as a foothold—and all the reasons to disbelieve it could be reconciled.

In this way science makes progress toward coherence—toward systems of ideas that fit together and support each other. The ideas that Earth orbits the Sun and that we can't feel smooth, uniform motion fit together very well, along with other ideas, and as these ideas were successful in making sense of the work, scientists became more and more sure of them. That's what happens: When ideas we choose to believe work, we become more and more committed to those choices. So we work hard to reconcile other ideas to agree with those commitments. Not all ideas and evidence come into place easily, but they can be reconciled—we can adjust our understanding of them so that they work with the system.

Eventually we are so committed to some foothold ideas that we call them scientific principles or laws of nature, and we accept them as "true." That's what *truth* means, in science: The truth is what fits into a coherent system of thought and experience. It doesn't come one fact at a time. Science is the refinement of everyday thinking, from adaptive, flexible, context-sensitive common sense to principled coherence.

The Role of Responsive Teaching in the Refinement of Student Thinking

In this chapter, we've argued and given examples to show how everyday thinking is rich in productive resources for learning in science and for learning as science. We've argued that everyday knowledge is variable with context—it's not a single coherent system but a diverse, extensive collection. Different parts of common sense say different things, some in conflict with the concepts and some aligned. For that reason, much of learning—by students as by scientists—involves searching through that collection for ways of thinking, learning what's in there and taking advantage of what it has to offer, sorting through it, and often reorganizing. We've argued that everyday reasoning starts to do that, again variably with context. When it seems appropriate, we work to articulate and distinguish specific meanings, look for alternative ways of thinking, consider evidence, and try to reconcile inconsistencies.

Finally, we've tried to call attention to how students understand and experience what is taking place. How people think depends on what kind of situation they understand themselves to be in, what they think they are doing (and why), and what students imagine science class to be.

Seeing the Science in Students' Thinking

It's often surprising to adults how easy it is to get students engaged in thinking and talking about questions in science. But it's very easy, especially with younger children. They're surrounded by the natural world every moment of their lives. How could they *not* think about it, explore it, and talk about it?

It doesn't happen only in school. Parents who are alert to such things will hear their kids and their friends chatting about anything from day and night, to air and breathing, to lightening and electricity, to ice and water. Or they see kids trying little experiments—not the miming of "experiments," when they get random liquids and objects and mix them up to make a mess, but simply trying things to see what happens, which the students might not even associate with science. A ball bounces in a funny way off the wall, and they try to figure out how to make it happen again; a rainbow appears on the wall, and they try to figure out where it's coming from; they see an insect on the window and it occurs to them to wonder how it can stick there, or what it's doing, or what it eats.

So what can school do? One thing it can do, unfortunately, is to convince them to quit that stuff, at least when it comes to science class, and start "doing it right." That's a well-documented problem for secondary students: By the time students reach high school, most have learned to separate what they learn in science from their common sense. There are many reasons for this, not just school, but there's good reason to believe that the usual practices of science teaching have been part of the problem.

But it's clear that school can help. Teachers who genuinely attend and respond to students' inquiry can help them learn to use what they know—what they know both about the natural world and about knowledge and reasoning— and build from it. Naturally, this is a challenge for secondary science teachers. By high school, not only have students likely learned to think that science and common sense are mutually exclusive, but there are great demands for teachers to move students through a collection of "right answers" that will be assessed on high-stakes tests. It is precisely for these reasons that secondary science teachers should take as their focus attending and responding to students' inquiry. With so much of current schooling and students' experiences with science in school standing in the way, the secondary science teacher may be the last opportunity for many students to learn to experience science as a refinement of everyday thinking.

On to the Cases

The next chapter is quick, just a brief introduction and overview of the case studies with some general information and suggestions for how to use them. Then we turn to the case studies themselves, in chapters 4–8.

Using the videos and transcripts (and the student work in Chapter 7), you're going to be watching and listening to students' thinking. The challenges will be to attend to and interpret what's going through students' minds, what they might be thinking and what they might be trying to convey. That's the focus, the students' thinking, and the purpose of the cases is practice at recognizing and considering how to respond to the beginnings of science. This chapter has been a primer in what sorts of things there will be to see: Everyday ideas, everyday approaches to reasoning, and the ways in which students may be joining the pursuit that is science.

This, we suggest, is a little-discussed and essential part of teaching. What we see and hear in students' thinking affects our judgments about methods and strategies, both on-the-fly during class and in planning. The more perceptive and insightful we are in attending to students' thinking, the more accurate our diagnoses of what they need and the better off we are in deciding what to do.

These decisions will come up along the way in discussing the case studies: If you notice something about the students' thinking, what might you then choose to do? We will have things to say about general guidelines for focusing on student inquiry, but we're going to hold off with them until Chapter 9.

Using the Case Studies

The next five chapters are the case studies. Each chapter includes (1) a quick introduction to the case, with suggestions for organizing how participants watch the video (or review the student work, in Chapter 7); (2) the teacher's written account of the class and analysis of the students' thinking; and (3) specific commentary and suggestions for facilitating conversations about the case study. The videos, video transcripts, and student work are included in the online materials (*www.nsta.org/publications/press/extras/responsive.aspx*). We strongly recommend printing transcripts. Have the group follow along with them as you watch video; participants can take notes about what they see and use them for reference during conversations.

This chapter provides a brief overview of the set of cases and provides four suggestions for facilitating discussions and one suggestion about the order in which to use the materials within a given chapter.

Overview of the Set

There are four case studies with video and one with students' written work. Feel free to skip around, reordering them to fit your course or seminar. But we recommend starting with the first one; in our experience, it is the easiest one for participants to identify and interpret students' ideas, and so it serves as a good introduction to these practices.

Chapter 4, The Owls and the Snakes (1), is a case study by Sarah Henson of her ninth-grade biology class. Students were asked to consider an interesting biological phenomenon: A species of owl shares its nest with a species of blind snake. Sarah asked students to discuss the nature of the relationship between the two species—How did they end up inhabiting the same nests?—and students argued about their hypothesized relationships. Her case study focuses on the students' reasoning in that discussion; we provide transcripts and video and a copy of the handout that Sarah gave her students.

Chapter 5, The Owls and the Snakes (2), is a case study by Izzy Kovach of her secondary self-contained special education biology class talking about the same phenomenon described above. After asking her students to discuss their hypothesized relationships between the snakes and owls, Izzy presented them with data that they used to provide evidence for or against the different hypotheses. Her case study focuses on the students' reasoning in that discussion; we provide video, transcripts, and reproductions of the data Izzy gave her students. We chose this case study and the previous one partly because they approach the same content, using the same scenario, but differ in interesting ways. While the student thinking in Izzy's case can be a little harder to interpret, it is valuable in showing the potential that students with learning disabilities have for engaging in scientific reasoning. Furthermore, this case pushes participants to listen more closely to student ideas *because* they are often difficult to interpret.

Chapter 6, The Rime of the Ancient Mariner, is based on a video from Jennifer Tanner's class, in which students were trying to interpret lines from the poem "Rime of the Ancient Mariner" by Samuel Taylor Coleridge:

Water, water everywhere and all the boards did shrink

Water, water everywhere, nor any drop to drink

Students worked to explain what the lines mean, in particular the mechanisms behind the shrinking of the boards, and the reason not to drink salt water. Dan Levin wrote the case study based on an interview with Jenny while the two watched the tape together following the class. We provide video and transcripts. We chose this case study for three reasons: First, during a short time interval, students express many ideas, some of which lend themselves to varying interpretations; second, this is our one case in which the science content is central to both physical and biological secondary science courses; and third, we find that the students' ideas usually stimulate discussions among participants about science content, which is something we like to encourage.

Chapter 7, Free-Falling Bodies (1), is a case study by Matt Reese, who used a set of questions to explore ninth-grade physics students' intuitive ideas about force and motion. The question set was developed based on discussions among the physics teachers in the research project. The questions ask students to think about what would occur in various physical scenarios in which objects fall. (For example, if one full and one empty water bottle are dropped from the top of a building at the same time, which lands first, and why?) Instead of video, this case study includes samples of student's written work that Matt discusses in his case study.

Chapter 8, Free-Falling Bodies (2), is a case study by David Hovan, who used the same question set in his ninth-grade physics class. This case study focuses on Dave's interactions with his students as they worked through the questions on the sheet and the subsequent whole-class discussion. We provide video and transcripts.

Suggestions for Using the Case Studies

As you watch and read the case studies, please focus first on interpreting and appreciating the substance of what the students are thinking. This implicit—and sometimes explicit—plea from us as facilitators to teachers and prospective teachers expresses the main goal we have when using these case studies. The suggestions that follow are geared toward that goal. Many people are tempted to focus instead on what the teacher is doing rather than the students, or on what the students aren't thinking rather than what they are, or on general features of the students' behavior rather than the substance of what they are saying. These are certainly important topics, and we do spend time on them in our workshops and seminars. Our core purpose in this collection, however, is helping participants attend to students' ideas and reasoning.

So, for the rest of this chapter, we will elaborate on four general suggestions about facilitation and one practical suggestion about ordering:

1. Temper the impulse to evaluate the teacher.
2. Focus on understanding the students' thinking as inquiry.
3. Support interpretations with specific evidence from the case.
4. Recognize but tolerate incompleteness and uncertainty.
5. And finally a practical suggestion: Watch the video before reading the teacher's account. Each case study comes with its own detailed facilitators' notes. Please consult them as well, particularly if you are preparing to lead a seminar or a class.

1. Temper the Impulse to Evaluate the Teacher

The greatest challenge we've found to productive conversations is people's compulsion to evaluate the teaching. In our workshops this happens again and again, unless we do something to forestall it. After just three to five minutes of video, participants begin finding fault: The teacher ignored one student or focused too much on another; the teacher hasn't had them conduct an experiment or clarified the question or given the students enough background information; the teacher hasn't shared some relevant data with the students; the teacher should first have them talk in groups, or draw diagrams, or record observations. Some of these criticisms may point to valid issues to consider, but there are several reasons to be cautious.

Quick Criticism Is Often Naïve

To an observer, it can seem perfectly clear what the teacher should do, but that's almost always because the observer has limited information. If it seems obvious when watching the video that the teacher should call on the girl who's raising her hand, it could be because we don't know that girl; maybe she's *always* raising her hand, and the teacher is trying to draw out a student who rarely participates. Someone's opinion that the teacher should use this technique or that, from a general sense of "best practices," may not be justified for this particular class for any of a number of reasons. Or, maybe, the teacher *does* use that technique, just not in these few minutes of video.

Rather than cast judgment, we should cultivate habits of asking why those choices might have seemed appropriate to the teacher. What might the teacher have been seeing and thinking, and what is the critic seeing and thinking that differs? What perceptions and interpretations of the students' reasoning underlie the teacher's actions and the critic's concerns? It's more difficult work to imagine what things might have looked like from the teacher's perspective, but it's important to do.

Even having much more information, particular choices in particular classes are always uncertain. Maybe if the teacher had chosen to conduct the experiment or shared some data more quickly, the students would have lost out on the rich discussion they were having; maybe if she'd organized them into groups, some would not have known what to do; maybe if she'd given more clarification it would have shifted their attention more toward her thinking than their own.

So rather than drawing conclusions about what the teacher *should have done*, we encourage participants to try to think in terms of possibilities, what the teacher *could have done*, recognizing all along that none of us has any way of knowing what the effects of any choice would have been. We speak of coming up with "menus of possibilities" for how teachers might respond, the metaphor of a menu to help us remember that there's always more than one reasonable way to proceed.

Quick Criticism Discourages Teachers From Letting Anyone Examine Their Practices

The second reason to temper the impulse to evaluate is that it can negatively affect the participants. Teaching is an uncertain craft, and teachers who are brave and generous enough to let others examine their practices are setting themselves up for criticism. Sharing one's own classroom video is not an easy thing to do, and sometimes it's the people least willing to do it themselves who are the most judgmental. We recommend that participants discuss the case study as if the teacher were in the room, because *teachers are in the room*, and they shouldn't leave the conversation thinking, "Whew, I'm never letting anyone watch me!" Our hope is that teachers and student teachers using these materials eventually begin to share video and student work from their own classes, without fearing that they will be judged and unconstructively criticized.

We recommend this nonjudgmental stance for facilitators and teachers as well, reflecting on their own teaching: Don't evaluate your actions by unattainable criteria. It is impossible to know how students will respond, so lessons won't generally "go as planned." Nor is it possible to follow every opportunity that comes up in class, so some will be lost. If teachers torment themselves for everything they missed or every choice they would have made differently, then examining their own teaching will be painful for reasons that simply aren't valid. Looking back, a teacher will *always* see things she hadn't noticed in class and think of other ways she might have acted. That's good! It will give her things to consider in planning ahead.

Evaluating the Teacher Draws Attention Away From the Students

We've suggested it's important to be careful and respectful about criticizing the teacher. But for our purposes, it's also important to be careful about *praising* the teacher. Evaluations of the *teaching*, whether favorable or unfavorable, sidetrack the discussion from focusing on the substance of the students' thinking.

To be clear: the teachers in our project worked hard to give students opportunities to express their ideas and reasoning and to try to attend and respond to their students' thinking. In that respect, we're proud of the teaching represented by these cases. But as much as we'd like to celebrate what the teachers are doing, we want to focus the conversations on what the students are doing. In principle, for our purposes, we *could* have included cases in which teachers dismissed or ignored students' incorrect ideas, as long as the classroom discussions included evidence of those ideas. That's why we try to redirect assessments of the teacher, even favorable ones, to the students: What perceptions and interpretations of the students' reasoning underlie the teacher's actions and the observers' assessments?

Avoiding judgmental evaluations of the teaching isn't the only reason to redirect discussions away from focusing on the teacher. And indeed, even if they're not being judgmental, people in our seminars tend to focus initially on the teacher's strategies. We expect many participants using these case studies will do the same, initially noticing the teachers and their methods, notably the format of the discussions. Of course, we're happy if case studies give teachers ideas for strategies. For this book to be of greater value, though, participants will need to shift their attention from what the teacher is doing to what the students are doing. The teachers didn't collect video snippets to demonstrate methods; they collected snippets to show student thinking. So, for example, you'll see more full-class discussions in these cases than you would by dropping in on the teachers' classes, where you'd be just as likely to see students writing, experimenting in small groups, discussing in pairs, and so on. This book features whole-class discussions simply because they are an efficient way to hear many students' ideas in a manageable (20–40 minute) video clip.

It's not because we think all science teaching should be in the form of full-class discussions!

Of course teachers will want help with thinking about how to implement various types of activities to open space for student thinking. Many excellent books and websites address these kinds of teaching methods. This book, by contrast, focuses on providing rich examples of students' thinking and materials for facilitating discussions about that thinking, filling a niche in which there isn't already an abundance of materials.

So, try to keep the focus on the students. It might help to encourage participants to view suggestions aimed at the teacher as arising from interpretations of the students' ideas. For example, when a participant thinks "she should have taught them about X first," it could be because something in the video makes the participant think the students don't know about X. So structure the conversation around that, around what the participant has seen or heard and how she or he has interpreted it. Then the group can move on to talk about ways to respond.

2. Focus on Understanding the Students' Thinking as Inquiry

By "focus on understanding students' thinking," we mean more than just attention to the particular conceptual ideas students express. We also encourage a focus on the components of scientific thinking discussed in Chapter 2: the students' sense of mechanism, their shopping for ideas and attention to clarity and consistency. How are they using and looking for evidence? How are they reasoning from what else they know? What sense are they making, and how are they articulating it?

For many people, paying that kind of attention makes a lot of sense in the abstract; they recognize those kinds of thinking to be what science is all about. But when they get down to cases, they focus instead on other things: How are the students behaving? How many of them actually speak or look like they're paying attention? These issues are certainly important, and of course participants will flag them and you'll talk about them. Our experience, though, is that most people have an easier time seeing these aspects of what's happening than they do thinking about the particular things students say. So, for example, in Chapter 6, when Grace says that salt dissolves in water and Andrew responds, "But not the salt water in the ocean," don't let yourself off the hook of trying to figure out what he might be thinking and why he might be thinking that, just because the students and Jenny (the teacher) don't seem to be paying attention to his idea. Our purpose in choosing these cases is precisely to help teachers and student teachers get practice in understanding what students say, in a space where the teachers can discuss their interpretations. Of course it's important whether the students are listening to Andrew, or whether Jenny is attending and responding to his ideas. But at least initially, we encourage you to focus the discussion on a harder task: using the data that is available, in that moment in the classroom, to think about Andrew's reasoning.

Another challenge for many people is analyzing what the students are thinking beyond an assessment of whether they are correct. Some experienced science educators get caught up in the hunt for misconceptions, as we discussed in Chapter 2, attending to student thinking in order to find its flaws. They notice the students' ideas and they compare them to scientists' ideas, looking for similarities and differences between students' and scientists' "conceptions" rather than looking at how students are engaging in inquiry. Sometimes, too, people want to talk about what the students are *not* saying or thinking, rather than on understanding what students *are* saying and thinking.

Our suggestion to focus on students' thinking means making a concerted effort to understand and appreciate the *students' sense* of what's happening. When a student says something that sounds strange, the challenge is to understand what he might mean by that and why he might think it was reasonable. Sometimes the best interpretation will be that he was just joking, or he was only mimicking knowledge he didn't really have; but sometimes it will be that he's onto something wonderful. One way we sometimes try to help teachers get started is by suggesting they imagine the students are *brilliant*, and therefore we should hang on their every word, trying to understand their meaning. For instance, when Andrew says, "not the salt water in the ocean," try taking it seriously in the way you would if we knew him to be gifted: What might he mean?

3. Support Interpretations With Specific Evidence From the Case

When participants are interpreting students' thinking, encourage them to make a point of identifying the particular statements or aspects of students' behavior that support the interpretation.

Often people's ideas about the students come from general expectations rather than from the case study itself. Case studies are valuable, however, because they allow participants to focus on the evidence at-hand, which sometimes defies expectations. In fact, running workshops on these, we commonly observe participants' expectations getting challenged by what they see. It's not unlike how we hope students will approach science: Check your expectations against the data at-hand, and be ready for the possibility that they will not match.

In our conversations, we focus closely on specific things students say, and it's not unusual or inappropriate to spend 10 minutes or more talking about a single statement, such as when Sarah Henson's student Aaron responds to another student's hypothesis for the relationship between the owls and snakes by saying, "I know what he's talking about, so it's 50-50." That may seem strange, to devote so much attention to a student's wording. In school, teachers clearly can't stop class to analyze every utterance. Nor, certainly, can they rewind and listen again, to see if maybe they misheard. But that's the whole point—to do something teachers can't do during class. A team of medical school students does similar things with a given piece of information from a medical case; the students debate its meaning and significance to the diagnosis, in ways they can't do in real time with patients, whom they'll see for a short time with no colleagues present.

We also like to compare what we do with student thinking to what scientists do with specimens. No one would find it strange to see a geologist poring at length over a single rock, or an entomologist over a moth, or a botanist over a leaf. Examining a specimen closely can help scientists develop new understandings. That's just what we hope to achieve in poring over moments of student thinking.

Typically, we find that participants, when first getting started, don't notice very much about the detailed substance of students' reasoning. As they progress, participants notice more and more, and they gain new appreciation for students' ideas, reasoning, and abilities.

4. Recognize but Tolerate Incompleteness and Uncertainty

The first part of this suggestion is to remember that a case study only tells you so much. The video portions vary from 20 to 40 minutes, which is a small sampling; this is why we call them "snippets." The teachers provide background information about the snippets, but there's only so much they can include, even about the preceding classes. Only so much information is available in the case study. More information might help participants interpret a student's thinking, or understand the teacher's interpretation. Even a flood of information, however, wouldn't eliminate the uncertainties of interpretation.

Nonetheless, we think it's important to proceed regardless of whether teachers feel they have enough information to make interpretations. Initially, some people balk at interpreting what a student meant, because they feel it's hopeless: "How can we *possibly* be sure?" One response to this concern is to think of science, where we're used to the idea that uncertainty cannot be completely eliminated. It's okay not to be sure! Another response is that it's often surprising how much progress a group can make interpreting student's thinking from the available evidence. And still another response: participants benefit from lingering and mulling over a student's comment just to consider the possibilities for what it might mean, in particular to discover possibilities beyond what people first noticed. Maybe a student's ridiculous-seeming comment actually has something to it. And when talking about the case study with colleagues, the main goal is to understand others' interpretations; it's not important that everyone agree.

5. Look at the Data First

We end with this practical suggestion, the easiest one to implement. By "the data," we refer to the evidence of student thinking in the video, transcripts, and student work. Have participants read the introduction to the case study for background information about the class, but hold off reading the rest of the case until *after* watching the video. That will let participants form their own impressions and come to their own interpretations, to practice seeing and hearing students' inquiry, which of course is the main point. If possible, participants should watch the video with colleagues, to hear a range of impressions. That's what we do in our workshops and seminars: we show a segment of video and ask participants to discuss what they saw in the students' inquiry.

After the discussion, participants should go back to the case study and read what the teacher had to say—what she was thinking during class, how she interpreted various student's ideas, what different ideas came up later (after the videotaped snippet). After reading, participants almost always see some things differently and some things the same; there's no one right set of interpretations and events to notice. As we've said, it's okay to disagree, but everyone should try to understand the rationale behind other people's interpretations.

As we think you'll see, or you may already know, video recording adds greatly to the sorts of discussions people can have about classroom interactions. The camera doesn't catch everything, not by any means, but it does provide a rich and immediate sense of the class. You'll be able to hear the tone in students' voices and see the expressions on some of their faces. It's not the same as being there, but in some ways it's better: You can play and replay the video, follow along in the transcript, and stop the action whenever you like.

The videos are captioned, so participants can choose to follow along on the screen or read along in the transcript. You'll notice that these are not professional recordings! In most cases, a member of the project staff visited the class and taped it with one or two home-quality digital cameras. Even if we were professional videographers, or could hire them, we might have chosen the approach we've taken, to be less intrusive in class and less "produced" in the final product. If participants are inspired to try recording themselves, perhaps with help from each other, that's great! That's how we got two of the four videos in this collection: Izzy and Sarah, along with the other members of the biology cohort of the project, decided to videotape themselves in their classrooms teaching symbiotic relationships through the study of the owls and snakes. We'll give a few tips on how to go about video recording in Chapter 9.

C HAPTER 4

The Owls and the Snakes (1)

This is the first in a pair of cases about classes on the same topic, a question developed by Izzy Kovach, one of the more experienced teachers in the project. She found an article about a "novel commensalism" wherein live, blind snakes live unharmed in screech owls' nests, and used it to create a question for student inquiry. Izzy's case study is in the next chapter. We start with this case, rather than Izzy's, because it shows students discussing the question when it is first introduced. Izzy's case study shows a class examining the evidence presented in the article to consider the various explanations that students have already proposed.

At the time of this class snippet, Sarah Henson was in her second year of classroom teaching. She attended the Masters Certification program at the University of Maryland, and received a teaching credential while teaching high school biology part-time. That program emphasized attention to student thinking, so it was an easy transition for her to join the research project[1] when she graduated.

Sarah was particularly interested in involving her students in scientific argumentation, and, as part of that goal, in helping them learn to listen and respond to each other's ideas. She heard about how Izzy had been using this question to do just that sort of thing, and decided to try it herself at the beginning of the school year—her first year as a full-time teacher.

The main data for this case study include the video and accompanying transcript (available at *www.nsta.org/publications/press/extras/responsive.aspx*). Sarah's written case study begins after Suggestions for Reading and Viewing. We recommend that a group studying the case study start by reading only the introduction of the case to get some background information about the class; stop after reading the handout, "A Mystery Relationship." Then read the transcript of the conversation, and/or watch at least some of the video, before continuing with the rest of Sarah's account. This gives participants a chance to recognize and interpret the students' thinking for themselves, before reading Sarah's perspective.

---

1. This research project is described in Chapter 1.

Suggestions for Reading and Viewing

Be sure to make copies of the transcript, included in full on the website. Even if you're watching the video, the transcript is useful for following along, for jotting notes, and for reference in conversations about the snippet with others.

Before we present the conversation that took place in Sarah's class, we usually show participants the handout she gave the students (Figure 4.1, p. 58), and provide time for them to discuss the relationship themselves. The snippet is 25 minutes long. When we use this case in pedagogy courses, seminars, and workshops, we stop reading or watching the students' conversation at two or three spots in order to encourage participants' close, careful examination of student thinking:

1. *Line 56, approximately 5 minutes in, when Michelle says, "No" and laughs.* We usually stop here and ask participants to discuss what has happened so far and to think about the following questions: How do you think it's going? What do you notice in students' ideas and reasoning? Does their thinking seem scientific?

2. *Line 114, about 11 minutes in, after Robert says, "Uh, it could be part of their nest..."* In this section, there are occasionally disagreements about what a student means. Such disagreements are a great opportunity to ask participants if there is any other evidence to draw on to determine what a student means.

3. *Line 155, when Michelle says, "It doesn't matter if your eyes are open."* Sometimes we stop it here too, and sometimes we just show the rest of the clip. Regardless of where we stop, we ask participants to consider the "menu of possibilities" of where the teacher might go next. What ideas might be worth following up on? How might the teacher structure the next part of the conversation, or the next activity, based on the ideas she has heard?

National Science Teachers Association

The Case Study: A Mystery Relationship

By Sarah Henson

Background

This is a case study from my second year teaching biology at a suburban high school in Maryland. This school had been closed for 20 years, but it recently reopened to handle the overflow in student population of neighboring schools. Now it has about 1,300 students, fairly equally mixed among African American, Latino, and Caucasian students, with a minority of Asian students. Students take eight classes per semester, which meet on alternating days for 85 minutes each. The school has met AYP every year in the three since it reopened.

When I started at the school, I was teaching part-time while working on my Masters degree at the University of Maryland. In my science pedagogy classes at Maryland, I had gotten interested in looking at how I could get my students to make scientific arguments, particularly to listen to each other's ideas and to respond to each other with scientific evidence. In one case study I wrote for my graduate program, I compared an "honors" biology class, with an "on-level" biology class during similar classroom discussions. (In my school "on-level" is a euphemism for lower academic track.)

During the discussions, I thought that the honors class was doing a lot better—certainly a lot more students were talking. When I went back and looked at both videos, however, I was surprised. Although the honors students were talking more, a lot of them were just repeating the same things, sort of "piling on" rather than considering the ideas critically. In the on-level class, fewer people were participating, but the ones who were seemed really to be listening to each other, responding with counter-arguments, and then posing their own ideas. I think that we often underestimate what on-level students can do in biology classes, and so we don't often engage them in the same challenging scientific inquiry that we do with our honors class. I decided that I really wanted to push argumentation in all my classes in the second year, and I really wanted to see what my on-level students, in particular, could do if they were asked to argue regularly.

This is a case study of a relatively small, on-level biology class that met for 85 minutes during the last period of every other day. It was composed of 10th and 11th graders who were taking biology for the first time, except for two seniors who were repeating the semester after failing last year.

This lesson was from the third class session at the very beginning of the school year. The first two class sessions were dedicated to experimental methods, so this was our first look at content specific to ecology, our first unit. I wanted students to have a first experience of scientific argumentation, and I hoped it would also get them starting to think about symbiotic relationships.

The Owls and the Snakes

The idea for this lesson came from Izzy Kovach, another teacher in the biology group organized by the people at University of Maryland. When I started working with the group in the summer, I heard about the conversation Izzy had led with her students about the curious relationship among the "owls and snakes." It seemed like a good way to get students to argue about a real biological question, and to draw on their experience to come up with explanations for the relationship. I decided not to introduce the vocabulary that the curriculum required (symbiosis, mutualism, commensalism, predator-prey, and parasitism) until after the students had discussed the relationship, thinking this would help them think without being tied to the particular words. I also thought this might help them associate the vocabulary with the particular relationships when they learned it afterward.

To start, I asked students to recall and share any background knowledge they had about owls and snakes. They provided information about snakes, such as what food they eat, that some are venomous, and that some are able to wrap themselves around their prey to constrict breathing. Information they provided about owls included things they eat, how much they can swivel their necks, that they are wise, and that they are nocturnal. In the course of the discussion on what the two organisms eat, students pointed out that they eat some of the same things (small rodents) and also that an owl could eat a snake. During this time, I just listened to the students' ideas, and tried not to correct them. I really wanted to begin to create an environment in which students felt comfortable sharing their ideas without fear of being judged as right or wrong.

We also talked a little bit about relationships in general. I wanted them to think about what it meant to have a relationship in the everyday sense. I think students have relationships with family members, friends, authority figures, and pets that can help them to think about biological relationships.

Finally, I gave students the handout presenting a "mystery relationship" between screech owls and snakes [p. 58]. I told them it was a real-life situation that scientists do not fully understand, and I gave the students three tasks: extract facts from the brief written scenario, use those facts to develop an argument that describes the relationship between the snakes and owls, and note any additional information they would like to know about the situation. I had them do this in writing, and then I started a class discussion to have students share, contest, and further develop their arguments.

The conversation took off! So many students had so many ideas to share that it was a challenge to keep track of it all. During the class, I felt like I had a hard time following all the arguments. I just tried to keep them talking, and to get them to listen and respond to each other. After a while, they kind of ran out of steam. Michelle even said, "I'm all argued out," and at that point I wasn't sure what to do. So for this case study, I decided to look more carefully at the transcript for the beginning of the discussion, to see if I could untangle some of the arguments that I had a hard time following in the moment.*

*This is a good point to stop reading, watch the video, and talk about the student thinking.

The Students' Ideas

The first idea I noticed was Diana's, who said, "The mother might not have noticed that the snakes wouldn't harm her eggs, so she just kind of let them stay." Avish pointed out that they were smaller than the eggs, which is great, because I think he was supporting Diana's idea by giving evidence that the snakes weren't harming anyone. Robert put forth two new ideas, saying that (1) maybe the snakes eat up eggshells or bugs that come around the nest, and (2) maybe the snakes gave off heat. I thought these gave us some good ways we could go, and I asked if anybody wanted to respond. Aaron spoke up.

> Aaron: It's kind of confusing, I know what he's talking about, so it's 50-50. I can understand that snakes protect it, by like acting like a shield from other predators, that want to steal the egg and eat it, so that the snake was in the nest, other predators won't go after the egg, since the snake is probably going to eat that other predator.
>
> Sarah: Ok.
>
> Aaron: So the owl would just leave it there and leave it alone to provide that extra shield.
>
> Sarah: Ok, so this is like- this is kind of a new argument, Aaron, right? You think that the snakes are up there for protection. They're protecting the eggs?

Figure 4.1

A Mystery Relationship

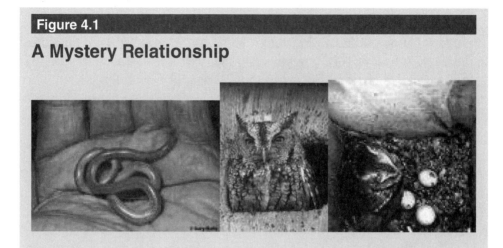

A biologist specializing in screech owls found a nest that contained both owl eggs and – of all things – snakes! While some snakes are known to eat bird eggs, these snakes were too small. They also had an unusual characteristic – they were naturally blind. As she watched the nest for a few days, the biologist noticed that the mother owl allowed the snakes to live in the nest unharmed. This seemed strange, since owls generally eat snakes or feed them to their young. The biologist had a hard time explaining this unexpected owl behavior.

Can you explain the relationship between the owl and the snakes?

Facts/Evidence:

Argument (create an argument about what you think is going on, based on the evidence you listed above):

What other information would help you solve this puzzle?

> Aaron: Yeah.

Initially, it seemed like Aaron was going to respond directly to Robert's argument. He said, "I know what he's talking about, so it's 50-50." I don't know what he meant by "50-50," but he said it often. Maybe it was Aaron's form of verbal stalling, like saying "Ummm." Maybe he was still processing what Robert said, forming his own response, or weighing the options.

But the rest of what Aaron had to say didn't talk about Robert's ideas at all, which makes me wonder if he'd really been listening. I think he was just making his own argument that the snakes were protectors, and wasn't really responding to Robert. I'm glad that Aaron was engaged and eager to share his own arguments; on the other hand the rest of the class didn't get to follow up on Robert's argument.

There was, however, a very interesting exchange around Aaron's idea about protection, and I remember being excited about it in the moment. I thought they were really beginning to question the legitimacy of some of the ideas.

> Sarah: Wh- who agrees or disagrees? Michelle?
>
> Michelle: I disagree because one, they're blind. And two they're smaller than the eggs so how are they really supposed to protect ...

Michelle's comment was in direct response to Aaron's argument. She clearly heard what Aaron said, and was attempting to disprove it by providing two facts (that the snakes are blind, and that they are smaller than the eggs). Perhaps because her counter-argument was so intelligible, Aaron was immediately ready to fire back with a defense. I encouraged the exchange, but tried to slow it down and track their ideas in writing on the board. This is most of what they said, with some intervening lines deleted so that it's easier to follow:

> Aaron: But since the snakes can pick up heat around other things, around the um, area, they can like detect um a prey nearby and pick it up and snap it up.
>
> Michelle: Um, but still, they're still small and we don't know if they're venomous or not, so how are they supposed to protect?
>
> Several moments later Michelle had something else to say.
>
> Michelle: We don't know what they can do, like, can they like, bite? Can they constrict? What are they going to do to protect?

> Aaron: They'll constrict. But I'm not sure about the biting part but I think they can detach, detach their jaw.... and make their mouth wider. But there's a 50-50 chance of killing themselves as well.

Again Aaron used his "50-50" phrase. Was he considering two possibilities—that the snakes can detach their jaws and either live or die in the process of doing so? It seems more likely to me that he was stalling again in order to give himself the time to weigh the implications of his previous comments and form what it was that he wanted to say.

Navarre got into the argument, suggesting that maybe if there were a lot of snakes, they could guard the nest, which I thought was great, but none of the students picked up on it. Robert reiterated his idea about the snakes eating the bugs that could do damage to the eggs, but he also responded to Michelle's counter-argument to Aaron earlier, saying that it was irrelevant whether or not the snakes were blind, because, "there are millions of animals that are blind, but eat other animals."

The next idea came from Bob and Navarre, who suggested that maybe the owls were just waiting for the snakes to get bigger so they could eat them. I'm not sure if they meant the parent owls would eat the snakes or the little owls would, but Robert didn't think much of that idea.

> Robert: I think if uh, the snakes were the species that got bigger, that'd probably either mean they were babies or they weren't fully mature, so I think that that would have been said here that they weren't fully mature snakes, you know?

This seemed pretty sensible. Robert was basically saying that these must be fully mature snakes, "otherwise that would have been said here." Aaron also had an objection to that idea, but it took him a while to get it out. The ideas seemed to come to him all of sudden, and he started talking before I called on him.

> Sarah: Aaron, what were you going to say?
>
> Aaron: I would have to disagree on the waiting for the snakes to get big.
>
> Sarah: Ok.
>
> Aaron: By that time, the snake might have moved on to- by a different place, just in case this attempt didn't sell.
>
> Sarah: Ok.

Aaron: So, if the snake was thinking ahead, like the owls going to take its life away, so it wants to um, move on.

I'm not really sure what Aaron was saying here, I think maybe he was thinking about the snake weighing its options. I don't know what he meant by "in case this attempt didn't sell," but maybe he was thinking back to Robert's idea, and "not selling" would be like not succeeding in finding anything to eat. Then, if the snake was "thinking ahead," it could plan to get out of there before the owl ate it. He seemed to be thinking about a conscious decision on the part of the snakes.

I made a last call for initial arguments and Robert said "Um, I don't have a reason for it, but snakes lose their skins every several months." Even though he did not present this information in the form of an argument that helped to explain the relationship, he thought it was important enough to bring into the discussion. I liked that at the time, and I liked it again later when I watched the tape. I also thought it was great that he said "I don't have a reason for it," by which I think he meant that he *recognized* that he was only providing a piece of information, not reasoning.

I think the importance of Robert's comment here is twofold. First, it demonstrates an atmosphere of collective problem solving, where individuals are willing to put forth pieces of information, even if their ideas are not fully formed. This requires an environment where students feel comfortable sharing even when they don't have a fully formed or "correct" idea. Second, this type of participation gets to the very heart of our scientific culture, which is dependent upon peer involvement, upon students like Robert who are willing to share information as well as to hear what others have to say about it.

I gave students a chance to respond to Robert's idea, and Michelle and Navarre had new things to say. The discussion eventually came back to Robert, where he built on his initial thought.

Sarah: Ok, so we have a new factor to throw in. How might that affect things?

Robert: I don't know yet, it's more complicated.

Sarah: Anybody else? (Aside when student comes into the room) How-who's got an idea? How would snakes shedding their skin play into this?

Michelle: When they shed their skin, don't they get bigger?

The Owls and the Snakes (1)

> Sarah: When they shed their skin, do they get bigger? Why do they shed their skin?
>
> Navarre: That is kind of disgusting. They just start to like go, skin just crawls off them as they go...
>
> Sarah: So I think that it has something to do with growth, that they try to- they get too big for their skin and they- it plays a role in their shedding.
>
> Robert: It becomes part of their nest, because different animals build different...(disruption to remind the class to be respectful to others).
> Uh it could be part of the nest because different animals uses different things to build their nest and it could be possible that it becomes part of the owl's nest.

Maybe just hearing his peers discuss different aspects of the idea aloud gave Robert some time to think, and helped him recognize what role this piece of information may have in the situation. He ended up suggesting that the owls would benefit from having the snakes there by using their skin to help construct (or repair) their nests. To me, this was a pretty interesting idea, because unlike all of the other ideas, it suggested that the owls were benefiting from something that the snakes *produce*, and not just their potential as food or for protection. It's a sensible idea, and there are examples of this sort of thing in the natural world, for example, in the way ants protect aphids that produce "honeydew" that the ants can eat.

I continued following along with the things I had asked them to write down on the handout. The handout asked, "What other information would help you solve this puzzle?" I really wanted the students to ask questions that would help them figure out the relationship, but I found that I needed to guide them to do this. For example, Diana asked, "How many snakes were in the nest?" When I asked her why that was important to know, she responded, "Because you'd know like how many snakes are like on the eggs and stuff." I pressed her to explain what that would make her say about the relationship, but she didn't have a ready answer. Maybe she was thinking that if there were a lot of snakes it might support Navarre's earlier idea that multiple snakes could work together to provide protection for the owl eggs.

Mostly, students had questions about how the owls or the biologist knew the snakes were blind (a discussion I had started as an example of a question). Robert had an interesting question that he tied to his earlier argument. He wanted to know what the snakes eat, or how they're eating. As with Diana, I pressed him on how that was going to affect what he thought. Again, I've taken out some of the intervening lines to try to capture Robert's whole thought.

> Sarah: Ok, how's that going to- Robert, make an argument about that. How's that going to affect what you think?
>
> Robert: Because we're going to find out about the snakes depending on that.
>
> Sarah: So, do you think the first one is depending on the second one? Or do you think the second one is-
>
> Robert: Well, I mean, it's not for sure but it just leads … It just kind of leads …. might not be exact but you know it could … it's just one-one reason. Because if the- if the owl built its nest around the snakes ... we know that the owl wanted to be around the snakes.
>
> Sarah: Ok.
>
> Robert: They're staying, and the owl let them stay, then obviously the snakes are depending on the owl.

I don't think it's exactly clear from Roberts' explanation how he thought that knowing what the snakes eat would help him answer the question; he only said that it suggests that the owls "wanted to be around the snakes" and that "snakes are depending on the owl." Earlier he'd thought the snakes might eat insects in the nest that could damage the eggs, and he might have been trying to support that idea.

I never did tell the students the "right" answer, mostly because I didn't know myself at the time. (I hadn't yet read the paper that Izzy found). Also, I didn't want that to be the focus of the conversation—getting to an official answer. I wanted them to get started at having a science talk, to listen to each other, to challenge and support others' ideas. I think they did that pretty well, and that's what I was hoping for. After the discussion, I presented the vocabulary of biological relationships that we're expected to teach in the curriculum (symbiosis, mutualism, commensalism, parasitism, predator-prey), and asked them to apply the terms to the ideas that had come up in the discussion.

Reflections

Like I said, I found everything kind of hard to follow during the class, although I had a sense that there were a lot of good ideas, and even some responses to ideas and the beginnings of arguments. As I continue to teach, I hope to get better at that, keeping up with the action, hearing ideas and being able to respond on the fly. Watching later, I was all the more impressed. These were on-level students, and this was our first try at having this kind of conversation. I especially like the interaction between Aaron and Michelle about the snakes as protectors, and I think it shows the potential for productive scientific discourse among students.

At the same time, I could see that some of the students would pose new arguments instead of directly responding to the argument at-hand, like when Aaron gave his own idea instead of responding to Robert's. That's something to work on. Maybe Aaron and other students are so preoccupied with their own thoughts that they have trouble listening to others. I tried to display the arguments at hand at the front of the classroom, to help students focus on it, but it might help to have students talk with scrap paper at hand, to keep track of their arguments, and to write down their ideas they want to bring up later. In general, I try to encourage students to write down ideas, to give a little "wait-time" to people who might be thinking more slowly.

Additionally, is there a way, and would it be productive, to hold students responsible for actually hearing what their peers are saying? While we had previously discussed being respectful to each other, were the students aware that when one of their peers is talking, the expectation is not just that they be quiet, but also that they be listening and considering the idea being presented?

Facilitators' Notes

Please see the general notes for facilitators in Chapter 3. Here we'll provide specific comments and suggestions with respect to discussing the video at the recommended stopping points, the rest of the snippet, and the teacher's case study. Our purpose here isn't to present a thorough analysis of the snippet but to give a sense of possible topics and issues that might arise or that a facilitator might bring up.

What Is the Nature of the Relationship Between the Owls and the Snakes?

Often, especially if we have 90 minutes or more to spend on the case study, we will have participants discuss what they think is the nature of the relationship between the owls and the snakes before they see what students said. (Later in this chapter, we explain what researchers think, and we provide the citation to the article for people to read if interested.) Sometimes we distribute the

handout Sarah uses in the class, to pose the question; other times we have just described the question in words. We haven't noticed a difference in the teachers' thinking about the question, but the handout often generates discussion about instruction, even before the teachers see the video of the students talking about it. For this reason, it might make sense to wait until you show the video to provide the handout, as the focus on instruction may distract participants from their *own* ideas and reasoning. If you do use the handout, it might make sense to remind participants up front that they'll have time to discuss instruction at a later point, as it relates to the student ideas in the video.

Suggestions of Possible Relationships

The initial suggestions of possible relationships are usually similar to what the students talk about in the case study. It usually comes up that the snakes might be eating parasites in the nest that could harm the eggs. Someone typically suggests that the snakes are somehow scaring off predators or that the owls might be keeping the snakes for the new hatchlings to eat. People usually challenge these last two ideas by asking what the snakes get out of it, which can lead to a discussion about whether or not the snakes need to get something out of it. We try to help keep track of the arguments by writing them on the board or on an easel.

The only problem we've encountered is when some participants have made suggestions others find laughable, such as that the owls are keeping the snakes as pets. It's as important in workshops as it is in class that everyone feels safe and respected, so we make a point of considering the ideas seriously. And there are other reasons for taking these ideas seriously; they are not so far-fetched. For example, we've pointed out there are documented cases of cross-species companionship in the natural world, such as an orangutan treating a cat as a "pet."

Use of Vocabulary

Especially if there are experienced biology teachers, we begin to hear some of the vocabulary that people read in textbooks. When this happens, we often write the words on the board, and ask people to explain what they mean.

The vocabulary that comes up most often are the terms *symbiosis*, *mutualism*, and *parasitism*. People sometimes remember that there can be a relationship in which one organism benefits but the other does not, and they often come up with examples, but few people know the biologists' term (*commensalism*) unless they've already taught the material. There's usually some discussion of whether there's a distinction between *symbiosis* and *mutualism*.[2] When this comes up, we usually try to move participants toward consensus on what words we should use *for our discussion*, regardless of their "official" meaning.

---

2. *Symbiosis* is usually used as a general term for any kind of biological relationship among species in which at least one species benefits from the relationship by improving its reproductive fitness. *Mutualism* refers to a relationship in which both species benefit.

Sometimes this discussion of vocabulary prompts a conversation about how important the vocabulary is, or whether it's important at all. One option is to hold off on this conversation until after watching at least part of the video, so it can be grounded in what the students actually do and say. When we have had the conversation, most people generally say that it's not that important for thinking about relationships, but it usually also comes up that this vocabulary might be important for scientists to communicate with each other; it always comes up that the vocabulary is probably required for exams.

Questions of Evidence

If we go on for a while, people start to ask questions of the facilitator to try to figure out the relationship. How do the snakes get there? What happens when the eggs hatch? What do the owls eat?

Often someone points out that it's difficult to resolve the discussion without more information. We acknowledge this limitation, but point out that it often happens in fieldwork that a journal is incomplete; perhaps the researcher who found the snakes was there to study some other aspect of screech owls, so this was a new discovery. It would be a genuine, reasonable objective for ecologists to think about what further information would help resolve the question, and so it seems like a reasonable thing for students to do in a classroom, whether or not they find "the answer." We might also provide further "known" information, such as screech owls' diets or the heights of the nests in the trees. Another possibility would be to introduce further data from the research paper itself (see Chapter 5).

How Did This Relationship "Come to Be"?

A further interesting avenue to explore is how such a relationship "came to be." This can promote a discussion of mechanisms of evolution, and can be useful for helping nonbiologists to hear how biologists think within an evolutionary framework.

This is the kind of question a biologist would consider. Considering plausible evolutionary mechanisms is an important part of what many biologists do, and should be an important part of science learning and teaching even when the topic is not explicitly about evolution. Having this discussion with teachers can model a kind of discussion that they might have with their own students.

What Researchers Say About the Relationship

The title of the article is "Live Blind Snakes (*Leptotyphlops dulcis*) in Eastern Screech Owl (*Otus asio*) Nests: A Novel Commensalism."[3] When the "correct answer" is revealed, or participants read the article, many are often unconvinced that it is *not* a mutualistic relationship; they think that the authors have not provided evidence to exclude mutualism. The authors argue for commensalism

---

3. See notes section for the full citation.

because the snakes would be able to get food elsewhere in the ground and trees and thus are not getting any novel benefit. However, participants have argued that the snake may be receiving a benefit that the researchers are not detecting, such as protection from some subterranean predator. (The snakes usually burrow underground). Furthermore, the authors themselves suggest that since the snakes will climb trees, they might benefit temporarily when there are declining food supplies in their usual habitat.

We think that's wonderful when participants feel entitled to argue with the scientists' conclusions, and we like to point that out. It is something, we think, to value in students as well.

The Discussion to Line 56

Opening the Conversation

We usually stop the recording at line 56, approximately five minutes in, when Michelle says, "No" and laughs. We ask participants how they think it's going, what they notice in students' ideas and reasoning, and what they see in the students' thinking that seems like the beginnings of scientific inquiry. Perhaps because there are quite a few student ideas in the first five minutes, or perhaps because we emphasize the attention to student thinking in our prompt, people frequently hear lots of ideas in these first few minutes.

Emphasizing the Substance of Students' Ideas and Reasoning

Often, however, people also want to say something about what the teacher is doing (or not doing). In this case, people usually comment positively on Sarah's nondirective style; some people want to point out that she reacts differently to Diana's question (challenging her argument) than Robert's (getting him to articulate his ideas).

We try to steer the conversation away from discussion about Sarah's moves at this point, assuring participants that we will get back to that discussion. Instead, we try to reorient them toward focusing on the students' ideas and reasoning. For example, if a participant says, "The teacher should have given Diana more of a chance to speak," we might ask, "What might Diana be thinking; what might she have said?" Likewise, if a participant says, "Sarah's doing a great job," we will ask, "What do you hear in the students' thinking that makes you say that?"

It also commonly happens early in the conversation that participants comment on students' engagement. In some cases these comments are positive; participants are impressed that several students begin speaking and offer ideas quickly. In other cases, the comments are negative; they point out that only a few students are participating. We acknowledge that student engagement is an important thing to pay attention to, but we emphasize that what we are doing here is focusing on the *substance of student ideas*. Teachers have a lot of practice in noticing who is engaged and who is not; they have much less practice in listening for substance.

In some workshops, participants have commented on this case (and other cases in this collection) that there is little student-student interaction; most of the exchanges are between a student and the teacher. If this comes up before we have had a chance to consider the students' ideas, we try to hold off that discussion until we move to ideas for instruction. This is an important observation; after all, we *do* want students to talk to each other rather than only communicate through the teacher. After we have discussed the substance of students' ideas, we come back to this issue and explore it a little. How do we understand the pattern of talk we see in this case? Is it simply that students and the teacher are unfamiliar with other possible ways of interacting in classrooms? In terms of instructional moves, how might a teacher respond instructionally if she noticed this during her class and perceived it as a problem?

Pressing for Specificity

Another common tendency, especially if this is the first case study they see, is that participants make general statements about how the students are doing, and we try to press them to include examples from the transcript to support what they are saying. For instance, if someone says, "I like what Robert said," we would ask them to interpret specifically what they understand him to be saying, and what they like about it.

Interpreting the Substance in the Students' Thinking

We often use this case study first because it is so rich in student ideas and reasoning. Many of these are easy to spot in this clip, and participants always have a lot to say. Our main intent in this is to cultivate close attention to what students say in these conversations, even if it is not possible from the evidence available to come to clear interpretations. (If this is the first time we are using a case study, we might remind participants: Pretend you know the students to be gifted; assume there is some wonderful meaning behind their words and we're trying to figure out what it might be.)

As we mentioned, in the first part of the transcript, people usually pick up on Diana's idea in line 2 that "the mother might have noticed that the snakes wouldn't harm her eggs, so she just kind of let them stay," and the way she argues with Sarah to defend it, such as in lines 10 and 12 where she points out that they "weren't taking up no room" and that "they didn't eat her eggs or anything." Some people notice that Avish supports her argument by pointing out that the snakes are "smaller than the eggs," implying that they're too small to do any harm.

Robert's ideas beginning in line 16 usually draw a lot of attention. He suggests two possibilities: (1) That the snakes eat up the eggshells or bugs and (2) that they give off heat to keep the eggs warm. People usually interpret him to be saying that the snake is helping the owl in some way by either eating up bugs or waste that could damage the eggs or babies, or providing warmth to help the eggs develop. (This is supported by his elaboration in line 65). Some people claim that his argument is stronger than Diana's because he's thinking about the possible benefit that the snake could provide the owl, while Diana doesn't assume benefit to either the owl or the snakes. When we hear this, we take it as an opportunity to create discussion around the claim. Do others agree that Robert's argument is stronger? If so, how is it stronger? Is it stronger scientifically? Or is it stronger because it seems to align with what Sarah apparently wants her students to do (come up with a symbiotic relationship in which one or the other organism benefits)?

Aaron's comment in line 30 is interesting. In responding to Robert's comment in line 16, he mentions that, "It's kind of confusing. I know what he's talking about, so it's 50-50," and he goes on to say that he thinks the snakes might be protecting the nest from predators. There is usually a conversation about what he means by "It's 50-50," and if there isn't, we bring it up, for the simple reason that it's a puzzling thing to say, and if a student says something puzzling it's worth taking a bit of time to try to figure out what he means. Some people don't think he means anything at all, and someone usually points out that he uses the same phrase in line 53 in a different context. In her case study, Sarah also suggests that this doesn't mean anything—she says it's a stock phrase that he often used in the class.

That has been the standard interpretation, although in one discussion, someone suggested that Aaron was reacting to Sarah. She had asked if anyone wants to respond to Robert's argument, noting that the idea of the snakes giving off heat had already been shot down; Robert pointed out that the snakes were cold-blooded animals, and Sarah mentioned that they might not have heat to spare. The alternate interpretation is that when Aaron says "it's 50-50," he is saying that he agrees with *one of Robert's two ideas*; he then goes on to argue in favor of what he *thinks* is one of Robert's ideas (that the snake is protecting the nest from predators that will damage the eggs), although he seems to have misinterpreted Robert's idea. We let this topic play out as it does; it is not important (and it is probably not possible) to settle on a "correct" interpretation of what Aaron really means.

Michelle, in line 36, disagrees with Aaron, saying that the snakes are blind and too small to protect the eggs. As one preservice teacher candidate interpreted it: "So the fact that they're smaller gives her evidence to refute [Aaron's] suggestion that this is acting like a shield from other predators." If no one points to Michelle's disagreement, we bring it up and ask participants what they think of it, because it's a good example of a student listening to and responding to another student's idea—Sarah's stated goal.

Often someone notices that Aaron counters in line 41 that the snakes can "pick up heat around other things" and can "detect a prey nearby and snap it up." Michelle seems to accept that argument, although she's not convinced that the snakes can protect. "But still," she says in line 50, "They're small and we don't know if they're venomous or not, so how are they going to protect?" Again, someone usually mentions this exchange, but we bring it up if no one does, again as examples of how students are starting to hear and respond to each other's reasoning.

Aaron's response in line 53 that "They'll constrict" usually gets a laugh, perhaps because of his tone and timing (students laugh on the tape, particularly Michelle). We prompt for serious consideration—what was he thinking? Secondarily, we might ask people what they think is so funny about Aaron's response. That people laugh might be reflective of what they understand Aaron to be thinking or why they think he states that here.

People tend to take the other part of Aaron's response more seriously. In one workshop a teacher pointed out that he has a reasonable response to Michelle's concern about their size when he says they can detach their jaw: "So [Aaron] didn't agree that size matters because [he] thought that they have this ability to, like, super-detach their jaw and make their mouth wider."

Moving From Interpretations to Ideas for Instruction

After the discussion about the exchange with Aaron and Michelle, we often open the floor for ideas for instruction that are grounded in interpretations of student thinking. We ask the participants to think not in terms of what the teacher *should do* or *should have done,* rather, what the teacher *might do* next, or what she *might have done* in response to particular student ideas. What is the "menu of possibilities"? Frequent general suggestions for what Sarah *might do* next include

- Let the discussion go on longer, (after all, it just started!) on the sense that it's going well—we ask participants to articulate what's going well about it, if they haven't already.
- Give students the vocabulary to attach to the ideas they are generating, on the sense that the ideas they are generating connect to the target vocabulary—we ask for examples, which can generate more discussion about whether the ideas really reflect the scientific terms.
- Ask students what information they'll need to solve the puzzle. We ask what they anticipate students might say if asked that question; some participants note that they've already started to ask for information.

- Keep track of the arguments and the evidence on the board, on the sense that there are many ideas in the air, or to model good practice. (Often someone suggests that Sarah seems to be doing this off-camera.)

While some participants think the discussion "just started," others can be impatient to see "where it's going to go," arguing that it can't go on through this "idea generation" phase forever. Someone usually mentions the way that Sarah seems to argue with Diana, and perhaps she might have instead opened it up to the class to say what they think about Diana's idea. Sarah does try to get students to argue with each other, but she doesn't seem to be encouraging them to talk to each other without going through her. It has been suggested that she might provide more "wait time" after a student speaks to try to get other students to respond, or that she might explicitly tell students that she wants them to speak to each other (perhaps doing the discussion in small groups first to give them these opportunities).

When we have distributed the handout that Sarah used in her class, instead of just describing the question to participants, there is sometimes concern that it presents the situation in terms of a single nest, and thus does not key students into thinking about how there might be a mutually beneficial relationship that was found among most members of the owl and snake species. The fact that Diana's response does not seem to relate to an ecological relationship, but instead an anthropomorphic relationship like a person might have with a squirrel who lives in the trees of the yard, ("They're not hurting anything so she just let them stay,") is often given as an example of how the handout may be misleading. In this case, the argument goes, Diana is not thinking about a populationwide relationship partly because of the way the handout is written.

A nice option here is to return the focus to Diana's response, since the comment allows a different interpretation of her thinking. Given the task she's been asked to do, is it a reasonable response? Another option is to ask participants if there are other places where they see students considering the evolutionary benefits of the relationship. Either way, it is worth discussing possible ways to draw attention to the fact that the phenomenon is really about *populations* and not an isolated case. Are there other student ideas that she can draw upon to emphasize this point? One option may be for her to ask the students how they think the situation would be different if this were only observed once, versus being observed in most owl nests.

Throughout, we try to deflect *evaluations* of the teacher, favorable or critical, toward neutral discussions about possibilities for instruction and how they might influence student thinking. In any teaching moment there are many possibilities for how to proceed, no one of which is "correct," and the purpose of these conversations is to consider what those possibilities are. As well, in most of our uses of these cases, we are moving toward the participants bringing in tape from *their* classes, and we try to frame conversations in that way; we don't want people to be reticent to present because they are afraid of being criticized.

The Discussion to Line 114

There are several places in this portion of the discussion we see as important for participants to consider—more important than proceeding to the rest of the video. Usually our workshops and seminars don't go past this segment of the transcript.

Navarre and Robert's Ideas

The first thing that people typically mention in this segment is Navarre's question in line 58: "Can't there be multiple snakes that guard around the nest?" A participant noted, "In line 58 [Navarre] suggests that maybe there are multiple snakes and so even though they're small, having many of them together could be good defense like on something larger."

Especially since the students are often responding to ideas they have heard much earlier in the discussion, it's useful to ask participants what they think Navarre is doing here. Is he coming up with a new argument, or is he responding to something he heard earlier? The general interpretation here is that he is supporting Aaron's "protection" argument by suggesting how the snakes could protect the nest, even though they're small.

In line 65, Robert elaborates on his argument about bugs causing disease and probably breaking the eggs, but he also mentions the possibility that the snakes are eating the eggs. (People generally interpret him to mean eating the eggshells so they don't deteriorate, attract bugs, and cause disease.) Furthermore, he jumps into the argument about whether or not the snakes being blind matters—pointing out that "It's not really relevant because there are millions of animals that are blind, but eat other animals." Participants are usually very impressed with the "relevance" argument, and with Robert in general. It's important to try to get out in the open what participants think is so impressive about the relevance argument. While it might be obvious to some people, it's not necessarily obvious to everyone. Especially because some participants frequently talk more than others, we want their interpretations and impressions of the value of student ideas to be as explicit as possible. This gives others opportunities to agree or disagree, which we like to encourage, especially when the interpretations of students' ideas and their value are not necessarily clear.

"The Owl Is Just Trying to Wait for the Snakes to Get Bigger So It Can Eat Them"

Bob brings up a new argument in line 73, that "the owl is just trying to wait for the snakes to get bigger so it can eat them," and Robert responds to this argument in line 82, by saying that if the snakes were a species that got bigger, it probably would have said that in the background information that Sarah gave them. This usually creates a lively discussion about whether or not Robert is appealing to the information that Sarah gave them as an authority in a way that is not authentic to science. (If nobody brings it up, we do.) The usual interpretation is that what Robert is doing is not really scientific. Here's one person's suggestion that what Robert is doing is problematic and inauthentic.

> I was sort of concerned about that. I mean you would think Robert was thinking more like a student than a scientist right? He was sort of thinking like this is the way things are presented in school, like they would have told us it was baby snakes if they wanted to think about baby snakes …. So Robert says "you know what, I think that would have been said here if they weren't fully mature snakes," and then at 88 he says it again like "otherwise it would be said here," so he's really determined to stick to this handout that he's got as like authoritative … like a worksheet that we get in science class has certain implications, it's not merely just observations but like they would have said something else if they wanted us to think about something else.

On the other hand, occasionally someone suggests that he's making an assumption that he thinks he's reading someone's research, and in that sense, he is making some assumptions that are reasonable:

> If you're reading somebody else's research they would generally have, you know, waited or looked into and figured out whether or not the snakes were baby snakes or not and then when they were summarizing it for their article or whatever sort of whatever they wanted to present to the scientific community, they would say they were baby snakes if they were baby snakes.

There is generally agreement that Robert is appealing to the handout as the authority here. The disagreement is whether or not what he's doing is bad or otherwise inauthentic to science.

The ways in which students perceive the authority of the teacher or the textbook is an important aspect of how they understand science, and we think this is a useful opportunity to bring issues of participants' perspective on students' understandings of science to the surface. So we find this disagreement productive, and if it doesn't come up on its own, we usually bring it up, either by prompting for further views about Robert's comment or by mentioning the ideas we've heard in other workshops.

Aaron also disagrees with "waiting for the snakes to get bigger," although typically people don't bring it up, probably because it's hard to figure out what he's talking about. For that reason in particular, we usually ask what he might mean by "if this attempt didn't sell," if nobody brings it up. One possibility is that he is anthropomorphizing the snakes and assuming that if the snake doesn't get some benefit than it would leave before it got big. (Perhaps he's thinking about the food snakes would get from eating predators that come around the nest—his earlier argument). It is especially important that teachers work to understand students who have difficulty making themselves understood.

"I Don't Have a Reason for It …"

One interesting idea in this segment is when Robert mentions that he doesn't "have a reason for it, but snakes lose their skins every several months," after Sarah asks if there are any more ideas. We (and Sarah in her case study) think this is interesting especially because in saying "I don't have a reason for it," it seems that Robert understands that this is simply a fact, and not an argument based on the fact. In fact he says that he doesn't know yet how it will affect things, because "it's more complicated." As Sarah points out in her case study, he does generate an argument that involves this piece of information as the conversation goes on. We point to this idea too if none of the participants mention it.

Often, however, it's at this point that participants think that the discussion has lost some steam, and that it might be appropriate for the teacher to do something else. As one participant said:

> Well, I think because they are coming up with more ideas like um, the latest idea was the shedding of the skin and stuff and seeing how that affects, like if that's part of the mass, I don't know. I feel like they're at a point where they can't defend their arguments from the beginning, now they're trying to come up with new ideas but I feel like they should stick to like the beginning ground and try to argue that.

Not everyone always agrees that the discussion has lost steam. Some participants think that although the students don't seem to be defending their arguments from the beginning, they may do so if given more time. While this is a nice place to move on to the "menu of possibilities" of ideas for instruction, we suggest first asking if there is agreement that the students are no longer being productive. If there is disagreement, we ask that participants be specific in what they hear the students saying that suggests they are still being productive.

Moving From Interpretations to Ideas for Instruction

Interpretations of student reasoning lead to possible ideas for instruction. One possibility is to ask Aaron what he means by "if this attempt didn't sell." Sarah does respond to Aaron's overall argument, but it's not clear what he means by this, and it might be important to his argument. Another suggestion is that Sarah ask students to respond to each other more. For example, in line 67, when Diana asks, "Do snakes have ears?" Sarah responds to the question herself by explaining that Robert's point above neutralizes the importance of the snakes' abilities to detect things around them. Instead, she might ask Diana to explain why that question is important, or if she's responding to what Robert said.

Overall, when considering what Sarah might do next, two possibilities predominate in our workshop. One is that Sarah could carefully outline the arguments that are on the table to distinguish the fully formed arguments from some of the other comments that are coming out. Another possibility is that she could move on to what she intended to do next, according to the worksheet, which is to ask the students what other questions they have, or what new information they would need to solve the puzzle.

We suggest continuing to press for other possibilities until there are no more suggestions. Some people take longer than others to speak up, and we want to capture their ideas, as well as those of the more talkative people. After all, there are other possibilities that most participants don't even consider. For example, Sarah continuously responds to student ideas, such that the discourse pattern goes Sarah-student, Sarah-student. Sarah might instead just not say anything in some cases, for example, when Diana asks, "Do snakes have ears?" and see if a student responds. Perhaps another student will ask why that question is important.

The Rest of the Snippet

In most workshops and pedagogy courses, that's as far as we get, partly because we usually spend a lot of time at the beginning of the class talking about the question itself, and partly because participants find a lot to talk about in the first two segments. One option, if you have more then one session, is to spend the first session discussing the question, (perhaps using some of the data provided in chapter 5) and then the second session on the transcript.

Students' Questions

Sarah begins this snippet by asking a question of her own. We'll discuss this later, but first we'll address some of the students' questions, how they might be interpreted, and how facilitators might respond to the interpretations.

In line 158, Navarre asks how the snakes can find anything for their food if they're blind. An appropriate move here is to ask participants why they think Navarre is asking this question. He doesn't say so, but it may be that he's actually responding to Robert's argument that the snakes are eating bugs in the nest, and not asking a question he had written down at the beginning of class. In that sense his question suggests that he's thinking of a counterargument to Robert's. Another possible interpretation is that this was the question he had written down at the beginning of class and he was just asking this question about the snakes in general—not assuming at the time that they were eating bugs in the nest. Navarre's question may be what prompts Rachel in line 164 to suggest that "They might eat just the nasty stuff that the owl feeds to the babies," which Diana adds to with the suggestion that they "might smell it," which responds to Navarre's question.

In line 176 Bob asks, "what happened when the eggs hatched?" We want to know what participants think of this question. We think it is a wonderful question because it would answer whether the snakes are being kept for food for the babies, but no students follow up on it. Navarre, Aaron, and Michelle ask some questions, but they follow in quick succession and not much discussion ensues. In line 192 Diana asks if all snakes were blind or just those. Sarah asks Diana how that information will help her, and Diana struggles to respond. Sarah gives her some help getting started, and Diana says in line 202 that if the whole species of snakes were blind, then it would mean, "it's common, that you just know that they're blind. But if you just know that it was just those ones inside the nest ...." Diana doesn't finish her thought, so it's unclear why she thinks it's important to know if this is something that happens with the whole species or if this is a one-time event.

Again, we'd like for participants to consider why Diana might be asking this question. One possible interpretation is that she is thinking that the snakes' blindness has some significance if it is a specieswide characteristic, but not if it is just the snakes in the nest. This interpretation would lend some support to the participants' argument that the handout itself was not clear enough for the students to reason in the way that Sarah wanted them to.

In line 208, Michelle asks, "How did the scientist know the snakes were blind?" A student suggests that they can tell by the eyes in lines 210–214, but a little later in the discussion Michelle disagrees, saying that, "When she said the eyes are grey, that can't really tell you because if the snake is shedding, don't their eyes turn like a misty blue?" There is some nice evidence here that Michelle is listening to and responding to the student's idea, but again, it's not clear why the students think this question is important.

Another example of this occurs in line 216, when Diana asks, "How many snakes were in the nest?" Sarah asks her why that question is important, and Diana responds that, "Because you'd know like how many snakes are like on the eggs and stuff." Sarah tries to get Diana to explain: "What would that make you say? What would that lead you to believe if there were a lot versus a little?" and even opens it up to the rest of the class. Again, however, no one is able to make it clear how that information would help answer the question. We suggest asking participants what they think Diana was getting at. Often, the perception is that Diana and the other students don't really know why they're asking these questions, especially since many of the students don't finish their thoughts. Another possibility, however, is that Diana is considering Navarre's earlier argument, that a large number of snakes might be protecting the nest by acting as a team.

Rachel says in line 223 that, "If there were only like three it might be a mistake in there, but if there's like twenty then obviously that's (inaudible). She doesn't finish her thought, but we would ask participants what they think she might be getting at. It's possible that she is thinking of something like what Diana seems to be getting at in line 192. That is, she's suggesting that the question will help them determine if this is a common relationship that has some meaning for the owls and the snakes, or if it's just something that happened once.

Robert has some questions that do appear to give him information that he would need to determine the relationship between the owls and snakes. He asks, in lines 235–237, "What do the snakes eat? How are they eating? ... and uh, who's their prey?" When Sarah asks him how that's going to affect what he thinks, he eventually says that it would tell us that the snakes are depending on the owl in some way. The usual interpretation is that he is expecting that if the snakes eat something that is found in the owl's nest (like eggshells, insects, or things the mother owl feeds the babies—all things that were mentioned earlier), then he could understand how the relationship benefits the snake. If no one brings up Robert's question, we would, because we think it demonstrates a good example of a student connecting his question to an earlier argument.

What Happened at the End of the Class and the Menu of Possibilities

Regardless of how much of the video we show, participants want to know what happens next. We tell them what Sarah did: She introduced the vocabulary that is called for by the curriculum and discussed examples with the students about what kinds of relationships were implied by their arguments. Considering what Sarah did next can lead to disagreements about whether or not this is what she should have done, or whether it makes more sense to do something different; for example, (if participants know of the data from the paper) possibly giving the students the data now. While considering "the menu of possibilities" for instructional responses is important, we try, again, to make sure the conversation is grounded in the ideas that the students bring up.

Discussing Sarah's Case Study

Structuring the Discussion

We have always shown and talked about the video, at least through line 114, before people read Sarah's case study. Showing the video first, we think, helps the case seem more real. It also gives workshop participants the chance to form their own ideas about what is happening. Often their ideas align with Sarah's.

We have approached the analysis of Sarah's case study in two ways. One way is to have participants discuss the case study in a subsequent class or seminar. During this conversation, we prompt participants to pay attention to the teachers' interpretations in discussing the case. Rather than focus first on what she does as the teacher, we ask participants to focus on what she sees and hears. What are the interpretations she makes that motivate her to respond? How do her responses fit with her interpretations?

There is not always time to have such a conversation, however. Another option is to have participants, especially if they are students in a methods class, read the case study and transcript and prepare a written analysis focusing on (1) student ideas they noticed that they think are particularly important, (2) how Sarah interpreted the student ideas that she heard, (3) places where they disagree with Sarah's interpretations, and (4) their own "menu of possibilities" for how Sarah might have responded to particular student ideas, or where she might go next. Although much of this analysis (particularly parts 1 and 4) might have happened in the conversation during the video, doing this assignment gives each participant an individual opportunity to do some analysis. Thus, if a few participants have dominated the conversation, others now have an opportunity to express their thoughts. A short follow-up discussion, after participants have read and commented on the case study, can then bring in some of the interpretations or ideas for instruction that were not discussed the first time around, especially if there was not time to watch the entire class on video.

"My Students Would Never Do This"

Often, people want to hear more about the background of the class. What expectations for student and teacher talk have been established? Have they had these kinds of conversations before? For many, it is surprising that "on-level" students are so well behaved, are attentive to each others' ideas, and seem comfortable arguing with each other. Often people feel that this sort of conversation could not happen in their own classes, and they want to know what was special about these circumstances. We try to deflect the perception that this was anomalous, mostly by simply telling participants that we have several examples of these kinds of productive conversations from high school and middle school classrooms. We argue that secondary students rarely have the opportunity to engage in these kinds of conversations, and it is important to give them such opportunities. When these conversations do occur, it is important to listen to the students and take their ideas seriously.

C HAPTER 5

The Owls and the Snakes (2)

anet "Izzy" Kovach was the author of the owls-and-snakes question Sarah used in her teaching (discussed in Chapter 4), and this is a case study of student thinking in one of Izzy's own classes. Izzy, we should say, was a "ringer," a highly experienced teacher with an unusual set of qualifications—including certification in special education, social studies, *and* science, and experience working in an alternative program for students with substance abuse problems. So she's a little different from the teachers in other cases in this book. We include this case to have an example of work in special education: Izzy's was a "self-contained" class for students with a wide range of diagnosed special needs.

As Izzy describes in her case study, she had used this owls and snakes story many times before. This year she planned to take it further, bringing in data from the research article itself to see if the students could use the evidence to draw conclusions about the various relationships that they had proposed.

The main data for this case study are the transcript, the data Izzy shared with the students, and the video. Izzy's case study begins after "Suggestions for Reading and Viewing." The video and the transcript are available at *www.nsta.org/publications/press/extras/responsive.aspx*.

Suggestions for Reading and Viewing

Be sure to make copies of the transcript. Even if you're watching the video, the transcript is useful for following along, for jotting notes, and for referring back to particular snippets during conversations about this class. Additionally, the transcript makes clear what data Izzy was referring to during the conversation.

When we use this case study in courses or workshops, we usually describe the curious owl-snake relationship and pose the question for participants to discuss it themselves, before we present the conversation that took place in Izzy's class (unless of course they've seen Sarah's case in Chapter 4). We have participants read the first part of Izzy's case study, stopping before the section "Students' Use of the Evidence." We then present the conversation, stopping at several spots in order to encourage participants' close, careful examination of student thinking:

1. *Line 54, approximately 8 minutes in, when Max and Cameron respond affirmatively to Izzy's question, "And are blind snakes capable of burrowing?"* We've found this is a good stopping point to ask participants: How do you think it's going? What do you notice in students' ideas and reasoning? Does their thinking seem scientific?

2. *Line 191, about 21 minutes in, when Kevin says, "True."* Again, we check in: What do you notice in the students' thinking? Do you see anything new in this segment, compared to the first?

3. We've rarely gotten further than line 191, but there are still things to talk about if you run the video to the end, as we discuss in this chapter. Regardless of where we stop, we ask participants to consider the "menu of possibilities" of how Izzy might respond. What ideas might be worth further attention? How might Izzy structure the next part of the conversation, or the next activity, based on the ideas she has heard?

The Case Study: Using "The Owls and the Snakes" to Teach the "Well-Designed Investigation"

By Janet "Izzy" Kovach

Introduction

A dozen years ago I stumbled across an interesting story about screech owls bringing a specific species of snakes, which are naturally blind, to their nests and allowing the snakes to live with them unharmed, for some unknown reason. It was in a "nature puzzlers" book, which a colleague had donated to me when he was cleaning his closet. At the time, I was looking for an engaging first-day-of-class activity, and I incorporated the case into a list of "unanswered questions" faced by biologists. I then filed the book away in my closet, perhaps to pick up again whenever I decided to retire.

I forgot about the story after that, always on a quest for a better season opener, until about three years ago when I made a move to a new high school. As I unearthed and repacked the book, I wondered if naturalists had ever come up with a reason for the owls' unusual behavior. But I never gave thought to using it until it was time to introduce the concept of symbiosis to my new self-contained biology class of 10th graders in special education[1]. The students had been struggling with the surfeit of vocabulary in the biology curriculum's introductory ecology unit while I had been struggling to find a way to encourage them to take ownership of all these new terms instead of simply trying to memorize a glossary list.

Aha! Why not give them an intriguing nonpredatory relationship between two species that are usually considered mutual enemies and ask them to figure out what might be going on? Better yet, why not use a case where a "correct" answer has not been established, so students need not be intimidated by being wrong? It was time to dust off "The Owls and Snakes" once again.

Each time I used the case, I was gratified by the students' engagement and their willingness to hypothesize all kinds of likely interactions. Classes generally agreed, in the end, that each species probably benefited from the nesting arrangement (e.g., owls may provide a safe haven for the blind snakes in return

---

1. There were 12 students in the class. The IEP primary code breakdown was as follows: Six students were diagnosed with "specific learning disability," three with autism, one with speak/language disability, one with "other health impairment" (Attention Deficit Disorder), and one with severe emotional disability.

for protection of the owls' eggs from intruders). Even better, when the specific vocabulary for symbiotic relationships was introduced, they seemed to have an easy time transferring the terms to match the interactions they had suggested as plausible, and they used the terminology freely and appropriately.

In fact, the lesson always worked so well and was so engaging that it struck me that it could be extended for another purpose. Here was a question asked by real scientists who were doing real science to find reasoned explanations. And my students were genuinely interested in finding an answer, as well. What a great way to introduce the concept of the "Well-Designed Investigation"[2] without starting with the off-putting vocabulary of *variables* and *controls* and the artificiality of creating an experimental design around some meaningless question about pill bugs and temperature or daphnia and caffeine.

The Lesson

I introduced the lesson as in years past. Following a lengthy and lively discussion of what students already knew about snakes and owls, I gave them a very short synopsis of the case and posed the question, "What is the relationship between the screech owls and the blind snakes?" After establishing a list on the board of "what we know for sure" from the synopsis, students worked in pairs to come up with hypotheses to explain the relationship. They seemed very comfortable with the term "hypothesis," knowing the usual definition of "an educated guess." Additionally, in order to get them thinking about the design of an investigation and useful data, I asked them to list other pieces of evidence that would help them solve the puzzle, explain how that information would help them evaluate what was happening, and devise a way to prove that their hypothesis was correct. Some student written responses fell back on the need to consult experts:

"I would like to know more about why blind snakes live with owls."

"I would read about how the owls live with blind snakes online or in a book."

Most students, though, generated their own approaches to gathering useful evidence for evaluating their hypotheses. I had given a handout in class, asking students for their hypotheses, and what evidence they would need to support their hypotheses. Here are two of what I consider to be the better responses (from handouts completed in class):

---

2. The "Well-Designed Investigation" is the language used in my school district for what is generally thought of as experimental scientific method. Teachers are required by the state to teach this vocabulary and it is assessed on the statewide biology test, which students must pass in order to graduate.

- *Hypothesis:* "The owl is keeping them for its baby food that when the owlet's hatch they will eat the blind snakes as a first meal."
- *How would you prove that your hypothesis is correct?* "I would need to see the owlets' hatch, and see how they interact with the blind snakes. The owlets would be feeding on the snakes. The number of snakes would begin to disappear."

- *Hypothesis:* "The owl is either using the snake for protection of the eggs or stored food for the eggs when they hatch."
- *What else would you like to know?* "To know if the snakes are protecting the nest, the biologist can put mice or rats in the nest so the biologist can see what would happen to the mice or rats."

So right from the first day, students were developing ideas for experimental designs that would result in measurable outcomes to verify their predictions. We spent the following class refining the hypotheses and compiling a class list of possible explanations for the strange animal behavior. Anything that fit the initial data was accepted. Here are the hypotheses we had in the list:

- The snakes are going to be baby food (for owlets).
- The owls are giving snakes a place to live ("compassion").
- The snakes are protecting the eggs, nest, or owls from enemies.
- The snakes and owls are protecting each other.

We spent the next period with a traditional curricular presentation of symbiosis versus predator/prey relationships and the standard definitions for mutualism, commensalism, and parasitism. Students spontaneously began applying the terms to their understanding of the snake/owl association, (along the line of "So that's what the owls were up to!") and we were able to formally attach a label to each of our hypotheses. I thought the students' spontaneous connection of the vocabulary to the case of the owls and snakes was wonderful, because students were taking ownership of the vocabulary, and using it to make their arguments. One student (Kevin) was adamant that the relationship was *initially* commensalistic (because the blind snake was provided a safe place to live), but would be transformed to predator/prey once the owl eggs hatched. Another student wondered, then, would that mean it really was a mutualistic relationship since both sides benefited at least some of the time?

It would have been difficult to move the lesson beyond this point if I had not been able to locate a published field study of the snake/owl relationship that provided real data for the class to analyze. Now the class had the opportunity to evaluate their hypotheses on the basis of evidence—the heart of real science. Without revealing the authors' conclusions, I inserted summaries of their observations and experimental data, one snippet at a time, into the next day's lesson. After each piece of new information, I asked the students how it impacted their understanding of the relationship. While some of the language and statistical evidence was well outside their comfort zone, the students were invested in discovering what was going on and willing to work at understanding the information in order to assess its relevance. Through the course of the discussion, the students displayed some sophisticated scientific thinking, as well as falling into some common intellectual traps.*

*This is a good point to stop reading, watch the video, and talk about student thinking.

Students' Use of the Evidence

To start the class, I showed the students their hypotheses from the day before and then started showing them the data so we could talk about it, one piece at a time:

- *Evidence #1: The blind snakes are normally fossorial, but they have been observed climbing trees to reach nests of ants.*

Initially, after I put up this slide, we spent a little time talking about the meaning of the word *fossorial*, and the students were

able to read its meaning from the context. Josh had a question about whether a *nest* was the appropriate term for where ants live. His question was a little off track from the discussion, but I really wanted to encourage students to talk, so I was trying not to "stamp out" any ideas, even if they seemed tangential.

I turned the conversation around to whether or not this evidence was useful for evaluating our hypotheses. Adrian said it was, because it showed that the owls could enter the nest on their own, but I wasn't clear about why he thought that was important. He said, "If the owls and snakes ever turn against each other, they could use that as an advantage for like, uhhh, battle and stuff." It seems like he was thinking that the snakes' mobility gave them another way, "an advantage" in dealing with the owls, but I'm not sure if he was thinking about how that could be used to evaluate the hypotheses.

National Science Teachers Association

Maybe he thought that the snakes' added mobility would make them difficult prey for the owls to catch.

Josh had an idea about how the evidence could be used to support a hypothesis.

> Josh: Don't snakes eat ants, and ants might like to, like when a baby gets born, when it hatches, ants will probably swarm around it and eat it, so same thing; it'll eat ants and other pests would [cut off].

> Izzy: Oh. Ok, so if ants are living in the owl's nest, maybe the snake is eating those ants and that helps the eggs. Interesting. So which of these ideas would that support Josh?

> Josh: They're protecting the nest from ants.

I put up the second piece of evidence, and asked if it gave us any information that would help us to support one of the ideas or get rid of one.

- *Evidence #2: 89% of the blind snakes in the nests are still alive when the fledglings leave the nest; the remaining 11% were found dead—of these, only one was partially eaten.*

Max immediately recognized what this meant.

> Max: Get rid of the predator-prey relationship.

> Izzy: Because?

> Max: Because only 11% of them are found half eaten. But only one was eaten.

> Izzy: Ok, and it-ok only one was eaten out of all the snakes that they found and most of them were alive.

> Max: Uh huh.

> Izzy: Alright, so that certainly doesn't sound like they're being saved for food. Because, what would you expect if they were-how many would you expect to find alive after the owls left the nest?

> Max: None.

In general, I thought the students were doing a pretty good job of reasoning with the evidence. Like I said, though, I noticed some pitfalls in their arguing, such as cases in which they were selectively ignoring some evidence—trying to justify a hypothesis with supporting evidence while ignoring nonsupporting evidence. I saw an example of this with the third piece of evidence I put up.

- *Evidence #3: Young nesting owls will eat both dead and live snakes put into their nest by researchers. However, live snakes that can quickly burrow into nest debris are not eaten.*

    Cameron: So my hypothesis was true.

    Izzy: Which hypothesis?

    Cameron: The snakes-the little owlettes hatch, they eat the snakes.

    Izzy: Ok, so that supports the predator-prey idea, but we have that other piece of evidence that they're still alive. So what must those snakes be doing? Those little-those live blind snakes that-that are put into the nest.

    Alex: Practicing for hunting?

    Izzy: Well, but, if they're-if they're practicing for hunting are they very successful?

    Kevin: Not really.

    Izzy: Not really. So, what are those snakes doing to stay alive, according to this?

    Josh: Burrowing.

    Izzy: Burrowing. And are blind snakes capable of burrowing?

    Max: Uh-huh.

    Cameron: Yes.

Here, Cameron picked up on the evidence that blind snakes put in nests by researchers will be eaten, which he took as evidence that his hypothesis was supported—that the snakes were being saved as food for the baby owls when they hatched. I challenged him a little to remind him of the previous evidence (that most snakes are still alive when the baby owls leave the nest) and asked what he thought the blind snakes were doing. Alex said that they were "practicing for hunting." I didn't really understand what he meant at the time. Possibly he was mixing up "owls" and "snakes" (like all of us, myself included, did throughout the discussion) and he was saying that the snakes were used as hunting practice for the baby owls (even though they generally didn't catch them). Josh pointed out that the snakes were probably burrowing to stay alive, and Cameron agreed, although I'm not sure if he really understood the implications of the data—that owls will eat the snakes, but the snakes usually burrow into the nest too quickly to be eaten, which essentially argues against a simple predator-prey model.

The next piece of evidence was about what the blind snakes eat, and I expected that it would solidify an argument in favor of the hypothesis that the snakes protected the nests from insects that could harm the eggs somehow.

- *Evidence #4: Blind snakes normally eat the soft-bodied larvae of insects they find in underground ant or termite nests.*

Kevin surprised me, however, by constructing an argument that did not support any particular hypothesis, but instead synthesized a new hypothesis using some of the evidence.

> Kevin: I think it's a little bit of both of commensalism and predator and prey.
>
> Izzy: So you're jumping right-this-is this giving you information to make that decision.
>
> Kevin: Yeah.
>
> Izzy: Why do you say commensalism, predator and prey?
>
> Kevin: Um, because well commensalism because, uh, the owl knows that the, um, that it would clean up the, the nest. Like from getting damaged or something, like, and if it was to get damaged then the, uh, there won't be any eggs to-to be, like, hatching from the nest.
>
> Izzy: So what would be damaging the eggs?
>
> Kevin: The insects.
>
> Izzy: Ok, so if there are insects in the nest it would damage the eggs-
>
> Kevin: Or-or at least do some, like, like termites they eat-they eat wood.

Izzy: Mmmhmmm...

Kevin: So-

Izzy: That's a good point.

Kevin: They could break off the branch or whatever.

Izzy: Oh! Think about that. The nest would fall to the ground.

Kevin: And then like predator-prey because it's like if the blind snake wasn't able to somehow get through underneath the mess, then they'll be eaten.

Rather than assuming that there was only one kind of relationship, Kevin was drawing on the evidence that (1) the snakes will occasionally get eaten, (2) they eat insects that could hurt the eggs (or cause the nest to fall to the ground), and (3) the snakes could "get underneath the mess," so they would be eaten. Based on this evidence, Kevin argued that it was "a little bit of both of commensalism and predator and prey."

With the next piece of evidence, Kevin saw corroborating support for the hypothesis that the snakes protect the eggs.

- *Evidence #5: Table of arthropods found in the debris of owl nests (species known to be eaten by blind snakes are marked by asterisks.)*

    Izzy: So what does this, what does this tell me?

    Kevin: Normally different animals live in the nest that the blind snakes eat.

    Izzy: Ok, so this confirms your idea, right?

    Kevin: Yup.

Other students also suggested that the evidence supported another of their hypotheses: that the owls provide the snakes a safe place to live.

    Izzy: Yeah, so there're insects there that they will eat. So which hypothesis does that support, Jeff?

    Jeff: Both?

    Aryton: No, the second one does.

Izzy: (reading hypothesis two from whiteboard): The owls are providing the snakes a safe place to live. Is it a safe place? Or a place with food?

Jeff: Place with food.

Izzy: I guess that makes it safe, right? So, are the snakes getting something out of this relationship too?

Alex: Yeah, food.

Despite Aryton's odd way of phrasing it, "the second one does," I took him to mean that the evidence supported the hypothesis that the owls are providing the snakes a safe place to live.

As Kevin did with the previous piece of evidence, Josh used the next piece of evidence to support the argument that the snakes were helping the owls in some way.

- *Evidence #6: Table of nestling growth rate and fledging weight in nests with snakes present and nests with snakes absent.*

Josh: It looks like the snakes do more helping. They're not as fat when they need to fly and then they—they grow really fast.

Izzy: They grow really fast and they can fly away at an earlier-at an earlier size. At a quick-so they're-they're leaving the nest more quickly. Good point. Not only are they growing faster but they're leaving the nest sooner. So they must-that's a good sign that they're healthy. So, Max, is that support for this?

Max: Yeah.

Izzy: That the snakes are protecting the eggs.

I thought this was one of the more difficult pieces of data to understand, but Josh interpreted it pretty quickly, pointing out that when the snakes are present, the baby owls grow faster and are able to fly at a lower weight. I think his use of the term *fat* is meant to suggest that because they are not as fat when they fly, they can fly better.

By the end of the discussion, the students were nearly evenly split between supporting the relationship as mutualism or commensalism (with the owl as the beneficiary). Of course, they were also curious to know what conclusion the biologists had reached, so I gave them the full copy of the journal article. Half of the class felt vindicated by the authors' defense of commensalism, with the usual bravado of those backed up by authority:

Kevin: I was right ... Yup, I'm right .... I'm always right.

But I was pleased to see that the opposition was not ready to just drop its own thinking in the face of expert opinion.

Josh: Can they prove they're really not helping the snake?

Izzy: Can they prove-well what-how would they have to prove that it's not helping the snake? How would you-how would you go about proving that the snake is-is not being helped?

Josh: Well those snakes are blind. I don't think they can find anything. And up there in that nest, they're safe and get free meals.

Although Josh didn't really answer my question of how he could prove that the snake is not being helped, he continued to develop his argument that the snakes were actually getting a benefit, because it was easier for them to find food in the nest and be safe from predators.

As a final activity to underscore the role scientists play in critically evaluating each other's research and the ongoing nature of the investigation process, I charged the students with devising a way to determine which group of snakes were better off—those on the ground or those in the owl nests. Seven of the 12 students were invested enough in the analysis process to suggest methods for deciding if the relationship was mutualism or commensalism. Some of these were simply a rationale for why snakes would be at an advantage on the ground or in a nest:

- *Snakes are better off on the ground because they can move better.*
- *Snakes are better off on the ground because they feel safe.*
- *The nest because they have protection.*

However, many students recognized the need for quantifiable data collection to support their claims:

- *Check the number of predators in the nest and the number of predators on the ground.*
- *You can see how many foods are on the ground and how many are in the nest.*

- *I would be looking for how much food the snakes would be eating. I would also be looking for how they move. It can sometimes tell how they are feeling.*
- *See if the insects in the nest, if the snakes like them better than the ones on the ground.*
- *The size of the snake.*

Reflection

At the end of this five-day (50-minute periods) lesson sequence, I was satisfied that the time had been well spent. Not only did I hear a classroom full of engaged students, I felt that I had evidence of sophisticated scientific thinking and authentic participation in inquiry. Still the bottom line in today's data-driven classroom is assessment numbers, and all I had generated was taped conversations with students.

Therefore I felt compelled to look at my students' performance on countywide administered semester exams, specifically at items purported to assess scientific thinking. I also compared their scores to those of 21 other students in biology classes in which I had only used the snake/owl relationship as a five-minute warm-up activity to introduce symbiosis.

The data was disheartening. While scores on these items were low (average 59% correct), they were higher than the average for the entire test (47%). However, they were not notably higher than the scores of students who did not participate in this five-day sequence. So did I waste valuable teaching time when I could have been covering more of the information on the test? If so, how do I reconcile that with calls for authentic, inquiry-based education and with my own sense from what students were thinking that this had been a really productive exercise to that end?

Perhaps the real concern should be with the test-driven assessment practices fueled by the expectations of "No Child Left Behind." Special education students in my district score notoriously low on exams—a 47% average is not unusual! The multiple layers of knowledge and reasoning necessary to answer test questions (background information, analysis of data, facility with language) make test-taking a daunting task for students with exceptionalities, akin to the difficulties faced by nonnative English speakers. Maybe the tests are not an adequate measure of students' science learning.

I believe that more meaningful (albeit more difficult to quantify) data on student learning can be derived from tools such as the video/transcript generated by this class. Including students' participation in such discussions as part of a student portfolio, we could more meaningfully assess what our students know and are able to do. In this case, my students demonstrated the ability to recognize evidence and design controlled investigations. They interpreted complex data sets and used them to refine their ideas. They recognized flaws in their own thinking and made revisions. These are the things I hope to see from my students in science class!

Our district's curriculum claims to put a very high premium on learning that science is a dynamic process of discovery. This does not match up well to a static, standardized testing regime. Analysis and evaluation of evidence are central to participating in science, and are not adequately assessed by the tests. It's time to take a hard look at how we assess students' science learning.

Facilitators' Notes

Please see the general notes for facilitators in Chapter 3. Here we'll provide specific comments and suggestions with respect to discussing the case at the recommended stopping points, the rest of the snippet, and the teacher's case study. Our purpose here isn't to present a thorough analysis of the snippet but to give a sense of possible topics that might arise or that a facilitator might bring up.

What Is the Nature of the Relationship Between the Owls and the Snakes?

Often, especially if we have 90 minutes or more to spend on the case study, we will have participants discuss what they think is the nature of the relationship between the owls and the snakes. In the previous chapter, we discussed how we facilitate this discussion and the kinds of things that come up. One difference between these two cases, however, is that Izzy gave the students the data, whereas Sarah did not. With this case, therefore, we give participants an opportunity to reason with the data themselves, so that they can compare their own thinking to the students' thinking.

One interesting question participants have asked is, "Do the owls bring the snakes to the trees or the snakes crawl up there?" The first piece of evidence says that blind snakes are observed climbing trees, but it's never clear if they do that to reach the nests or if the owls bring them there. People think this is important; the argument is that if the snakes went to the nest on their own, then it might be evidence for mutualism, as they would seem to be going for "choicer" food. On the other hand, if the owls bring the snakes there, it would not necessarily support a mutualism argument because the snakes are not choosing to go to the owls' nests.

The Discussion to Line 54

Opening the Conversation

We usually stop the recording at line 54, approximately eight minutes in, when Max and Cameron respond affirmatively to Izzy's question, "And are blind snakes capable of burrowing?" We ask participants how they think it's going, what they notice in students' ideas and reasoning, and what they see in the students' thinking that seems scientific.

Emphasizing the Substance of Students' Ideas and Reasoning

Often, people first want to talk about what Izzy is doing (or not doing) or the nature of the activity. Here, people usually comment positively on how Izzy has set up the activity, and what a great way it is to get students thinking about using evidence. At this point, we try to steer the conversation away from discussion about Izzy or her methods, trying instead to focus participants on the students' ideas and reasoning. For example, if a participant says, "This is a great way to get students to think about the relationship between evidence and hypotheses," we might say, "What is it that you hear that makes you say the students are thinking about that relationship?"

It also commonly happens early in the conversation that participants comment on students' engagement, especially when we've shown the video. This is particularly problematic in Izzy's case study, which takes place in a self-contained special education classroom where several students appear not to be participating or even following what's going on. Some students have their heads down on the table, and one (Max) is rocking back and forth.

There's no question that it is important for students to be engaged, and we acknowledge that it may be problem. But, we emphasize, we chose this clip for the student ideas it puts on display. So, once the point is made about student engagement, we work to refocus the discussion on student thinking. (Sometimes, if engagement issues continue to dominate the discussion, we have pressed the point that while it is important to help the unengaged students, it is also important to work meaningfully with the students who are engaged. As well, we note, it may be difficult to assess these students' engagement, based on their physical behavior.)

Pressing for Specificity

Another common tendency is for participants to make general statements about how the students are doing, and we try to press them to include examples from the transcript to support what they are saying. For instance, if someone says,

"I like what Josh is doing in line 12," we ask them to interpret specifically what they understand Josh to be saying, and what they like about it.

Interpreting the Substance in the Students' Thinking

We rarely use this case study as our first one, primarily because some of the student ideas are difficult to interpret. This is a special education classroom, and some of the students in the class have disabilities related to language use. Often it seems as though a student *has* an idea, but it can be difficult to understand what it is. By the same token, the students' difficulty in expressing themselves makes it more important to listen carefully in order to interpret what they are trying to say, and participants who have already had some practice may be in a better position to study the transcript for meaning.

For example, Adrian responds very quickly to Izzy's question in line 20 about whether the first piece of data (that the snakes are normally fossorial but can climb trees to reach ant nests) can be used to evaluate the hypotheses. He says that we can "use it to evaluate." Someone usually mentions what Adrian says at the beginning of the discussion, and the general consensus is that he hasn't really constructed an answer to how the data can be used to evaluate a hypothesis; he is treating the question as a "yes or no" question, without realizing that he needs to explain his answer. As one participant put it, Adrian is approaching the question as "low-hanging fruit"—one in which he can give a simple one-word answer without putting too much thought into it.

We've pointed out Adrian's statement in line 21, "The snakes are capable of climbing up trees, and they can get to the nests on their own." What can we say about Adrian's reasoning there? In response to this prompt, people often interpret him to make an important distinction; one teacher remarked that Adrian's comment "suggests something about the relationship, like [that the snakes are] a voluntary participant in whatever is going on."

Pushing even further, we ask participants to think about what Adrian means in line 23 when he says, "And if owls and snakes ever turn against each other, they could use that as an advantage for like, uh, battle and stuff." Again, the perception is generally that Adrian is not thinking about how the data could be used to evaluate the hypotheses, but someone usually interprets him to be continuing to support the idea that the snakes have some agency in the relationship. It seems to some that he might be trying to reject the predator-prey hypothesis; that is, the snakes' ability to climb trees might suggest that they could easily escape from the owls and thus are not easy prey.

Josh's comments in lines 25 and 27 are usually not the first thing mentioned, perhaps because it is very clear from what he says that he is making an argument that the snakes could be protecting the baby owls from ants and other pests that might harm them. If no one mentions Josh's idea, we ask about it, and the consensus is usually the same as what Izzy mentions in her case study, that Josh is clearly using evidence to support a hypothesis. Interestingly, it has been suggested that Adrian's comment might have prompted Josh's idea. Perhaps Adrian's comment that the snakes are voluntarily going to the nests helped Josh think that there might be something in the nests that benefits the snakes.

Max's statement in lines 29 and 31 is very interesting, and if no one brings it up, we do. He says, "We can get rid of the predator-prey relationship ... because there's only 11% of them were found half eaten, but only one was eaten." He has incorrectly summarized the slide, which says, that *11% were found dead* and *1 snake was found half-eaten*. When we ask about his meaning, participants seldom notice that he has incorrectly summarized the slide and instead focus on what appears to be his overall argument—that since most of the snakes were *not* eaten, we can "get rid of the predator-prey relationship." One option here is to draw participants' attention to what Max actually says; does his incorrect summary mean that he has not appropriately interpreted the data? When we have done this, most participants are unconcerned with his summary. They argue that despite his misstatement, he has used his overall interpretation (that most of the snakes are not dead) to support an argument against the predator-prey hypothesis. We also like to draw focus to Max's idea because we believe it suggests that he is demonstrating an important understanding of science—that claims are made on the basis of a preponderance of evidence, although some discrepant or anomalous data may be present.

Participants also often mention Cameron's comment in line 37: "Well, I was gonna say the-because of the dead-uh the dead blind snakes-thinking they were picky about their food, because they'll eat live ones." What does Cameron mean here? Why was he "gonna say the...are picky about their food" and then change his mind? Is he doing some good scientific reasoning? Although what he says is a little confusing, it is generally agreed that he is saying that he thought the *owls* are picky about their food because the previous data suggested to him that the "half eaten" snake was a dead one. He had his hand up as Izzy was introducing the next set of data, so this is likely what he "was gonna say." However, hearing that new data, he decides that "it doesn't seem that way."

If someone doesn't bring this point up, we do, mostly because it suggests beginnings of scientific inquiry that require close listening and interpretation to recognize. Many participants point out that he is not using the evidence to consider the hypotheses available, and so they don't think he is reasoning with the data. However, participants who focus on how Cameron is *trying to make sense* of the data disagree. Even though he is not doing what Izzy wants him to do, he is doing some sensible thinking and being metacognitive about his own ideas. As one participant put it:

[H]e's shown this marvelous bit of scientific reasoning—[he] has this idea from the beginning of (line 39) that maybe the owls are picky, they'll only eat dead snakes—they won't eat live snakes. Right, because you know I think everybody sort of has some familiarity with this, like some animals will only eat like live food that they catch and they won't eat dead food and some won't eat dead things and only live things. But, then he hears the rest of the data and he like he evaluates his own hypothesis and he compares it to the data and it doesn't fit and so he rejects his own hypothesis.

Another interesting thing happens shortly after that in this discussion. Cameron keys on the piece of evidence that says that the baby owls will eat live blind snakes *if they can catch them* to argue that his hypothesis is true—that the baby owls will eat the snakes if they can catch them. Although he appears to miss the other evidence that (a) most snakes found in the nest are alive, and(b) live blind snakes can burrow into the nest, he seems to understand the nature of the activity, as one participant noted:

He gets that whole "well-designed investigation concept," that I started off with a hypothesis, now I have evidence, and now the point is to see if the evidence makes my hypothesis true or false, and I found something that sort of agreed, and so now I made a conclusion, my hypothesis was true.

In response to Cameron's idea, Izzy asks him to consider the other evidence, that most of the snakes are still alive, and asks what those snakes must be doing. Alex says "practicing for hunting." We ask about this idea, too, because it seems like an odd response to the question of what the snakes are doing. Reading it carefully in context, participants generally agree that Alex is referring to what *the owls* are doing, and not the snakes, reasoning, "I think he was thinking about the owls, or owlettes, are keeping the snakes for practicing for hunting."

Another participant said, "Maybe he's saying that the snakes are practice for hunting, the snakes are just practice." Some special education teachers who have seen this case have suggested that this might also reflect language difficulties, specifically over syntax and word endings. Alex might have been *trying* to say the snakes are *practice* not *practicing*.

This happens frequently throughout the discussion, that the students (and Izzy also!) often refer to the owls, when they likely mean the snakes, or vice versa. This makes it all the more important that participants try to interpret what the student might be saying in context, because the students often use the wrong word. If Alex does mean the owls, then he's doing something very interesting—he's proposing a new hypothesis, based on his reading of the data. One possibility is to ask participants to consider the alternative here. What if Alex does mean the snakes? Is there some way to understand why he might be saying that? Is he just confused?

Moving From Interpretations to Ideas for Instruction

After we have discussed the student thinking up to line 54, we ask participants to think about ideas for instruction, asking them to ground ideas for instruction in what they've heard so far. As always, we try to forestall criticism or praise of the teacher; we ask participants to think not in terms of what the teacher *should do* or *should have done,* but rather what the teacher *might do* next, or what she *might have done* in response to particular student ideas. What is the "menu of possibilities"? Since we don't generally use this case first, this point does not generally need much discussion.

Most frequently, the first item on the menu is what participants assume Izzy will do, namely to continue on to the next piece of evidence. Another frequent suggestion is that she might halt her established procedure to have a discussion about how data should be used to evaluate a hypotheses, since we have heard students both considering the preponderance of evidence (as Max does in line 31), and keying on the aspects of data that fit with their hypotheses (as Cameron does in lines 39–45). How can Izzy help students to see the distinction in the reasoning here? Working from the same interpretation of student reasoning, some participants have thought she could stop and ask students which hypothesis is supported by the preponderance of data that they have seen so far. Does the evidence so far support one hypothesis over the others?

The Discussion to Line 191

Sometimes someone points out the tangential conversation that starts in line 68 when Josh asks if a caterpillar counts as a larvae. (He did something similar earlier in the discussion when he asked whether the place where ants live should be called a nest). Often people argue that his question isn't related to the overall conversation about whether the evidence can be used to evaluate the hypotheses; others occasionally see something positive in what they think he's doing. As one participant said,

> You know, we often talk about how high schoolers will learn something in class and then they just won't relate it to a different problem. In this case, he's actually seeking out something that he thinks it's related to, it's a living thing—it shows him trying to achieve a particular understanding, and connect the conversation to something he knows about.

Often someone points out that this is one of the few times in the conversation when the students speak to each other directly, without going through Izzy. Max says, "It's a living thing, actually," and Josh responds, "Well, larvae are living."

We give time to this topic if someone raises it: What do people think of Josh's question? What does Max mean with his statement that "it's a living thing," and why does he think it's a response to Josh's question?

Every time we've used this case, someone notices the exchange between Kevin and Izzy in lines 77 to 94. Kevin seems to be doing something that no one else has done up until this point. The usual interpretation is that he's keying on the data showing that most of the snakes are not eaten but some are. One participant surmised,

> [He's saying that] If the blind snakes weren't able to get through then they'll be eaten. Like if that's true, some of them might get eaten but some of them are protecting the nest, then it is like a combination of commensalism and predator-prey.

We think this exchange is worth talking about because Kevin has decided the evidence suggests a combination of two hypotheses, and that seems like a sensible thing to do. Relationships in the natural world are often complex! Think of the way house cats will sometimes toy with a rodent before letting it go. In this case, the relationship could be thought of as commensalistic, because the cat is "practicing for hunting" while the rodent is not necessarily being harmed. Other times, however, the cat will eat the rodent.

One thing that is unclear to many people about Kevin's comment is why he insists that one aspect of the relationship is commensalistic rather than mutualistic. A participant stated, "I'm not entirely convinced why he's saying it's commensalism because he talks about how the owl benefits, but he's not specifically saying the snakes are getting nothing out of it."

Additionally, there's often some disagreement about what Kevin means when he says that the snakes would "clean up" the nest. In the class, Izzy appears to assume that he means that the snakes are cleaning up the nest like a maid would clean a house. However, one participant pointed out that he may be using "cleaning up" in a different way based on what the evidence suggests the snakes are doing:

> I feel like when he uses that phrase "cleaning up" I don't think he means it in the sense that like you know the way he cleans his room I think it's more of like the way cops would clean up a street or something—like in order to improve the security of the nest.

We think this is a very productive place to stop and talk about what a student means. Why is Kevin claiming that it is both commensalism and predator-prey? Why does he think it's commensalism and not mutualism? Is that clear? How is he using the term *cleaning up*? All of these are productive questions we might ask to help focus participants on Kevin's meaning. Here as often, it is hard to be confident about an interpretation; still, we are trying to cultivate practices of close attention to students' meaning. What participants decide in any particular seminar or workshop is not as important as their considering the matter closely.

Another place we like to focus attention is the conversation that follows the sixth piece of data. What do the candidates hear in the students' reasoning with this data? Someone usually points out Josh's comment in line 165:

> So I mean isn't he getting at mutualism because snakes are helping? The owls are having an increased growth rate, and the snakes are surviving also so isn't that kind of what he's thinking over?

While most people agree that Josh is seeing in the data that the faster nestling growth rate, and the lower weight at first flight, means that the snakes are benefiting the owls, there is often disagreement over whether or not he thinks that this supports mutualism as the participant above argued. Josh does not seem to make an argument that the snakes are benefiting, only that they're helping the owls. When the discussion comes up, we like to ask if people think that Josh is supporting a particular kind of relationship. It may be that participants read into his statement that he thinks the snakes are benefiting, so it's worth stopping and giving them an opportunity to check their own assumptions.

Kevin's comments in lines 186 and 188 are a little unexpected, and so it's worth drawing participants' attention to what goes on here. Kevin states that he disagrees that it is an example of mutualism, but reiterates his comment that it's an example of both "predator-prey and commensalism." His comment in response to Izzy's question "you don't think the snakes are really getting anything out of it?" is surprising though, because he says "yeah, but what are the owls getting out of it?" This seems surprising because his explanation before that the snakes were protecting the nests seems clear and sensible. So what is Kevin thinking here? Is he mixing up the owls and snakes (in name only) as others have done? Participants point out that this is unlikely because he appears in line 191 to accept Josh's explanation that the owls "get to be more healthy." So we may have to reconsider what Kevin was thinking, when he says it is commensalism; who does he think is benefiting, and why does he think the other species is not benefiting?

Moving From Interpretations to Ideas for Instruction

Again, after we have discussed the student thinking in this case study, we invite participants to think about a menu of possible ideas for instruction, asking them to ground ideas for instruction in students' ideas and reasoning.

One frequent suggestion is to ask Kevin to explain more about who he thinks is benefiting in the relationship, and who is not, because participants often think he has become less clear as the conversation has gone on. Other possibilities usually come up as well. Given that Izzy has discussed all of the data with the students, asked them to suggest what kind of relationship they think the evidence supports, and heard a variety of ideas, she might ask the students to write down what kind of relationship they think the data supports, and to explain why they think the data supports this relationship. After all, only a few students (primarily Max, Josh, and Kevin) have made clear explicit arguments. It might be useful to "check in" on everyone else's thinking at this point in the discussion. Another frequently suggested possibility is to tell the students what the researchers concluded, and see what they think of this conclusion. This may be valuable, because it will let the students see how scientists have evaluated the evidence, and show them that their own arguments resemble those constructed by scientists.

We suggest continuing to press for other possibilities until there are no more suggestions. Some people take longer than others to speak up, and we want to capture everyone's ideas. After all, there are other possibilities that most participants don't even consider. For example, Izzy continuously responds to student ideas, such that the discourse pattern usually goes Izzy/student/Izzy/student. She might work to push students to respond to each other's ideas directly. For example, in line 165, Josh has made a fairly sophisticated inference from the data. But do other students understand the inference? Izzy's move here is to repeat Josh's idea and mark it as a "good point," but she might ask if anyone else can explain what Josh said, and explain how the evidence shows that "the snakes do more helping."

The Rest of the Snippet

In most workshops and pedagogy courses, that's as far as we get, partly because we usually spend a lot of time at the beginning of the class talking about the snake/owl question itself, and partly because the first two segments are fairly long. If you do want to go further, the rest of the transcript is provided. Since we don't usually get to this part, participants usually want to know what happens at the end of the class. We usually tell them, especially if we want to ask them to anticipate how the students might respond.

At the end of the class, Izzy gives the students the article and asks them to look through it to find out what the authors conclude about the relationship. If we do get this far, we hope that participants notice the discussion between Josh and Izzy in lines 303 to 308 after it is established that the authors conclude that it is a commensalistic relationship. If they don't, we bring it up because we think Josh is doing some good things—he's questioning the findings of the scientists and suggesting why they might not be correct.

Josh asks if the authors can prove that the owls "are not really helping the snake." When Izzy asks how you would go about proving that the snake is not being helped, Josh says "Well those snakes are blind. I don't think they can find anything, and if they're in the nests they're safe and get free meals." One way to look at his comment here (especially if you're looking for deficits in students' thinking) is to notice that Josh is not really responding to Izzy's question about what evidence would support the commensalism theory. Another way to look at it, however, is to see the theory that Josh is offering for why the scientists might not be correct. That is, he is suggesting that since the snakes are blind, their presence in the nests makes it easier for them to find food than if they were on the ground. We like this exchange because we think it's important for students to question the authority of scientists, and Josh makes a valid point that could possibly be tested. In fact, it's not at all clear from the article why the authors have rejected mutualism. They appear to assume that the snakes are receiving no benefit—since many snakes of the species never live in owls' nests. They find food on the ground, and they can also find food in the nests.

Discussing Izzy's Case Study

We have always shown and talked about the video, at least through line 54, before people read Izzy's own analysis in her case study. Showing the video first, we think, helps the case seem more real. It also gives workshop participants the chance to form their own ideas about what is happening. Often their ideas align with Izzy's.

One option is to have participants discuss the case study in a subsequent class or seminar. During this conversation, we prompt participants to pay attention to Izzy's interpretations in discussing the case. Rather than focus first on what she does as the teacher, we ask participants to focus on what she sees and hears. What are the interpretations that motivate her to respond? How do her responses fit with her interpretations?

The final section in Izzy's case study, Reflection, can be useful for stimulating a conversation about what we should be thinking about in assessing our students' learning. Izzy expresses some dismay about how her students did on questions related to the Well-Designed Investigation on the exam, and articulates her struggles in reconciling her students' test performance with her experience leading the discussion.

A discussion about Izzy's concerns could be productive. How do other teachers reconcile what they hear from their students with what they see on exams? Do they join Izzy in questioning the role of their own "summative" assessments and the connection of these assessments with what students can be heard and seen doing? We think Izzy's honest expression of ambivalence in this case study can provide an opportunity for other teachers to question the alignment between what they care about students doing in science class, what they hear in their students' ideas and reasoning, and how their students perform on standardized measures of achievement. We encourage participants to bring in examples of video and student work from their own classes, in order to address these questions in their own context. In this way, analysis of what students are learning is focused not only on what they have "mastered" by the time the test comes around, but on how they're engaged in authentic scientific activity.

CHAPTER 6

The Rime of the Ancient Mariner

This case study documents what happened in Jenny Tanner's 10th-grade biology class when she showed her students a stanza from Samuel Taylor Coleridge's poem "The Rime of the Ancient Mariner," and asked them to explain what they thought it was describing.

> *Water, water everywhere and all the boards did shrink*
> *Water, water everywhere, nor any drop to drink*

The high school biology curriculum guide that is used in Jenny's district suggests this activity, and places it after students have studied processes of diffusion and osmosis. It is intended to give students an opportunity to apply their understanding of osmosis and associated vocabulary (e.g., hypertonic and hypotonic solutions) to their interpretation of the poem. Jenny had seen a video of another teacher in the project leading a discussion about the poem, and she was interested in trying it herself, but with a twist: Instead of having the discussion when the curriculum guide suggested, she decided to explore how her students might reason about the mechanisms at work *before* she introduced them to osmosis and the associated terminology.

The main data are the transcript and video of the class session. Dan Levin wrote the case study based on his recorded conversations with Jenny, in which she discussed her interpretations of the students' thinking as she watched the video and read the transcript. The case study begins after Suggestions for Reading and Viewing.

Suggestions for Reading and Viewing

We present the case starting with some background about the class and lesson. The transcript and video can be found on the website. We suggest you read the beginning of Jenny's case study, just up until the section titled Getting Started. Then watch the video, while following along in the transcript, before you read the rest of Jenny's account. By doing things in this order, you get the chance to recognize and interpret the students' thinking for yourself, before you find out what Jenny saw and heard.

The video snippet is 19 minutes long. Be sure to make copies of the transcript, which is useful for following along, for jotting notes, and for reference in discussion with others. When we use this case in seminars and workshops, we stop reading or watching the students' conversation at two or three spots in order to encourage participants' close, careful examination of student thinking:

1. *Line 102, approximately 6 minutes in, when Rachel says, "and then ... cause didn't you say that—."* We usually stop here and ask participants to discuss what has happened so far and to think about the following questions: How do you think it's going? What do you notice in students' ideas and reasoning? For this case study, this stopping place is also a great opportunity to ask candidates to think about what Jenny might do next with what she has heard. Several times we have used this case study when time was very limited. (It can be a good one for that, because it's shorter than the others, and there are a lot of student ideas in a short period of time.) When this happens, we often just describe what has happened in the conversation through line 102 and start watching with Jenny's response to Rachel, saying that the students have focused in on the fact that you can't drink salt water because it makes you dehydrated. Starting there lets participants get to the end of the conversation, which gives them a chance to see the most interesting ideas and how the class co-constructs them.

2. *Line 210, about 11 minutes in, after Tilson says, "Like water moves from high—high density place to a low density place."* Here we stop and ask similar questions. How is it going now? What do you notice in the students' ideas and reasoning? Do they seem to be thinking scientifically?

3. From here we usually play it out to the end, and ask the same questions again. When there's been enough talk about the students and how they're thinking, we ask participants for thoughts about the menu of possibilities for how the teacher might respond.

The Case Study: The Rime of the Ancient Mariner

By Daniel Levin and Jennifer Tanner

Background

This class occurred during Jenny's third year teaching biology at a suburban high school in Maryland. The school had about 2,700 students that year, with a population fairly equally mixed among African American, Latino, Caucasian, African, and Asian students. This was an "honors" biology class for 10th-grade students. Although honors biology was generally offered to high-achieving 9th-grade students, this section was offered to 10th graders who had performed well in the 9th-grade physical science class that they had taken the previous year.

Jenny had not tried to lead a discussion about "The Rime of the Ancient Mariner" before. She didn't even know that it was in the curriculum guide, which she rarely used, because most of what it recommended was just "simple, worksheet-oriented activities" that didn't give students opportunities to reason about interesting phenomena. Jenny was interested to see what would happen if her students discussed the poem, having seen and been impressed by a video of a conversation about the poem from another teachers' class. A discussion around the poem might be a useful way to elicit students' understanding and reasoning about water transport.

One of the things that had come up in the teachers' discussions about many of the videos[1], however, was that students often treated vocabulary they had learned as the answer, without paying much attention to the mechanisms that were represented by the terminology. For example, one student Lexi, in the conversation from the other teacher's class, identified that the poem was about osmosis, but she could not do much more than that.

> Lexi: Doesn't it have to do with osmosis though?
>
> Teacher: Okay, so what does it have to do with osmosis?
>
> Lexi: Meaning, uh, the water ... Like, doesn't it kinda mean, like the water inside the boards left out the boards and then it shrank?

---

1. These discussions occurred as part of our NSF-funded project *What Influences Teachers' Modifications of Curriculum?* (see Chapter 1). As part of that project, teachers watched video of classroom conversations and analyzed the student thinking in evidence.

Teacher: Why would it do that?

Lexi: I ... (shakes her head)

In that class, the teacher had introduced the concept of *osmosis*—and the students had done several activities that demonstrated how water flows from high to low concentration across a selectively permeable membrane— before they discussed the poem. Jenny thought that it would be interesting to see how students reasoned about the poem before she introduced the term and the idea. The students had talked and read about diffusion and about membrane semipermeability, but not yet about osmosis. Jenny thought that discussing the poem might create an opportunity for students to construct an understanding of osmosis, and she planned to follow it with a homework assignment on the topic.

At the beginning of the lesson, Jenny projected the two famous lines from "The Rime of the Ancient Mariner" on the screen, and she asked a student to read them aloud. She told the students that the lines were from a poem, written from the perspective of a man lost at sea. She asked them to think about what the poem meant and to write their interpretations down in their notebooks. She then gave students a few minutes to write, after which she asked them to share their interpretations with the rest of the class.*

*This is a good point to stop reading, watch the video, and talk about the student thinking.

Getting Started

A few weeks later, Jenny and Dan watched the video and Jenny pointed out some of the things she remembered noticing during the class and what she noticed now. During class, she was surprised that the first comments, from Moyatu and Rachel, focused not on what was going on in the particular setting, but instead what it meant for human populations globally. In retrospect, however, while this wasn't what she had been looking for, she realized that Moyatu and Rachel were both answering her question, "As you read this poem, what do you think of?" in a reasonable and sensible way. They may have expected that the poem was a starter for a conversation about global environmental and health issues, and not realized that Jenny wanted to have a discussion about the mechanisms behind the phenomenon described in the poem.

Andrew's interpretation of the setting provided an opportunity for Jenny to push students to reason about the mechanism behind why we can't drink salt water. Andrew said you couldn't drink it, "because it's not good for you," and "it's gross," and Brian said it was because of the salt, which would "dehydrate you" and was "bad." This set the stage for the conversation Jenny wanted to have about *why* drinking salt water causes dehydration. The conversation shifted briefly, however, when Tilson explained his interpretation of the poem.

> Jenny: Alright, Tilson, what do you think? You gonna expand on Brian's thought? ... No?
>
> Tilson: I think it's talking about a boat, and how the boards on the boat shrinks when there's no water.
>
> Jenny: When there's no water the boards of the boat would shrink?
>
> Tilson: Yeah.
>
> Jenny: Why would that happen?
>
> Grace: The water expands the wood.
>
> Tilson: The water expands.
>
> Jenny: Is there water or is there not water?

During class, Jenny thought Tilson just didn't understand the situation and thought "there was no water," but watching the video later, she wasn't sure of that interpretation, partly from what he had to say later in the discussion. Maybe Tilson was thinking that there was no water because he was thinking of the boards of the deck, which may not be completely immersed in water and "when there's no water" meant the times when there was no water touching the boards.

Hearing the exchange later, Jenny also noticed Grace's comment, "The water expands the wood." What was she thinking? Probably, she was thinking of her own everyday experience with wood swelling in water. She may have been following off of Tilson's comment that there was "no water." That is, if there were water, the boards would swell, so if there were no water, this would explain why the boards would shrink. Jenny realized that she didn't really know what Tilson or Grace was saying, and had only assumed at the time that the comments were based on a mistaken assumption.

Jenny interrupted with a question: Why was it bad for shipwrecked people to drink salt water? Rachel suggested two possibilities: that it "messes with your brain chemistry" or that "it dehydrates you so much that you die." Sensing that the conversation was back on track about "what Brian said" about salt and dehydration, Jenny continued to pursue it. As the conversation proceeded, Jenny noticed several kinds of comments. Some of the students continued to focus only on the fact that drinking salt water *was* bad and not *why*. For example, students mentioned that salt water, would "make you sick" and "was dirty." Hawaney mentioned again that salt water "makes you thirsty" and "dehydrates you," but she didn't explain why, and Andrew continued to assert that salt water was bad.

Jenny heard other students beginning to think about why. She noticed some students were thinking of the salt absorbing water, as a way to explain why it would cause dehydration. Grace was the first to say that "the salt absorbs the water." Moyatu seemed to be thinking of something similar, (lines 68–70), when she described how a little bit of water "becomes solid" when it is combined with a large amount of salt. Brian said this idea the most clearly.

> Brian: If you drink salt water, and the salt water like goes into your body, then the water's already in your body and the salt water, or just like the different molecules of salt—salt molecules kind of absorb water in your body and it will dehydrate you.

Other students, Jenny noticed, seemed to be thinking of a chemical reaction between salt and water, rather than a physical absorption.

> Rachel: I mean, I guess it would be some kind of chemical process where it wouldn't exactly be water anymore, it would be like a form that your body couldn't use.

Hawaney said something similar.

> Hawaney: Since water is just like H_2O and, salt water's like a different kind of a different kind of compound than water...

Jenny thought that these students were beginning to think of something important, how salt water might be chemically different from water.

Still other ideas focused on the salt itself, independent of water. For example, Haja suggested that it was "bad for your heart." Discussing this later, Jenny thought that in these cases students were probably focusing on the fact that salt contained sodium and they knew that too much sodium was a problem. As Brian said, "sodium is good for you, but like if you take too much in at a time it just messes you up."

Grace referred to salt as a solvent, but when she elaborated on what she meant, it was clear to Jenny at the time that she was thinking of what she knew about the role of salt in melting ice. Although she didn't elaborate on what the melting phenomenon might have to do with why it's not good to drink water, Jenny pointed out during the interview that Grace was trying to visualize what the salt might be doing to the water in the body. Perhaps seizing on Grace's mention of the term, "solvent," Rachel suggested that because water was a solvent it would break up the NaCl into sodium and chloride molecules. Like Grace, Rachel didn't seem quite sure how this would contribute to the problem of drinking salt water. Nevertheless, Jenny's sense of the conversation was that many of the students were beginning to draw on what they already knew about salt and water to reason about the problem.

"The NaCl Might Attract Stuff From the Boards"

Although she noticed some positive things in the students' ideas and reasoning, Jenny reported that she felt quite a bit of tension during this early part of the conversation. She was pleased that the students were curious and were coming up with a lot of ideas, but the conversation was unfocused, and she did not want to direct it. The students were generating a lot of ideas, but they seemed to bounce from one to another, without really listening to each other, even though some of the ideas seemed sensible and could have helped the group to make progress.

Hoping to encourage a more coherent conversation that moved toward a well-articulated mechanism, Jenny decided to see if the other part of the poem would provide an easier situation for the students to reason about. She suggested they "look at a couple lines here," and repeated the second part of that stanza—"and all the boards did shrink." In the interview, Jenny explained her thinking about her instructional move here. She thought that the same explanation of why you can't drink salt water would help explain why the boards shrink, and so if the students were able to visualize the shrinking boards, then maybe it would help them explain why it's bad to drink salt water.

Jenny was pleased with how the conversation developed from there. Students continued to draw on their prior knowledge, both about things that they had seen (such as Metzy's comment that the salt would "eat" the boards) and things that they had learned in class (e.g., Rachel's idea that the water's polarity might allow it to "react" with the salt and thus be broken apart).

More than that, Jenny appreciated how much they were listening to and trying to make sense of each other's ideas. For example, Moyatu was not satisfied with Metzy's comment about the salt eating the board, and both Moyatu and Haja were uncertain whether Rachel's drum explanation made sense. Even more impressively, Brian questioned the premise of the entire conversation.

Brian: I thought if you put water on like wood it swells.

Students: Yeah!

Metzy: Oh yeah, what if that happens?

Jenny also pointed out in the interview that students were beginning to generate mechanisms that could describe the *movement* of water, which could be productive for understanding how salt causes dehydration, that is, how it causes the movement of water away from parts of the body that need it. She was excited, for example, about Rachel's description of the drum.

Rachel: Well, I know that um if you take a drum that's too tight, and you put water on it, or sometimes you like hold it like over a fire, then it'll tighten, so I think like maybe if it evaporates...

Jenny saw Rachel drawing on her experience with drums to suggest a process (evaporation) that she knew could cause things to get smaller. Additionally, Rachel's explanation pointed toward a new possibility—that there might be water inside of things like drums (or wood) that could move out. Jenny decided to make that idea explicit for the class to consider.

Jenny: Yeah, so Rachel's saying, I think, it's getting smaller cause the water's evaporating.

Rachel: And, I guess if the—like if the water molecules are in with the water where the water's going to evaporate and the molecules are in the wood?

Jenny: So the wa-water inside the wood would evaporate.

When Jenny asked other students if that made sense to them, she got a mix of reactions.

Students: Sure ... no ... depends ... yeah ... well ... if it's ... if it rains ...

Andrew: Depends on if it's been dried out or not.

Andrew: I mean if it's—if it's not been like—

Brian: Oh!

Andrew:—if it just came off a tree or something then it probably does have water

Jenny: Alright, so if we just cut the tree then it's got water in it.

> Brian: Okay. So the tree-so wood comes from trees—(Laughter—Jenny: Good) and the tree, and trees need water in order to uh survive, when you cut the tree down and make the uh, wood, there's still water left inside of it, but when you put it in salt water the salt water will evaporate the actual water inside of it.

Jenny noticed two things about this exchange later. First, it seemed clear to her that Brian was trying to use the idea that there might be water inside the wood (an idea that Rachel brought up initially in line 157) to reason about why the water might move. He noted that "when you cut the tree down and make the wood, there's still water left inside of it," and drew on Rachel's mechanism of "evaporation" to suggest why the water inside the wood would move out (and presumably cause the boards to shrink). Second, Jenny noticed Andrew's sensible point that whether or not there was water in the wood "depends" on the state of the wood. This seemed like productive scientific reasoning—Andrew showed recognition that phenomena in the natural world are contingent upon the particular conditions.

Finally, it was in this section of the conversation that the first mention of concentration came up, although the students referred to it as "density."

> Toan: Well the NaCl might like attract stuff from the boards and then like water flows from the boards where it's dense to like less dense...
>
> Jenny: So the board becomes less dense because—
>
> Toan: Like there are holes on the board...

Here Jenny interpreted Toan to be saying that the water was more dense inside the boards than outside and so it "flowed" from inside the boards to outside. This mention of density was the first evidence of the students considering differences in the composition of different kinds of water that could lead to the movement of water. Naturally, this consideration can be seen as productive in that it is part of the "right answer" (i.e., the mechanism of osmosis). Additionally, however, it provides important detail that can elucidate other possible mechanisms, such as how evaporation occurs.

"Maybe It's Like the Other Way Around"

The issue of density continued to come up, mostly from Tilson, who said, "Doesn't water go to a place with lower density?" Although she was still working to hear and understand her students' ideas, Jenny was determined to have her students make progress. In fact, hearing the beginnings of it, she started wanting them to settle on the idea of osmosis, because they needed to end up there eventually, and she wanted them to have the satisfaction of coming up with the idea themselves. Directing the conversation, Jenny asked Tilson what he had said earlier about density, and he gave her a surprise.

Jenny: What did you say earlier?

Tilson: Osmosis

Jenny: What's that?

Tilson: Like water moves from high—high density place to a low density place

Jenny: So water's moving from a high-density place to a low-density place?

Students: (lots of voices—inaudible)

Jenny: Alright so we talked a—so diffusion, what's that?

Watching the video, Jenny saw Tilson leafing through his book, something she hadn't noticed during class and it occurred to her that the assignment for that evening's textbook reading was on the board. Something else that surprised her, watching the video, was that she had mentioned diffusion, a topic they had already discussed. She thought that Tilson had brought it up. Either way, it provided a new thing for the students to think about.

Listening during class, Jenny had thought the students "got it"—that they understood water moved from high concentration to low and were putting that together with the earlier conversation about there being water in the boards. Watching the video during the interview, however, she wasn't so sure that she understood what Brian was thinking in particular.

Brian: Well, maybe it's like the other way around, so if the water like molecules move from high density to low density...the ocean.

Jenny: So where they gonna go? Where--What's going to happen to the water?

(Bryan and other students suggest it will leave the wood).

Bryan: It's gonna go from the wood ... out like any hole in the wood.

Jenny: Why would it go from the wood into the ocean?

> Brian: Because it's going from a lower concentration to a higher concentration. You just reverse it.

Listening to what Brian said at first, Jenny assumed he was saying that water density is "high" inside the wood and "low" in the ocean and so it moved from high concentration to low, just like they had learned for diffusion. Later, however, he said that water is going from "low" inside the wood to "high" in the ocean and, "You just reverse it." Jenny was surprised by this. Was he now contradicting himself? Or was he referring to salt and not water when he said "lower" and "higher" concentration here? And what was he thinking of reversing? Was this just a rule he was memorizing?

And not everyone was okay with the explanation anyhow. Using the example of oxygen in the lungs, Rachel seemed to be saying that if they were talking about something moving *out*, it would have to be something that was moving from higher density to low.

> Rachel: Isn't it because like, okay if the example is like oxygen going into the water because there's more like, like a higher density of oxygen in the water, so it would be like, going from like, the ship where there's like maybe 10 water molecules to the ocean where there's like a million. It's by—it's moving to a higher density place from a lower one. It...
>
> Jenny: So it goes from a lower density place to a higher density place? What's diffusion?
>
> Rachel: Okay! Yeah! Then would it be—
>
> Brian: Diffusion of cells from a higher concentration.

Jenny corrected Brian's use of "cells" to "molecules," and Brian and Hiba together said it was from high to low.

> Rachel: Yeah. See, yeah I feel like they, like they move in the direction where there's more space—so like it doesn't really make sense to me because...

Jenny thought this was terrific! Rachel seemed confused, but confused in a very productive way, insisting that the explanation should make sense. She didn't understand why the water molecules would "move in a direction where there's more space" because they had learned from studying diffusion that molecules move from higher to lower concentration. Jenny reminded them of earlier conversations about oxygen in the lungs, and guided them to similar reasoning about water in the boards. As they followed her, she switched to challenging that reasoning, asking students to explain how there could be a higher concentration of water in the board when it's in the "big old ocean." Very quietly, Grace said, "because the water in the ocean is salt, and the—so it's NaCl and the water in the boards is just H_2O." This was a distinction that Jenny had been hoping for, and so she asked Grace to repeat it.

> Grace: The water in the ocean is a mixture of NaCl and H_2O but the water in the board is just H_2O so that's a higher concentration.

"So that's a higher concentration." Grace had made a distinction that Jenny hadn't heard before, that it was a higher concentration of water when there was no salt than when there was salt. Brian followed up with a long explanation that clarified what Grace had said

> Brian: So if you took like a—if you took like a drop of salt water and compared it to a drop of just regular water, there'd be more of the regular water in the regular water because there's also salt in the salt water so the salt water has a lower concentration of water since it's mixed with the salt, so the water molecules would move to the outside of the board where there's a lower concentration.

With this statement Brian was able to clarify, in his own words, why water would move out of the boards. What's more, he had managed to create a model, using the idea of the amount of salt that would be in "regular" water versus the amount of salt that would be in salt water. Jenny was particularly impressed with this, because when she and her colleagues taught osmosis, they would show students a model of a semipermeable membrane (such as a piece of dialysis tubing) inside of a beaker, varying the concentration of salt inside and outside of the beaker. Here, Brian had created his own model, which Jenny felt she could return to when the class reviewed osmosis in detail.

From here, it was just a short step for the students to apply this understanding to the mechanisms for dehydration. Several students, including Brian, Ann, Metzy, Haja, and Andrew, seemed to understand that water would go out of the body's cells if a person drank salt water, thus causing dehydration. Jenny thought it was worth checking to see what everyone else understood, however, and so she asked the students again to write down their thoughts on the meaning of the stanza, for her to collect after the lesson.

Reflections

It's cut off on the video included with the book, but immediately after the discussion, Jenny turned to Dan and said, "Wow. That was amazing!" He asked her later in the interview what she liked so much about it, and it took her a long time to figure out specifically what she liked. Eventually, it came around to three things. First, she loved that the students were listening to each other's ideas, and because of this they seemed to construct their understanding of what was going on as a group. Second, the room had a bustle of enthusiasm and participation, and even those who weren't speaking seemed engaged in what was going on. Finally, she loved how invested the students were in making sure the answer made sense; Rachel was unhappy with an explanation that was inconsistent with what she knew about diffusion, and Brian's final description placed the mechanism in his language that he and others could understand.

For Jenny, the session was a surprise. With only a little guidance from her, the students had collectively arrived at a sensible explanation for the stanzas for "The Rime of the Ancient Mariner."

Facilitators' Notes

Please see the general notes for facilitators in Chapter 3. Here we'll provide specific comments and suggestions for discussing the video at the recommended stopping points, as well as for discussing the case study. Our purpose here isn't to present a thorough analysis of the snippet but to give a sense of possible topics and issues that might arise or that a facilitator might bring up.

Interpreting the Poem

We don't usually ask participants to interpret the poem themselves before watching the case study. First, we usually have a group of mostly biology teachers, and to them, the poem is obviously about osmosis. Even if this is not obvious, it becomes so when participants read the beginning of Jenny's case study (before watching the video). Additionally, questions about the content often come up as we watch the video. In some cases, physical science teachers who have not taught about osmosis admit that they're not quite sure about "how it works," which usually leads to others in the group explaining the mechanism of osmosis.

It often happens that people agree with Brian's thought (line 137), "I thought if you put wood in water it swells," in questioning the premise that the boards shrink. In one showing of this case study, we heard the following exchange:

Alex: I like this [Brian's comment] because this is confusing to me, because it's not really clear to me that the boards would really shrink at all.

Ryan: Right. I mean it's clearly part of ... it's a poem.

Zeke: Why wouldn't it be starting with salt water? Salt water before and after—the boat's in salt water. Do you understand what I mean? If the salt water...

Dan: The question of whether the boards really do have freshwater in them.

Alex: It's—unless it's going from freshwater to salt water, exactly, why would water be going in or out because the concentration of the salt water that's inside the board is the same concentration as the salt water that's outside the board?

When these questions come up, we allow time for participants to consider them, because we think it's productive for teachers to think about science that arises out of students' ideas. It helps the teachers to understand the ideas better themselves; it helps them appreciate the quality of student reasoning, and it gives them the opportunity to think about how they might respond. Depending on the group, we might leave the topic open—if it won't prevent participants from continuing to focus on student thinking. Often, though, we have helped them resolve the science in a way that is consistent with the premise, such as offering that they could take it as an empirical fact that boards shrink, in boats at sea.

The Discussion to Line 102

Opening the Conversation

If we have time to start from the beginning, we stop the recording at line 102, approximately five minutes in, when Rachel says, "and then ... 'cause didn't you say that—." We ask participants how they think it's going, what they notice in students' ideas and reasoning, and what they see in the students' thinking that seems like the beginnings of scientific inquiry.

Emphasizing the Substance of Students' Thinking and Pressing for Specificity

Even when participants have already had experience discussing case studies, it's typical for some to begin with comments about what Jenny is doing, such as to applaud how she is drawing out students' ideas and pushing them to explain why salt water would cause dehydration. We try to steer the beginning of the conversation away from Jenny's moves, reminding participants that we try to focus on instruction after we have considered the students' ideas. Instead, we try to reorient them toward the students' ideas and reasoning. What and how are they thinking about the boards' shrinking? How are they doing?

It's very common, as it is in other case studies, for participants to begin with general comments about the students' thinking, such as that students are "drawing on their prior knowledge." We welcome the contributions but press for evidence: "Can you point to a specific instance where you hear a student drawing on prior knowledge?" Of course, there are many instances they could choose, and people have no trouble finding examples: Moyatu and Rachel's knowledge of the problems with water resources, Brian's idea in line 17 (picked up by the other students) that salt causes dehydration, Haja's idea that salt is "bad for your heart," Rachel's idea that sodium "can't actually be in water by itself," Grace's idea of salt breaking down ice into water, Rachel's use of the term *solvent*, or Grace's use of the term *dissolve*, or Moyatu's interesting question, "If you put a little bit of water and a lot of salt, the water becomes solid, doesn't it?"

One option here is to ask participants to talk about what they mean by "prior knowledge." Some of these ideas are things students have heard as disconnected information (salt is bad for your heart), seen in other classes (sodium can't be in water by itself), or learned from everyday experiences (water becomes "solid" with a lot of salt). Are all of these equally valuable as prior knowledge?

When, as is typical, participants commend students' use of terminology, we take a moment to ask about that. What do participants like about it? Are they just happy to hear terminology from the course, or do they hear the students trying to come up with substantive explanations that involve these concepts? Grace and Rachel certainly seemed to be trying to use the idea of water as a solvent to reason through the problem in lines 93–102, and it's worth trying to push participants beyond the fact that they're using the vocabulary toward what they're *doing* with the vocabulary. What are Grace and Rachel trying to say?

Interpreting the Substance in the Students' Thinking

That this is an honors biology class and that students contribute from the beginning tends to impress teachers. People get the sense that the students are very bright. Still, it's often easier for participants to hear what they imagine to be deficits in students' thinking than it is to hear the possibility or sensibility in their ideas. For example, when participants begin to focus on specific ideas, someone usually mentions Moyatu's and Rachel's comments about drinkable water in the background, and judges them to be "off track." However, in some cases, others have pointed out (as Jenny mentioned in the interview for her case study) that this is not an unreasonable thing to say if they've simply been asked "as you guys look at these words, what do you think of?" without being asked to think specifically about *how* they should interpret it. This is an important point, and if no one brings it up, we often ask about it, by saying something like, "If you just think about how Moyatu and Rachel are interpreting the poem, how might they see their interpretations as sensible?"

Another typical pattern, in response to the question, "What do you notice in students' ideas and reasoning?" is for someone to say, "I like what Rachel is doing." When we hear this, we follow up by asking, "What is it that Rachel is doing?" "What do you like about it?" And more specifically, "Can you point to a particular line where you see Rachel doing that? With these prompts, someone usually mentions that Rachel seems to be genuinely trying to figure out what's going on, drawing on everything she knows about the problem. The idea in line 55 is usually given as an example. Drawing on what she has likely learned about "chemical processes" in middle school, Rachel wonders if the salt in the water "wouldn't exactly be water anymore, it would be like a form that your body couldn't use."

And then, of course, there are other specific ideas in the transcript to ask about if no one brings them up. What is the distinction that Rachel is making in line 41 about how drinking salt water can affect people? Why does Andrew, in line 59, say in response to Grace's statement that salt dissolves in water, "But not the salt water in the ocean?" Does he believe that salt is not dissolved? Why might he think that? And what might Brian be imagining in line 89 when he talks about "different molecules of salt?" If participants don't key in on some of these ideas, we bring them up.

Finally, it can be useful to draw attention to the exchange between Tilson, Jenny, and Grace in lines 21–29, something Jenny commented on in her interview. Participants have never brought up, maybe because it is so difficult to interpret. For this reason though, it is exactly the kind of exchange that we like to focus on, to see the *substance* of students' thinking even when it is not obvious. Why would Tilson say, "the boards on the boat shrinks when there's no water"? Is he just misreading the poem, or is he considering some particular kind of scenario? And why would Grace respond to Jenny's question about why that would happen by saying "the water expands the wood"? One interpretation for Grace's response is that she's thinking about something she has seen, that water expands wood, and so she considers Tilson's claim that the wood shrinks when there's no water as the opposite situation. That still doesn't explain why Tilson would say "when there's no water," when the poem clearly says that there is water everywhere. Jenny's interpretation is in the case study, but she had the benefit of hearing Tilson throughout the whole discussion.

Moving From Interpretations to Ideas for Instruction

After participants have a chance to talk about the discussion up to line 102 we ask them to think about what Jenny might do next. What is the "menu of possibilities?" Naturally, this depends largely on how people think it is going and what ideas (if any) they think are worth focusing on some more. Frequent general suggestions for what Jenny *might do* next include:

- Let the discussion go on longer and contine to push students for a mechanism for dehydration, as she has been doing. We usually ask participants why they think it's worth continuing in this vein. Usually, it's because they see value in the students' ideas, particularly what Metzy and Brian brought up, about salt absorbing water, and Rachel's idea that the salt in some way changes water so it's not really water any more. A related idea is that Jenny could continue to pull on these ideas in particular. *How* does the salt absorb water, and how does it change it?

- Have students write down some of their ideas on the board. This often comes from people who think that some of the students are not catching some of the most interesting ideas from their peers. One teacher participant said, "Yeah, I think it's easier for the other students to understand what their fellow students have said [when it's written on the board], especially if they're all facing forward and talking to the teacher." In other instances this comes from people who are intrigued by Rachel and Brian's descriptions of salt and water on the molecular level, and would like Rachel or Brian to expand on what they're talking about so that the other students could see how they are thinking about the molecules.

- Return to the poem and have students consider the first lines (about the boards shrinking). The interpretation here is that the students aren't making progress, possibly because they feel as though it is enough to say that drinking salt water causes dehydration, and the other lines might force them to think more about the mechanism. This is a particularly interesting suggestion because it is exactly what Jenny does. It suggests that some of the participants hear the conversation as Jenny did and that there's a certain shared rationality about how to proceed.

- Guide students more. This is in direct contrast to the suggestions above. This idea usually comes from participants who are frustrated with the discussion and hear the students making little progress. One participant referred to the conversation as "hide the peanut," where the teacher knows the answer and is making students "find it" without her help. Suggestions include telling them to think about what they know about diffusion, or even explaining osmosis at this point.

Of course our perspective is different than that expressed in the last suggestion. We see Jenny as trying to accomplish much more than finding that peanut. She was trying to engage the students in scientific reasoning, and there is evidence that's what they were doing. For that reason, we see this as an essential thing to address, participants' taking the goal of science class as arrival at canonical ideas. Much of our purpose in these case studies is that teachers and prospective teachers see and aim for more than canonical correctness in students' reasoning, and this presents an opportunity for conversation: What are the beginnings of scientific thinking in evidence here? How might instruction build on those beginnings? Typically other teachers challenge the idea that Jenny should guide the conversation more, and we facilitate and participate. If nobody does, however, we offer our own respectful disagreement with the assumptions behind that idea, and in any case we do not pretend to be neutral on the matter. At the same time, it is important not to impose our views on teachers; our purpose is only that they see the possibility of a different perspective.

We continue to remind participants to consider the menu of possibilities not as evaluations of the teacher, favorable or critical, but rather neutral suggestions about possibilities for instruction and how they might influence student thinking. Any of these suggestions could be considered reasonable possibilities and may lead to different outcomes. The point is that the teacher has had to make choices in the moment—choices which seemed reasonable to her at the time. Notably, Jenny, like all the other teachers we have worked with, will often come up with other possibilities of what they could have done. We want to emphasize to people who are going to be conducting their own case studies that they shouldn't think of these possibilities as moves they should have made, but rather as different approaches they might have taken, or could consider in similar circumstances in the future.

The Discussion to Line 210

There are several places in this portion of the discussion we see as important for participants to consider. As we mentioned above, if time is limited we generally start with this segment, from line 102 to line 210, because it is so rich in evidence of student thinking.

As in the previous section of video, it is common for participants to focus on particular students and what they're doing. Here, people usually mention Brian. Again, we try to push people to articulate what they like about what Brian is doing, and what in particular they interpret him to be doing or saying that they think is valuable. Usually someone mentions his good humor, such as in line 104, when he asks "Is this English class or biology class?" and the way in which he seems to be trying to make sense of the situation. One participant noted:

> He would say something, and if he didn't get it, he would sit back, and he would let it digest and like, come back, like, "wait a second. So, that doesn't make sense. So maybe let me think about it."

Participants are often also impressed with the way Brian appears to be listening to and following up on other students' ideas. For example, someone pointed to line 198, where he picks up on Sam's idea a few lines earlier about the role of water as the universal solvent: "He was collaborating. Probably trying to, um, trying to use what Sam originally said and then try to help."

We appreciate these comments and usually press for more about the substance of his collaborating. What does Brian mean by "...if water is the universal solvent and like there's always so like—so much water inside the boards then like salt water goes into the boards as well the water is dissolving—is dissolving the salt and as it does that then there's no more water—"? This is a difficult line to interpret. Is he saying something that he thinks makes sense? Or is he just thinking aloud, trying to come up with an idea as he speaks? One interpretation is that he is saying that the water that is in the boards is completely taken up with the job of dissolving the salt, and so there is no more water. He gives up on his idea, so it's hard to know if he was planning to say "and that causes the boards to shrink." Some people use this tendency of Brian's to occasionally give up on his explanations as more evidence of his pursuit of a sensible answer (lines 19, 198, and 279). That is, he gives up on his responses because he becomes uncomfortable over whether or not they make sense.

Of course it's also worth going back and focusing on Sam's statement here too. She says, "Water's a universal solvent. So basically it dissolves trees, 'cause trees require water and sunlight for them to grow." Does she really think that water "dissolves trees"? And why does she say that is "'cause trees require water and sunlight for them to grow?" Usually people see this line as nonsensical. Of course water doesn't dissolve trees. Even the second part of Sam's statement would suggest this is not so. After all, if trees needed water to grow, why would water dissolve them? In one session, however, someone pointed out that the first part might be considered sensible, saying, "She could be picking up on what she knows about trees, that they have water in them, and if water is the universal solvent, then maybe it dissolves trees, and also the boards, causing them to shrink."

Much in the way we hope teachers consider how students are approaching questions in science, we think it is important for teacher educators to consider how teachers approach interpreting student thinking. In this instance, we appreciated how the participant was making an interpretation, and equally important, taking a stance of looking for the possible sense in what a student has to say. In this instance, too, another participant challenged the interpretation. These are the practices we hope to engender—that participants will try to interpret the student's meaning, and that others will consider whether or not those interpretations make sense.

"And All the Boards Did … 'Sink'?"

An interesting conversation to have is why the students start talking about the boards "sinking" rather than "shrinking," beginning with Brian's statement in line 116 that, "It would possibly just sink," and including Metzy's comment in line 135, "Like it's sinking …" Toan's comment in line 185 that water goes inside the board and "makes the boards heavy," suggests that he might be thinking about what causes the boards to sink (Jenny's response suggests that is how she understood him). Why would the students be thinking about the boards "sinking?" Are they simply misreading or mishearing the line of the poem, or do they have some reason for thinking that "sinking" makes more sense than "shrinking?" If no one brings this up, we do. Where has this idea of "sinking" come from?

"Maybe if It Evaporates …"

Rachel's comment in line 145 draws a lot of attention, and if it doesn't, we bring it up. It's not that difficult to understand what Rachel is saying, but it's helpful, when people notice it, to urge them to say what they think of it. To us, it's terrific that Rachel is using an experience that she has had with drums to think about how something might shrink. As we continue to read through this part of the transcript, it's useful to talk about whether Rachel and the other students are using the drum explanation as an *analogy,* that is, that the mechanism might be similar, or if they are thinking of evaporation as the possible mechanism by which the boards actually shrink. For example, in line 172, Brian talks about the water being in the trees, and says, "but when you put [the wood] in salt water the salt water will evaporate the actual water inside of it." Brian appears to be co-opting Rachel's language of evaporation, but how is he using the word *evaporation*? Does he really think the water is evaporating (which suggests he might not really understand evaporation)? Or is he just using the term as a placeholder for another word that he doesn't know? Participants usually see this as another example of Brian picking up on other students' ideas and using them to construct an explanation. Most don't think that he is actually referring to evaporation in terms of the mechanism by which liquid undergoes a phase change and becomes gas.

"It's Going to a Place of Lower Density"

The conversation in this section usually turns to a discussion of the students' use of the term *density*. This often starts with a general statement that the students are now talking about density, which puts them on "the right track" (that is, making progress toward the "correct" mechanism).

We usually use this as an opportunity to ask participants to look through the transcript and try to trace where the idea of density begins and how it develops.

The first mention is Toan's statement in lines 131 that, "the NaCl might like attract stuff from the boards and then like water flows from the boards where it's dense to like less dense." To most, this line seems pretty clear, it appears that Toan is thinking of the movement of water from a more dense area to a less dense area, an idea that could help make progress toward understanding a concentration gradient. Toan's next line, however, is confusing. What does he mean, "There are holes on the board," in response to Jenny asking for elaboration? Does he mean that the water is flowing out through holes in the board? In that case, what does he mean by holes? Is he thinking of large holes, or is he thinking of small microscopic holes, as one might conceive of in a semipermeable membrane? Alternatively, could Toan still be thinking about the board "sinking" rather than shrinking? After all, this is how Metzy might be interpreting his idea of holes in the board when she says, "Like it's sinking...Was that your question?—sinking?" in line 135. Similarly, Toan returns to the idea of sinking in line 185 when he says, "The water, like it goes inside the boards, makes the boards heavy." These are lines worth pointing toward if participants don't mention them, in order to try to get a better sense of what Toan is thinking about.

The next mention of density is Tilson's response to Rachel's point about evaporation. When Jenny asks, "why would the water evaporate?" Tilson replies that it is going to a place of lower density. Someone usually notices that Tilson picks up his textbook and looks through it when Jenny asks him to repeat it. The general interpretation is that Tilson has looked ahead in the text and seen information about osmosis, although some argue that this is something he already knows about water, maybe based on his understanding of evaporation. Later, Tilson's use of the word *osmosis* is evidence to support the former interpretation.

With the students talking about density, it is quite common for participants to object to the students use of the "wrong term"—using *density* instead of *concentration*. Some find this puzzling, considering that Tilson appears to have looked osmosis up in the textbook, where he likely saw the term *concentration*, and considering too that the students were familiar with the term *concentration* from their earlier discussion about diffusion. (In fact, they switch to using the term *concentration* when Jenny asks them to remember about diffusion in line 213).

In one session, a participant had a thought about why the students might be using the term *density* in a sensible way.

> [W]e use the words interchangeably when you talk about like population density you're really talking about population concentration. It's not density in the sense of mass over volume. The mass of, you know, residents of [the city], right? You're talking about number in an area, which is concentration,

but we say population density, we use, you know, or traffic density. We use density as analogous to concentration in areas where people sort of understand what is going on. And so in 131 when the student says like, "NaCl might attract stuff from the boards and then water flows from the boards to like less dense." I mean I thought he was really coming up with that concept before diffusion was introduced and really early on he remembered this idea that water is going to go to something that's less dense and I think what's he's understanding is less concentrated.

In this interpretation, although the students know the term *concentration*, they revert to a common usage of the term *density*. There is usually a lively argument here about whether or not students should be using the correct word and whether or not Jenny should be correcting their usage. Steering the conversation away from what Jenny should be doing for the moment, we take this opportunity to nurture this debate about vocabulary. Does it matter that the students are using the term *density*? Why does it matter? The participants who argue for the use of the correct word make the point that the students will be tested on *osmosis*, and it may confuse them to hear the word *density*. Others point out that this is just the beginning of the series of lessons on osmosis, and it will not be complicated to inform the students of the correct term later. Like the participant above, they think it is fine that the students are using the term *density* (for now), as it expresses an idea consistent with common everyday usage.

Another interesting thing that happens during this discussion is that participants begin to question their own understanding of the differences between density and concentration. This is another example of how the students' ideas in this case study can be useful for engaging participants in deeper understanding of content.

These are just some of the issues that come up in this section, or that we think are worth bringing to participants' attention if no one mentions them. As usual, there are many more student ideas that call for interpretation. For example, what does Moyatu mean when she asks, in response to Brian's description of the salt water causing the non-salt water to evaporate, "But, but wouldn't it just absorb the water? Absorb the water because, because when the tree—when the tree actually has water it comes from the roots, but if you have wood, there's nothing for it to like ... absorb, so it just absorbs it"? And what is Tina talking about when she says, in response to Brian's suggestion that the water is dissolving the salt, "Um, well, you said that, you were asking why the tree like wouldn't be absorbing the water—the salt water. Um, maybe it could be the water and the salt has already just like combined, which would mean that the way—that the tree would just not want it ... (laughs) not want it, but it just doesn't take

124

it in"? These are examples of student thinking that we often bring up if no one mentions them and as time permits.

Moving From Interpretations to Ideas for Instruction

In deciding how much of the video to show, it's useful to factor in at least 10 minutes or so for talking about ideas for instruction based on the analysis of the student thinking. Interpretations of student reasoning lead to possible ideas for instruction. After participants have a chance to talk about the discussion up to line 210, we ask them to think about what Jenny might do next. What is the "menu of possibilities"? Are there particular ideas that are worth focusing more attention on?

As described above, there are usually a number of people who think it's important for students to understand the difference between *density* and *concentration,* as these terms relate to diffusion and osmosis. One possibility is that Jenny might engage students in describing what they mean by *density.* How do they understand density on the molecular level, and how do differences in density of molecules lead to movement of molecules?

Generally, ideas about what Jenny might do next reflect how people think the discussion is going. Usually, there are two groups of people. Those who feel as though Jenny is treating all responses as equally valid, and thus the students are continuing to flounder, argue that it would be worth giving them some greater direction, for example reminding them what they know about diffusion, and asking them to think about how to apply it here. Those who feel as though the students are making progress often would like to see things continue in this vein, and perhaps even think about the teacher taking on a less central role—maybe asking students to respond to each others' ideas instead of responding herself. Participants in this group often point out that Jenny has been somewhat directive. For example, she explicitly draws attention to Tilson's idea about the flow of water from high to low density in line 210, which he describes as "osmosis." From this point of view, Jenny is already drawing attention to ideas that could help students move toward the correct answer. One option she could take to have students think more scientifically is to have them address Tilson's idea, to see if they think it would explain what is described in the poem. For participants who are looking for more student-student interaction, the practice of paying attention to each other's ideas is at least as important as rapid progress toward the correct answer.

We suggest continuing to press for other possibilities until there are no more suggestions. Some people take longer than others to speak up, and we want to capture their ideas, as well as those of the more talkative people.

The Rest of the Snippet

If we have stopped the video at line 210, discussed the students' thinking, and asked participants to consider the menu of possibilities, the most salient feature of this part of the snippet is Jenny's direct move of introducing the idea of diffusion in line 213. One option is to stop quickly here, especially if it didn't align with any of the possibilities that were suggested, to ask people to predict how it might play out in how the students think about the problem. Alternatively, it might be useful to mention before restarting the video after 210 that we are going to watch the remainder of the video and consider the students' ideas before discussing how Jenny's move may have influenced it. After all, we want to remain focused on the students' thinking. Whichever way we choose to do it, a discussion about the menu of possibilities right before this instructional move brings it into focus. Surprisingly, when we have shown the video straight through from line 103, it's not obvious to everyone *who* brings up the idea of diffusion, just as it was not obvious to Jenny in the case study.

Discussions about student thinking in this part of the video usually begin with the ideas that are easiest to understand, and have come up in conversation before. For example, most participants notice that the students' language (e.g, Brian and Toan in lines 215–216) shifts from talking about density to talking about concentration, which most consider to be directly tied to the introduction of the term *diffusion*, in the context of which students had learned to use the term *concentration*. Usually if we've had the conversation about terminology previously, people don't notice that Brian reverts to using the term *density* in line 223. If we haven't had that conversation before (which is rare) this is a useful time to address it. Again, does it matter that the students have not been using *concentration* until now? If it matters, why does it matter? And does it matter that Brian reverts to using *density* in line 223? What does it tell us about Brian's understanding of density and concentration?

Other ideas are much more difficult to interpret, which provides a greater opportunity to practice interpreting students' unusual or unconventional thinking. For example, what is Metzy thinking when she responds to the "What is diffusion?" prompt by saying in line 220, it's "like when you mix something and it becomes unmixed?" or when she says "it's gonna be a big circle of water." People usually don't spontaneously begin talking about these ideas, probably not only because they are difficult to interpret, but also because they don't seem to be necessarily "on-track" toward the correct understanding. Focusing on these ideas is an opportunity not only to get participants to practice interpretation, but also to remind the group that our goal is not only to evaluate students' progress toward the correct answer, but also to *understand students' meaning*. This can help us understand *how* students are thinking. Is Metzy's thinking scientific? Unless we spend time unpacking and interpreting the seemingly unclear ideas, we don't necessarily know if they are productive in moving the group toward a correct mechanism, or even a coherent mechanism in general.

"Maybe It's Like the Other Way Around"

It's worth spending some time on Brian's idea, in line 223, when in response to Jenny's question of whether diffusion comes "into play here," he says, "maybe it's like the other way around, so if the water like molecules move from high density to low density... the ocean." The usual interpretation here is that Brian has "got it"—that he understands water moving from a place where it's more "dense" (on the boards) to where it's less "dense" (in the ocean). It's important here to draw attention to Brian's comment in line 233, if no one else brings it up. He says, "It's going from a lower concentration to a higher concentration. You just reverse it." What exactly is he saying is moving from lower to higher concentration? Salt? Water? It's not clear, and to many he seems to be saying something different from what he said in line 223. Does he think that water is more concentrated outside of the boards or inside? And does his reversion to the use of the term *concentration* tell us anything about his thinking? Is he actually using *density* and *concentration* differently? These are all questions that have come up when we have discussed Brian's ideas here.

"It Doesn't Really Make Sense to Me Because—"

Rachel's analogy to oxygen "going into" water usually draws attention, and it's worth spending some time trying to understand what she's saying. Her overall point seems to be that the water would be moving from low concentration to high concentration, but the analogy itself is not quite as clear, so we often ask if participants can imagine the situation she is imagining of oxygen "going into water." Is she thinking of water as having a higher concentration of oxygen than is outside the water?

One of the reasons to draw attention to this idea is because it helps participants to recognize how Rachel is trying to make sense of what she is hearing, and how that comes out in the way she participates. It's hard to know what she is planning to say in line 238, but based on her statement in line 247 it she seems that she is responding to Jenny's question about diffusion with a challenge. In line 247, she says clearly that "it doesn't really make sense" to her. Why doesn't it make sense to her? What does she mean when she says that she feels like "they move in the direction where there's more space?" One interpretation is that by "they" she's referring to molecules, and whether she's talking about oxygen or water molecules, the implication is that molecules *would* move in a direction where there's more space (as the students learned is true for diffusion). Thus Rachel is pointing out an unresolved problem: Isn't there more space for water *inside* the boards?

"There'd Be More of the Regular Water in the Regular Water"

Brian's comment beginning in line 274 usually draws the most positive attention. It is clear to almost everyone what he is saying about the relative concentration of salt in salt water versus in the water in the boards. It's important to spend some time discussing what people like about Brian's comment. The fact that the idea is also a "correct" understanding of the fundamentals of osmosis can focus attention only on the correctness. But there are other things to admire about Brian's move here, and it's worth drawing attention to those things.

Participants recognize many positive features here: Brian is again constructing an idea based on one that has come before—people point out that it was Grace who first described the difference in concentration of water between salt water and fresh water in line 270. Participants also appreciate the way in which Brian puts it in his own words, and creates a model by considering a "drop" of water with and without salt.

Although we try to maintain a focus on the substance of students thinking, the end of the video often leads to a discussion about participation. While some participants see the entire discussion as productive, many are concerned with "who understands." The argument is that, if the conversation is an assessment of who understands what, then there's not much that can be said about anyone other than Brian and Rachel and maybe a few other students. This can be used to transition to a conversation around what a teacher might do next. It can also be an opportunity to open up a conversation about what else might have been accomplished besides students "discovering" osmosis. After all, one of the possible instructional responses is to move to a more guided understanding of osmosis, possibly an explicit description of the model. So what does the discussion accomplish? Are there people who think it has value otherwise? Do others disagree?

What Happened Next and the Menu of Possibilities

We usually tell people that Jenny ended the class by having students return to their notebooks and write down how they interpreted the poem now. The class ended after that, so we ask participants to consider what a teacher might do next, in this case, with the evening to plan for the next class. There are a number of possible ways to respond and by hearing each other's ideas, teachers can access a deeper pool of possibilities than each alone would consider. We usually wait until the discussion of the menu of possibilities has gone on for a while before we tell participants what happened in the next class. The students went over the homework in the textbook, which introduced osmosis, and did a lab activity in which they looked at the changes in the mass of potatoes exposed to different salt solutions.

Discussing Jenny's Case Study

We have always shown and talked about the video before people read Jenny's case study. As we discussed, this is a complex and often subtle case study to analyze, and thus it requires some time to be used productively. If time is short, we focus on the discussion of the video more than we do on the case study. Since the case study covers the entire class, it's a little difficult to discuss without having watched the whole video. If there is time, we suggest approaching the analysis of Jenny's case study in the ways we describe in Chapter 3, talking or writing about how participants see the situation as Jenny describes it. (This is a little more complicated, however, since Dan actually wrote this case study based on an interview with Jenny.)

One option is to discuss how Jenny heard the ideas in the moment versus how she attended to them as she and Dan watched the video during the interview. For example, in the moment, she noted that she thought Tilson's comment in line 22 ("I think it's talking about a boat, and how the boards on the boat shrinks when there's no water") suggested that he just didn't understand the situation indicated by the poem. Watching the video during the interview, however, she thought he might be thinking that the boards on the deck were not immersed in the water. What do participants think of the difference in these two interpretations? Does one seem more accurate than the other? And if so, what does this tell us about the differences in how Jenny was listening to the ideas in the moment versus listening to them when she had more time to consider Tilson's possible meaning? This can lead to a more general discussion about how we listen to students in the moment and what watching the videos later can afford for our thinking about students' ideas.

"My Students Would Never Do This"

The case study describes the students as honors students, and most teachers recognize the willingness to participate that often characterizes upper level classes. Usually, by the time we show this video, participants have had enough experience watching the owls and snakes videos and observing classes to see that such discussions are not necessarily anomalous, that they can be found in high school and middle school classrooms even with students who are not labeled as "honors" or "gifted." If we consider the potential ideas and reasoning that *all* students bring to science class, then we should be creating opportunities for them to express their ideas and reasoning, and planning to attend and respond to their thinking.

CHAPTER 7
Free-Falling Bodies (1)

N inth grade students at two different schools worked on the same conceptual questions about freely falling objects, and this is the first of two case studies about what happened.

These questions were developed by the physics group in our research project. Unable to interpret the thinking underlying students' extremely brief responses to a textbook's questions about free fall, the teachers brainstormed conceptual questions intended to elicit students' conceptions and reasoning in more depth. We then compiled those questions into the "Free-Falling Bodies" question set (Figure 7.1, p. 133). In this case study, Matt Reese analyzes his students' written responses to the questions; in the next case study (Chapter 8), David Hovan describes what happened when he discussed the questions with individual students and with his whole class. We usually use Matt's case study first because we think it's easier for participants to analyze written work before examining video. Additionally, the questions are tricky, especially for participants with limited physics background, and we like to give participants an opportunity to think about the questions themselves (as discussed below). Exploring students' written work first, before moving on to the fast-paced conversations in Dave's class, can help teachers see how their own thinking compares to the students' responses.

The data for this case study is the students' written responses to the question set; these can be found at *www.nsta.org/publications/press/extras/responsive.aspx*. Matt's written case study begins after the Suggestions for Reading and Reviewing Student Work section. We recommend that participants start by reading only the introduction to Matt's case study, containing the background information about the class and the question set; then spend some time looking through the student work before continuing with the rest of Matt's account. This gives participants a chance to interpret the students' responses for themselves, before reading Matt's interpretations.

Suggestions for Reading and Reviewing Student Work

Be sure to copy the student work, included as a PDF file on the website, to share with the group. The file contains responses from six students, and each response is three pages long. The six students are identified by initials: JW, DD, SE, JF, CE, and CK. Matt explains in his case study why he chose these students.

The question set is shown in Figure 7.1. One option is to have participants work on the questions themselves, either individually or in small groups, so they can familiarize themselves with the conceptual terrain before looking at students' responses. This can be intimidating for people with limited physics background, however, so we usually hand out the student work right away. This allows people to talk about their own understanding of the questions in the context of interpreting the students' ideas. We have found that discussing the students' responses almost always leads to productive conversations about the science, as participants wrestle to reconcile their situation-specific intuitions with their understanding of the general physical principles.

We recommend providing 15–20 minutes for participants to look through the student work, prompting them to interpret what the students are thinking. It's important for participants to have something to write with. We encourage participants to highlight noteworthy student ideas and jot down their interpretations. We sometimes pair up participants or put them in small groups to begin talking about what they have read, but in our experience it is imperative that people have time to read the student responses individually first. The questions are complex and both the students' handwriting and the substance of their ideas are often not clear.

Figure 7.1

Free-Falling Bodies

1. A bowling ball and a small rock are dropped at the same time from the same height. Which one lands first? Here is a student's answer:

   STUDENT: "They land at the same time. If there were no air, the bowling ball would land first. But air resistance slows the bowling ball down, so they land together."

   Do you agree with the student's reasoning? Disagree? Explain.

2. A bowling ball and a small rock are dropped from the same height at the same time. Which one lands first if this experiment is done
   (a) on the Earth?
   (b) on the Moon (which has no air)?

   Be sure to explain your reasoning and to answer both (a) and (b).

3. To escape a burning building, a father drops his baby out the second-floor window, and at the same moment, the father lets himself fall out the window. They both land in a padded "person catcher" set up underneath the window by firefighters. Who, if either, lands first: the baby or the father? Explain your reasoning.

4. Two identical plastic soda bottles, one of them full of soda and the other completely empty, are dropped from the roof of this school at the same time. A student, when asked which object lands first, answers as follows:

   STUDENT: "We learned from those Galileo experiments that objects of different mass all fall at the same rate. So the full and empty bottle land at the same time."

   Do you agree? Disagree? Explain your reasoning.

5. A slippery ice cube is released from rest from the top of the ramp shown here. It slides without friction and reaches the bottom in one second. Then, a bigger, heavier ice cube is released from rest from the top, and slides without friction. Does it reach the bottom in less than a second? Exactly one second? More than one second? Explain your reasoning.

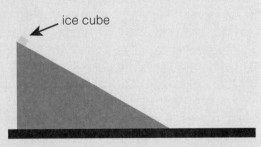

ice cube

The Case Study: Free-Falling Bodies (1)

By Matt Reese

Background

This case study describes student work collected during my fourth year teaching Honors Physics to ninth graders at a high school in suburban Maryland. This is not a "Conceptual Physics" class, which is offered to ninth graders at many high schools in Maryland, but a full-fledged physics course. The material is identical to a traditional high school physics course that many other students take their junior or senior year. This creates a challenge for the students because, for some, physics will be one of the most difficult courses they take in their entire high school career, and they have to take it while they are still adjusting to high school. Fortunately, my freshman physics classes are usually small, only about 20 students, so I have time to work one-on-one as needed with students who struggle.

At the time of this case study, the class had been studying inertia and gravity. We had done several things to explore inertia. Students had conducted a lab to explore the movement of objects with different masses being pushed by the same force, and I had done several demonstrations of inertia, including the classic "plate on a tablecloth" trick[1]. Students had read about Newton's first law, and we had a class discussion about inertia.

We had also spent considerable time discussing gravity, and we had done an experiment to show that all objects fall at the same rate. Over the years I have found this to be a difficult concept for students to grasp. Additionally, in previous years I have often purposely ignored air resistance and only given questions where it was not present, because so many students had trouble incorporating it into their understanding of falling objects. This year, however, I had shown students what happens when you drop a piece of paper and then ball it up and drop it again, and we had discussed the role that air resistance plays on falling objects.

Following the discussions of gravity and inertia, we moved on to a lab about Newton's second law, though we hadn't talked much about it in class. I realized during the lab that I wasn't quite sure what my students

---

1. When you quickly yank a tablecloth out from under a plate, the plate hardly moves, because its tendency not to change its motion—its inertia—makes it "resist" accelerating in response to the force exerted upon it by the tablecloth.

134

understood about inertia and gravity. I thought it was important for me to get a sense of what they understood at this point, before moving on to discuss Newton's second and third laws.

The "Free-Falling Bodies" Question Set

Dave Hovan[2] had used this question set the previous year, and he suggested that I try it. Dave thought that the questions did a good job probing students' understanding of free-falling bodies, and I was anxious to know what they understood about inertia and gravity. The questions elicit considerations of mass and air resistance with real-world examples, which could help me to understand how students considered these variables alongside their intuitive sense of how things fall.

I gave the question set to the students without reviewing anything we had learned about inertia, gravity, or Newton's second law. My students are very good at repeating back what I say in class, and I really wanted to see how they were thinking without using my words. I let them work in small groups, and I told them they were not being graded on correctness, but only on their ability to explain their thinking.

Reviewing the students' work afterward, I found that many students gave similar answers (probably because they were working on it together). I analyzed the students' responses to questions 1, 2, 4, and 5. I didn't analyze question 3 because I thought it was so similar to question 4. I grouped those answers and chose students at random to include in this case study. Therefore the responses in this study are fairly representative of my students as a whole. My goal was to analyze student responses to get a sense of what they understand about inertia and gravity, where they were struggling, and hopefully get a sense of why they were struggling.

Student Responses

Question 1: The Bowling Ball and the Rock

> *A bowling ball and a small rock are dropped at the same time from the same height. Which one lands first? Here is a student answer:*
>
> STUDENT: *"They land at the same time. If there were no air, the bowling ball would land first. But air resistance slows the bowling ball down, so they land together."*
>
> *Do you agree with the student's reasoning? Disagree? Explain.*

---

2. See Chapter 8.

Most of my students disagreed with the hypothetical student, though with some variation in how they explained their disagreement. CK wrote:

> I disagree because the reason they land at the same time is because gravity pushes all objects down at the same rate. The only reason the bowling ball doesn't land first is because it has more inertia, and resists gravity. Gravity then has more force and overcomes its inertia.

CK disagreed because, as he said, "gravity pushes all objects the same." He went on to include some detail of his understanding of how inertia applies to this situation. To CK, it was the ball's inertia rather than air resistance that "resists gravity" and presumably keeps it from speeding up faster than the rock. I think he was drawing from what he had learned in the class about more massive objects "resisting force," to reason that gravity must be pulling on the bowling ball more to overcome its greater inertia. As he said, "gravity then has more force and overcomes its inertia." This is a subtle concept, which many other students did not include in their responses.

A different kind of response was offered by JF:

> I disagree, because the bowling ball has more mass than the little rock and it didn't have to be air.

JF didn't write a lot, so it's difficult to know if he was disagreeing with the result, the reasoning, or both. When he said, "the bowling ball has more mass than the little rock," it suggests that he thought the bowling ball would land first (other things being equal), because it's heavier, but it's not really clear from what he wrote. More curious is the second part of the statement, "And it doesn't have to be air." What did he mean? I may be reading too much into this, but perhaps he was saying that the bowling ball would fall no faster than the rock *even if there were no air*. If this is what he meant, it suggests some understanding of inertia: A bowling ball falls no faster than a small rock, in the presence or absence of air, because its greater mass (and greater inertia) takes more force to drag it down—similar to what CK was saying.

Another student, JW, responded to the question with the following:

> Some of his reasoning is wrong. If there is no air resistance, both objects have the same acceleration when falling. Air resistance acts on very light objects with large surface area.

JW was the only student of the six I chose for this case study who focused on air resistance in this question. He had seen the experiment where I dropped a piece of paper and it fell very slowly, a phenomenon I had explained in terms of air resistance acting on the paper. Paper is very light and has a large surface area, two things the bowling ball does not have. JW wrote that "some of [the students'] reasoning is wrong," because he did not think air resistance would act on the bowling ball. It's not clear which part of the student's reasoning JW thought was *correct*.

Question 2: Falling on Earth vs. Moon

The second question brought in the complicating factor of dropping two objects on Earth and on the Moon.

> *A bowling ball and a small rock are dropped from the same height at the same time. Which one lands first if this experiment is done*
>
> *(a) on the Earth?*
>
> *(b) on the Moon (which has no air)?*
>
> *Be sure to explain your reasoning and to answer both (a) and (b).*

JW responded as follows:

> *(a) On Earth both may land at the same time. Because the objects are heavier, air resistance may not act on them.*
>
> *(b) They land at the same time. If there's no air there's no resistance. No matter the mass, they will fall at the same rate.*

JW's responses here are consistent with what he said in question one. Both the rock and ball are relatively heavy and he did not think air resistance acts on heavy objects. (He used the term *heavier*, and I assume he means they are heavier than an object that he has seen influenced by air resistance, like the paper in our demonstration.) In part b, he stated that if there were no air then they would land at the same time. We discussed in class that objects fall at the same rate, but we also saw an example of how air resistance factors in with light objects or objects with a large surface area. Based on JW's responses to these two questions, I think he understood the principle that gravity accelerates all objects equally regardless of the mass, and understood the role that air resistance plays with objects in real conditions. It's not clear from his responses, however, *why* he thought objects fall at the same rate. He did not express the sophisticated understanding that CK did, about the balance between inertia and the force of gravity.

Another student, SE, responded to question two as follows:

> (a) *Land at the same time*
> *+m = +i*
> *−m = −i*
> *acceleration is equal*
> (b) *bowling ball*
> *no air resistance.*
> *Bowling ball has more mass and nothing is slowing it down.*

These responses are so fragmented that it's really hard to know what SE was thinking, and I'm confused by her responses. SE apparently was writing down things that she learned in class in the first part. She wrote that they would land at the same time on Earth, and that acceleration is equal. This is material that we reviewed about the effect of gravity in the absence of air resistance. She also included two equations, which seem to make the point that more mass (+m) means more inertia (+i) and less mass (−m) means less inertia (−i). I'm pleased to see that she seemed to understand the relationship between mass and inertia, but I don't know that she understood *why* this fact would cause objects of different masses to land at the same time (e.g., the greater force of gravity on the more massive object cancels out its greater inertia). It's possible that she was basically repeating the hypothetical students' answer from the first question. Looking back at her response to the first question, this seems like a real possibility, because she agreed with the hypothetical student, writing, "I agree because the bowling ball has more mass than the rock making it land at the same time." I don't see evidence that SE was thinking through the question here other than to repeat parts of her reasoning from question 1.

SE's response to the second part is also confusing. She wrote that in the absence of air the bowling ball would fall first because it "has more mass and nothing is slowing it down." If she understood inertia as she seemed to based on her response to part a of question 2, then the more massive bowling ball would land no sooner than the light pebble because the ball's greater inertia means it takes longer to get moving. Here, she was focusing on the lack of air resistance to slow the ball down; but then why did she not mention air resistance in part *a*?

National Science Teachers Association

JF responded to question 2 as follows:

(a) the bowling ball because the more mass will cause it to drop faster (b) Neither, both would float.

JF's response to the first part of the question seems to confirm my thinking about his response in question 1. He thought that heavier objects fall faster. This would explain why he said he disagreed with the student in question 1. He did not agree that they would land at the same time. I think JF was disregarding what we learned about objects falling under the influence of gravity and relying on his intuition. It is intuitive to most people that heavier objects fall faster, because they regularly see this happen. However, JF did not mention the role of air resistance either, so he did not seem to be thinking about the demonstration we saw with the paper, which would explain why heavier objects tend to fall faster in the presence of air resistance.

JF's response to the second part reveals a confusion I saw in many students' responses. JF said that both objects would float; he seemed to be suggesting that neither would fall *at all,* perhaps because he was thinking that *no air means no gravity.* Until this lesson, I had never addressed the confusion about air and gravity specifically in class because I never realized students would think it. The first time I saw responses about no gravity without air I ignored them because I thought they were isolated responses, but this analysis has confirmed that this is a common confusion. Why do students think no air means no gravity? I'm not sure, but I think it's because of reading or watching TV programs about objects in space. When the question says, "on the Moon," it makes students think of space, which they have "learned" has *no air* and *no gravity.* This isn't entirely true; there is certainly gravity on the Moon or any celestial body, even ones without an atmosphere. Nevertheless, I have become aware that this is something I need to address.

Question 4: The Soda Bottles

Two identical plastic soda bottles, one of them full of soda and the other completely empty, are dropped from the roof of this school at the same time. A student, when asked which object lands first, answers as follows:

STUDENT: "We learned from those Galileo experiments that objects of different mass all fall at the same rate. So the full and empty bottle land at the same time."

Do you agree? Disagree? Explain your reasoning.

CE answered,

> *I disagree because if the full soda bottle is heavier than the empty one it is more likely that the more massive bottle will land faster. The empty one will not resist the air.*

CE's second sentence is very interesting, "the empty one will not resist the air." CE seemed to be thinking about how the air was affecting the bottle. In her mind, the more massive one would land first because it would not be affected by the air nearly as much as the less massive one; the more massive object could push through the air better. CE may have been applying what she saw in the demo where I dropped the textbook and a piece of paper at the same time. On a side note I have debated this question with other physics teachers. I believe CE is actually correct and the more massive soda bottle would land first because air resistance has less of an effect. In essence, the force due to gravity overwhelms the force due to air resistance *more* in the case of the full bottle than it does in the case of the empty bottle. Nevertheless, other physics teachers I've talked to have disagreed, arguing that because the bottles have the same shape, air resistance acts no differently on them. I think that if you think about it intuitively, you know the heavier one drops faster. This is because the force of air resistance counterbalances the downward force (mass times g) on the empty bottle more than it counterbalances the downward force on the full bottle.

DD also had an interesting answer to this question.

> *I agree because the higher mass will slow down to the lower masses rate. The full soda can will slow down to the rate of the empty one because more mass has less acceleration.*

We had spent quite a bit of time on the experiment with varying masses under the same force. Like many of my students, DD seemed to have grasped that greater mass has greater inertia and thus accelerates less quickly than lighter masses under the same force. However, DD was neglecting what we learned about gravity, that the more massive object also experiences a stronger gravitational force and therefore all objects accelerate the same under the force of gravity.

Question 5: The Ice Cubes

The final question in the question set is as follows:

> *A slippery ice cube is released from rest at the top of a ramp. It slides without friction and reaches the bottom in one second.*
>
> *Then, a bigger, heavier ice cube is released from rest at the top, and slides without friction. Does it reach the bottom in less than a second? Exactly one second? More than one second? Explain your reasoning.*

SE answered,

> *The heavier ice cube reaches the bottom in more than one second because it has more mass. Greater mass means less acceleration. Therefore, it takes longer for the ice cube to reach the bottom.*

I think this confirms that SE understood inertia as we discussed it in class. She wrote, "greater mass means less acceleration." So if she were thinking along the lines of the experiment we did in class, then if the same force were pushing or pulling the two ice cubes along a horizontal surface, the bigger ice cube would take longer to cover the same distance. The difficulty here is that gravity is the force pulling on the ice cubes, and gravity pulls on heavier objects more, resulting in the *same* acceleration for objects of different mass. Since SE's answer from question 2 suggests that she knew that heavier and lighter objects fall at the same rate under the influence of gravity, I wonder if the ramp keeps her from seeing that gravity is acting. I wonder what she would say if I asked her what force causes the ice cubes to slide down the ramp.

CK's response to question 1 suggested to me that he had a good understanding of the relationships among mass, inertia, and gravity. But for question 5 he responded as follows:

> *It would get to the bottom in more than one second. Since the first cube hit in one second the bigger one takes longer because it is heavier. When you use the same force, but increase the mass, the velocity and acceleration decrease, increasing time.*

CK's answer is very sensible and clear; it's similar to SE's response, but more specific: If both cubes were under the "same force" the more massive one would have more inertia and would then take longer to reach the bottom. In question 1, CK said that the force of gravity must be greater on the heavy ball so it can overcome its greater inertia. If the activity did not include the ice cube question I would feel confident that CK had a very strong understanding of the concept of inertia and how it relates to gravity. What about if the ramp is different? Again, I wonder if it somehow "shuts off" students' thinking about gravity because it seems more like a horizontal surface than it does like a free fall.

Reflections

My main goal for this part of the force unit was that my students would develop a strong understanding of inertia. I think there is evidence in these responses that many of the students, represented here by CK, DD, and SE, do demonstrate a strong understanding of inertia, particularly as it can explain what causes more massive objects to accelerate less under the influence of a particular force. CK was even able to apply his understanding of inertia to free fall, balancing it with gravitational force to explain why objects of different masses land at the same time. I was really impressed that a ninth grader could do this. This is a difficult concept, and I know there are many physics-trained people who don't understand this; they simply accept what Galileo told us, without understanding the reason. Although we had talked about gravity, about falling objects, and about the effect of air resistance on falling objects, it's pretty clear to me that inertia was what really stuck with my students, even though the other principles are applicable in this situation. Even those students who were having difficulty with the assignment were able to use the term *inertia* in at least some of the questions. Even when they applied it incorrectly, it was clear that they at least understood what they were applying, rather then just throwing in the word, hoping it would get them some credit. DD, for example, neglected the role of gravity in discussing the bottles, but demonstrated that she did understand that different masses are affected differently by a given force. She showed that she understood inertia without even using the word. Some might argue that she needed to use the vocabulary to show true understanding, but I would disagree. It is those students who can explain concepts in their own words without using the vocabulary who convince me that they have a strong understanding of the concept.

Many of my students would have benefited from taking a little more time to think before they wrote down a response. I think most of them wanted to answer quickly and just wrote down the first thing that came to mind, without thinking if it all fit together (like SE in question 2). On the other hand, JW and CK represent students who really seemed to be trying to figure out what would happen, and who tried to use the principles of inertia, gravity, and air resistance to explain why. For many of the others, however, inertia was fresh in their minds from the previous lessons, and they seemed to be trying to find a way to apply it to each question. Some might feel satisfied with this; it could be argued that the students are retaining something that they've been taught—in this case, demonstrating their understanding of inertia. I want more, however. Naturally, I want my students to retain what I've taught them, but I also want them to keep thinking about new situations. In the future, I plan to spend more time talking to my students as they work through these questions, as I saw Dave Hovan do with his class. I want to be there with them while they're working and have them explain their thinking to me. This will help me to understand where they're struggling and allow me to more adaptively push them to explain themselves clearly. I think it will also force them to think about what they're writing and consider whether or not it's coherent.

Facilitators' Notes

Please see the general notes for facilitators in Chapter 3. Here we'll provide specific comments and suggestions for discussing the question set and the student work.

Discussing the Questions: Question Set "Key"

The question set was designed to tap into students' conceptions about mass, air resistance, gravity, and inertia to reason about real-world (nonidealized) situations involving falling bodies. The questions are purposely nonstandard, to make it difficult for students to simply repeat rote responses.

As discussed above, we generally don't have participants work on the questions themselves before we get started. It's useful, however, for the facilitator to have a "key." So here, we summarize responses a physicist might provide. The facilitator can decide if and when to share these responses. Usually some variants of these come up during discussion of student work. Note that these are not necessarily "right answers," since ambiguities and contingencies allow for several possible right answers in many cases. What is most important is how participants reason through the responses and consider the relevant factors in each case.

Questions 1 and 2a

Question 2a directly asks about a bowling ball and a rock dropped on Earth. Galileo proposed that in the absence of air resistance, all freely falling objects descend with the same acceleration. This acceleration, caused by the force of gravity pulling the object down, does not depend on the object's mass. In the presence of air, however, collisions between air molecules and the object create an opposing force that pushes back on the object, "resisting" its motion.

So, for a falling object, air resistance is an upward force "resisting" the downward motion. For very light objects with great surface area, the effect of air resistance is obvious: Think of a flat piece of notebook paper falling, compared to the same piece of paper crumpled up. For very dense, compact objects like the bowling ball and the rock, however, the effect of air resistance is negligible unless they're moving very fast. Dropping the rock and bowling ball from a great enough height, and using a sensitive enough timer, one could theoretically measure the difference in the time it takes them to land. But for everyday drops, over a few feet or even 10 or 20 feet, they should appear to land at the same time because neither is appreciably affected by air resistance.

Question 1 asks about the hypothetical student's reasoning. The student says that the objects land at the same time, and adds: "If there were no air, the bowling ball would land first. But air resistance slows the bowling ball down, so they land together." If there were no air, as described above, the two would fall at the same time. If air resistance did reduce the bowling ball's downward acceleration, the rock would land first. The real reason that objects of different mass accelerate at the same rate under the influence of gravity (in the absence of air resistance!) is this: While a more massive object has more inertia and thus takes more force to be accelerated, gravity exerts more force on the object. For instance, if the bowling ball is 100 times as massive as the rock, the bowling ball is 100 times harder to accelerate; but gravity pulls the ball down with 100 times as much force. The greater gravitational force compensates for the greater inertia, causing the ball to accelerate down at the same rate as the rock.

Question 2b

In the absence of air, air resistance would not be a factor, and hence the two objects would land at the same time regardless of their mass.

Question 3

Falling from a second-floor window, neither the baby nor the father gains enough speed for air resistance to affect them significantly. They likely land at the same time, assuming they started falling from rest at the same time from the same height.

Question 4

Although at first glance this question resembles the previous one, there is a key difference: The two bottles have the same size and shape but very different densities (mass per volume), while the father and baby are very different sizes but have about the same density. Because the force of air resistance depends on size and shape, it acts equally strongly on both bottles. But that air resistance *force* has a greater *effect* on the empty bottle, because in general, a given force has more effect on a lighter (lower inertia) object than it has on a heavier (higher inertia) object. Intuitively, the full bottle can "plow through" the air resistance more effectively than the empty bottle can. So, air resistance takes away from the empty bottle's downward motion more than it takes away from the full bottle's downward motion. The full bottle therefore lands first, by a noticeable margin.

Question 5

If there were no friction, the key forces acting on each ice cube would be gravity pulling it along the ramp and air resistance. At the low speeds reached by the ice cubes, air resistance has little effect. So, as in question 1, 2, and 3, the objects fall at the same rate, because the greater gravitational force acting on the bigger object compensates for the bigger object's greater inertia.

Opening the Conversation About the Students' Work

Once participants have had some time to look through the student work, we open the conversation by asking, "What do you see in the students' thinking in their responses to these questions?" We encourage people to identify the statements that they're talking about by referring to the page numbers, student initials, and question number.

Emphasizing the Substance of Students' Thinking

One advantage of using written work rather than videotaped discussion is that the teacher is not seen, making it impossible for participants to focus on the teacher. This does not mean that participants initially focus on the student thinking, however. The question set itself tends to become a distraction, as people frequently comment on how they think it influences the students' responses. For example, someone usually brings up the way question 3 is worded, noting that it is confusing because most students are not likely to imagine this situation and accept that the father and the baby are falling out of the window "at the same moment." Comments like this usually stem from some unstated interpretation of what a student wrote, however, so we push for the interpretation that led to the concern. We ask, "Can you point to a particular student response that makes you think this is a question?" Someone usually mentions JF's response on page 11, as one participant brought up in a discussion, for example:

> [JF] in his or her answer says the baby goes out the window first, but the father then catches up. [JF] doesn't even have the concept of—or understood the question—of both falling at the same moment—it's as if the baby went first and the father catches up and that's why they land at the same time.

It is certainly worthwhile to have a discussion about whether the question set is misleading or ambiguous and how the teacher might respond, but not just yet. We try to keep the conversation focused on student conceptions and reasoning before turning to questions of appropriate responses or modifications. Otherwise there is a danger that the conversation becomes entirely about the question set—moving far from understanding the students' thinking. One way to handle this in this particular situation would be to ask the participant above something to the effect of, "based on JF's response to his or her vision of the question, what can we say about JF's ideas about how mass affects the rate of falling?" Moves like this can help to return the focus to the student's thinking and away from the perceived limitations of the question.

Encouraging Specificity

Another common tendency is for participants to make general claims about students' thinking, without pointing to specifics. For example, in one session, an early comment mentioned a particular student but did not point to the evidence to support the claim about that student:

> I think that there was just one student who used common sense to answer this question, I mean anyone, if they don't talk about inertia before, you tell them what the problem is, drop the can ... a full can of soda and an empty can of soda which one hits the ground first, anyone can answer that, but because they have this unit about inertia, they incorporate that into answering the question and they stop making sense of the question, so I think there was just one student that recognized that, and all the rest were just trying to connect it to the material [they learned] before and just continually forgetting about the real-life situation.

As with comments about the question set, these general comments are usually based on tacit specific interpretations of student thinking, and we press for specificity. Which student does the participant think is making sense? What does she take as evidence of sense-making? And what features of the other students' responses suggest that they are so focused on inertia that they "stop making sense of the question?"

Interpreting the Substance in the Students' Thinking

As participants begin to identify specific examples of student thinking, we push for interpretations of the students' ideas and reasoning and for explanations of why students may be thinking in certain ways. Often a student response to a particular question will lead the group to look for a similar or contrasting response from another student. Alternatively, the group might look at the same student's response to another question, to see, for example, if a student is consistent from one response to another. We don't have a particularly systematic way for doing this, but we recommend these general practices of comparing/contrasting (1) different students' responses to the same question and (2) the same students' responses to different questions.

These notes don't address every student response. Our purpose is to give a sense of possible topics and issues that might arise or that a facilitator might bring up as the group looks at the collection of student work.

Using Common Sense

Because the contrast between students who are thinking sensibly and those who are just writing down things they've heard is salient to many people, it's worth leveraging this contrast to get at the specifics of student thinking. For example, the participant above gave CE's response to question 4 as her example of a student who was using common sense. In response to that question, CE wrote, "I disagree because the full soda is heavier than the empty one its most likely that the more mass will land faster. The empty one won't resist the air." By contrast, someone usually points to TA's response to the same question, "I agree because that's what we learned in the Galileo experiments," as an example of not bringing in common sense. It's worth spending some time with examples like this to discuss what participants take as evidence of "common sense." Many participants have argued that the key phrase in CE's response is "The empty one won't resist the air"; not only does she seem to realize that air resistance is present, but she says the empty bottle "won't resist the air," suggesting that she's imagining air as an impediment to motion that a bottle must "resist" in order to fall. TA, by contrast, does not even explain his reasoning.

It's reasonable to have the group look at the other student responses through this lens of "making sense." What about JW's response to Question 5 (p. 3), for example? JW says, "A rule to pay attention to is..." Is JW simply repeating something he heard in class, or is he also drawing on common sense? And what about JF's response to Question 1 (p. 10), "I disagree, because the bowling ball has more mass than the little rock *and it didn't have to be air.*" Is JF giving a common sense response? This is particularly challenging to figure out because it's unclear what JF is saying. What does he disagree with? And what does he mean by "*and it didn't have to be air*"? In these tough-to-parse cases, participants often find it helpful to look at the students' other responses. For instance, people generally think JW used common sense throughout the question set, as evidenced (in part) by his pointing out that air resistance would "act on the empty bottle, as if it were affecting a feather, or a piece of paper." One gets the sense that JW is thinking of the "lightness" of the bottle, and visualizing it actually falling through the air like a feather. Looking at all of JW's responses raises another question, however: why does he not mention air resistance in response to question 5, when it's such an important factor in all of his other responses? Did his common sense about slid-ing ice cubes lead him *not* to consider air resistance, or did his reasoning not draw upon common sense at all? Can we even know based on what he *doesn't* say?

Gravity on the Moon and the Role of Air

The apparent confusion about whether air is needed for gravity to work, and about whether there's gravity on the Moon, usually comes up, and if it doesn't we focus participants on a student response where it does. For example, in response to question 2b, DD writes an equation that says "No gravity = Things can't fall." Why does DD say this? Does she really believe there is no gravity on the Moon, and if so, does the question's reminder that the Moon has no air relate to this belief? Similarly, SE mentions that if there is no gravity "than noth-ing would land," and JF says that "neither" would land. "[B]oth would float."

Participants are often surprised by this confusion. We recorded the follow-ing conversation in one session:

> Ryan: On page 4 the student said that there was no gravity on the Moon but he must have seen astronauts walking on the Moon they didn't fly away when they were walking on it.

Here Ryan interpreted DD to be saying that there is no gravity on the Moon, which he thought was inconsistent with what students would have seen. But Emily pointed out that the student also said the objects would fall, and the bowling ball would fall first.

> Emily: But he says that the bowling ball is going first and then there is no gravity "pulling it down" but the bowling ball is going first!

> Alex: The mass is greater so it falls faster even though there's no gravity.

> Ryan: So it's a contradiction.

> Emily: Yeah.

Participants also see this contradiction in SE's response on page 7. There are many avenues to explore here. Why might students be thinking that there is no gravity on the Moon? Are they confusing air and gravity and misreading the question, or do they actually believe that there is no gravity on the Moon? It's important to ask participants to look at the three responses (JF, DD, and SE) that suggest there is no gravity, because close analysis reveals differences in the students' thinking. JF simply states that there is no gravity and so both objects float. SE's initial answer clearly suggests that she thinks heavier things fall faster in the absence of air resistance, and she only addresses the issue of gravity parenthetically, as though hedging her bets. As the participants above note, she seems on the one hand to suggest that the bowling ball would fall first because it has more mass, even though she thinks there's no gravity and things can't fall! If no one brings up these differences, we do, because we think careful attention will show variation in the students' responses; they can't simply be classified as all thinking exactly the same thing about gravity on the Moon.

Mass, Inertia, and Acceleration

Students' understanding of the relationships among mass, inertia, and acceleration is usually a major topic of discussion. What do students understand about these variables and how are they applying their understanding to the questions? A defensible generalization is that the students understand that more massive objects have greater inertia, and that many of them have learned, perhaps from the lab they did previously, that a more massive object takes more force to make it accelerate at a given rate. One participant summarized this in discussing DD's response to question 5. About the more massive ice cube, DD had written,

> *It will reach the bottom in more than a second b/c there is more mass in the bigger ice cube. More mass is less acceleration so it goes slower than something with less mass.*

Commenting on DD's response here, Alex pointed out what he saw as the question.

> Alex: I mean it's interesting that [DD] states greater mass means less acceleration, which is true, in, in some contexts where if you have the same force, which is going back to how they did that lab, I mean he talks about it here, but the way they did that lab was they had a constant force and they just replaced the target mass with something heavier and heavier and he's observed that more mass equals less acceleration. But the important caveat is that then the force isn't changing, but here, it's the acceleration that's not changing.

This is one of the main places where the students' responses can lead to a discussion of the science, especially if participants do not have expertise in physics. The distinction Alex draws is not immediately obvious to some participants, and it's worth taking some time to help everyone get comfortable with the physics concepts. As Alex points out, the students' lab, where the *same* force pulled *different* masses, differs from free-fall questions, where the gravitational force "adjusts" to accelerate all objects at the same rate. Sometimes participants want to discuss *why* this is true of gravity and not other forces. One option is to ask if anyone can find a student who seems to understand this, drawing attention to CK's response to question 1 if no one else does.

Also worth flagging, if no one else does, are some other interesting ways in which students express their understanding of the relationships among mass, inertia, and acceleration. SE's use of equations to show the relationship between mass and inertia almost always gets mentioned. For example, in one session participants discussed SE's response to question 2a. They noted that she wrote that the bowling ball and rock land at the same time, but she then wrote the expressions +m = +i and −m = −i, followed by the mathematical symbol for *therefore "acceleration is equal."* One participant pointed out that while she expressed a "true concept" that greater mass has greater inertia, "it doesn't really explain how she gets from there to 'therefore' acceleration is equal." Looking at the other place where SE uses a mathematical expression, participants often express confusion. SE says that she agrees with the hypothetical student's reasoning to question 4 because *+m = −a and −m = +a and "they cancel each other out thus causing them to land at the same time."* SE's reasoning is hard to understand. What cancels what out? And how do they cause things to land at the same time? It's worth trying to figure out what SE is trying to say. One interpretation is that she thinks the greater gravitational force on the full bottle, which other things being equal would make it fall at a greater rate, is compensated for by that bottle's greater mass, which other things being equal would make it fall (accelerate) at a lower rate (+m = −a). Her choice of the phrase "canceling out" is odd though, and it's possible she means something different.

Moving From Interpretations to Ideas for Instruction

This case study provides an opportunity to remind participants that responsiveness encompasses not only in-the-moment instructional moves but also planning for the next class, for the next week, and for longer stretches of time. Teachers modify their instruction all the time. These modifications come in response to many things they notice in the classroom: how students behave, how motivated they are by certain kinds of activities, and so on. Modifications that are responsive to students' thinking, however, are most likely to be productive in helping students to learn science content and learn how to think scientifically. Thus, after the discussion of student work, we invite participants to discuss how Matt might respond based on the participants' interpretations of that work.

It's useful to address the general issues that came up. How, for example, might Matt encourage students to use their common sense and discourage them from just trying to use the vocabulary and concepts they have most recently been taught (but without deeper understanding)? Most practicing teachers acknowledge that they often face this issue in their classes. However, it's important to appreciate the challenge faced by the students, too. In many classes, they're *supposed* to simply repeat things they have heard from the teacher, and it might be asking a lot for them to switch their approach for one particular activity.

Participants often suggest that Matt could display to the entire class some of the responses that use common sense, particularly those from CE and JW but without identifying them, of course. Another suggestion is for Matt to be more specific in the future about what he expects. When he told students "they were not being graded on correctness, but only on their ability to explain their thinking," did they really believe him? And if so, had they practiced doing this enough to really understand what he meant by "explain your thinking?" And what might students think "explain your thinking" really means? To students who have rarely been asked to use their common sense, could "explain your thinking" sound like "use the stuff we've learned to explain your thinking? This is different from "use common sense," and may in fact be why so many of the students fell back on the idea from an earlier lab that more massive objects have greater inertia, but without fully integrating this idea into their own sense-making. As participants point out, this is not an incorrect idea, but it can lead students to disregard their productive intuitions about how objects fall. Outside of a physics class, would a student really think a heavy object takes longer to fall than a lighter object?

Another suggestion is that when students work on question sets like this, Matt might circulate around the room, emphasizing his point that he wants them to think sensibly about each scenario. Matt suggests this himself in his case study, and it seems to many participants that this could help keep students focused on using their intuition rather than falling back on their tendency to recite vocabulary they think the teacher expects.

And what of the common confusions about gravity on the Moon? Several participants have suggested that Matt might show students a video clip of astronauts moving on the Moon and lead a discussion about how their movement can be explained. This might provide an opportunity for the students to wrestle with the causal connections between air and gravity and the ways in which each affects movement on a celestial body.

Considering How the Questions Influence the Students' Responses

As we discussed, people often want to comment on the ways in which the question set itself might influence students' responses. This is a reasonable thing to discuss; all teachers construct or modify curricular materials, and it's important to think about how the structure and content of the materials might influence students' responses. However, we try to put off this discussion until after analyzing the students' ideas, for an important reason: The student responses are the "data" from which we can gain insight into how the wording of the questions influences students' answers. Teachers can *anticipate* how students might respond, of course, and this is a practice we encourage in lesson planning (see Chapter 9). However, looking at the student work tells us which expected responses actually occurred. Particularly for new teachers, seeing the students' responses can inform how they construct activities in the future.

Often, when participants raise concerns about the way a question is written, others step in to remind them of the purpose of the question set. For example, in one session, a participant complained about question 2, claiming that it "was kind of tricky—and they had to make the best of it to get an answer." Other participants were less concerned about whether the questions were "tricky." As one participant put it, "I think the point here is not to have the wrong-er right answer—I think the point here is to make them ... think and write down their thinking."

Additionally, it's important to remember that Matt particularly wanted to know what his students understood about inertia; he cared more about that than about the correctness or incorrectness of his students' answers.

Discussing Matt's Case Study

Finally, if we have time, we have participants read and discuss Matt's case study. Since Matt was focused primarily on his students' understanding of inertia, one possible topic of conversation is whether this focus influenced what he attended to in students' responses. Are there other facets of student thinking that he might have missed because he was looking for understanding of inertia?

One curious aspect of Matt's case study is his decision not to analyze students' responses to question 3, which he says is very similar to question 4. But do students give similar responses to those two questions? How do we decide which segments of student thinking to analyze? On the one hand, making *a priori* decisions about what to exclude can keep the analysis manageable and can focus attention on the responses expected to be most illuminating. On the other hand, the excluded data might contain interesting insights into students' thinking.

Of course, the goal is not to criticize Matt in any way. As we remind teachers, Matt is not with us to defend his choices. We can question those choices and consider what else Matt might have done, both in his teaching and in his analysis, but the point is for all of us to learn more about student thinking and to discuss the best ways to elicit and respond to students' ideas and reasoning.

CHAPTER 8
Free-Falling Bodies (2)

This case study describes what happened in David Hovan's ninth grade "Conceptual Physics" class when he asked students to answer the conceptual questions introduced in the previous chapter. While the students were working on the question set, Dave walked around the classroom listening to their ideas and helping them make sense of the physical situations described. He then brought the class together to discuss their responses.

The data for this case study are the video and transcript (available at *www.nsta.org/publications/press/extras/responsive.aspx*). The case study begins after Suggestions for Reading and Viewing. We recommend that you start by reading only Dave's introduction, to get background information about the class; stop before the heading, The Bowling Ball and the Rock. Then read the transcript of the conversation and watch some of the video, before continuing with the rest of Dave's account. This gives you a chance to recognize and interpret the students' thinking for yourself, before finding out what Dave saw and heard.

Suggestions for Reading and Viewing

Be sure to make copies of the transcript, included in full on the website. Even if you're watching the video, the transcript is useful for following along, jotting notes, and referencing in conversations about the snippet with others.

Chapter 7 contains the complete question set. If the group hasn't already used that case study, one option is to have participants work on the questions themselves, individually or in small groups, to explore the ideas before hearing students' responses. This can be intimidating for people with a limited physics background, however, so we usually give the group the student work right away. We have found that discussing students' responses almost always leads to productive conversations about the science, as participants wrestle with their own understanding of the physical principles.

This snippet is 30 minutes long. When we use this case in pedagogy courses, seminars, and workshops, we stop reading or watching the students' conversation at two or three spots, in order to encourage close examination of student thinking:

1. *Line 74, approximately five and a half minutes in, after Tiera says, "So they're going to hit at the same time?"* Since Dave talks with individual students in this section, it is a great opportunity to look at individual

students' reasoning in detail. We begin with our usual prompts, asking participants how they think it's going, what they notice in students' ideas and reasoning, and what they see in the students' thinking that seems like the beginnings of scientific inquiry.

2. *Lines 88–204.* Little substantive discussion occurs between lines 74 and 88, so we usually skip over that part. If we have plenty of time, we continue playing the video from here to line 204, after the class finishes discussing question 3. Again, we ask participants to focus on the students' thinking before moving on to the possibilities for instruction.

3. *The Rest of the Snippet.* Many interesting student ideas come up in the discussion of questions 4 and 5, so if time is limited, one option is to skip from line 74 to line 204. Since questions 1 and 2 receive attention in the first part of the video, skipping to line 204 allows the group to focus on students' thinking about more of the questions.

The Case Study: Free-Falling Bodies (2)

By David Hovan

Introduction

The course I teach, Conceptual Physics, uses Dr. Arthur Eisenkraft's *Active Physics* textbook. During the school year described in this case study, my first lesson on free fall used part of the "Your 'At Rest' Weight" activity from this book. When I talked about this lesson with the other teachers and the facilitators in the physics group, those of us who used this text agreed that the lesson instructs students to follow a linear, step-by-step recipe designed to help them discover the physics principles that determine the motion of free-falling objects. Unfortunately, the text is written at a level that is incomprehensible to many of my freshman students. It's extremely wordy, and uses advanced vocabulary that they struggle with.

Rather than having them work on the activity in groups and risk losing their attention because of frustrations with the text and other distractions, I decided we would go through the lesson as a class. I led them through the instructions, performing demonstrations that involved dropping objects with different masses and surface areas, and asked the students questions to get them engaged in a discussion about the kinematics and dynamics of free-falling bodies. My demonstrations, questions, and explanations got very little response, however, and I found myself repeatedly explaining and demonstrating the principles of free fall. I heard little from the students to give me evidence that they were making sense of the material.

I talked about my frustrations with our physics group. One of the physics educators from the Maryland group volunteered to create a question set that would synthesize several of the ideas from the *Active Physics* activity and from our conversations, but in a more open-ended way, to try to better elicit my ninth graders' ideas about falling objects. The emphasis on students' own explanations in this activity is a clear diversion from a traditional, theoretical lesson with selected demonstrations of free-falling objects. I decided to use this question set to reintroduce the motion of free-falling objects several weeks after I taught the lesson from the *Active Physics* text, because very few of my students remembered the principles discussed in the first lesson anyway. I used this new lesson to both ensure the students were more likely to be thinking rather than memorizing and to take an informal survey of what ideas they had developed from my previous classes, other classes, or their own experiences. In an effort to maximize the number of sincere contributions and creativity, I tried to create the least threatening environment I possibly could by telling them repeatedly that I would not take off points for "incorrect" answers. After I said this, one girl asked, "Does that mean there's no right or wrong answer?" I thought it would be dishonest to confirm this—after all, in each case there are answers that a physicist would give—but I didn't want them to be inhibited by their sense that they might be wrong, so I said, "I want you to think about what would happen ... you're not going to lose points for giving a wrong answer. I just want you to think about what's gonna happen and explain why."

The Modified Lesson on Free Fall

As just mentioned, the question set[1] is a modification to the activity "Your 'At Rest' Weight" from the *Active Physics* text. Its purpose is to elicit student ideas about free fall before they study weight as the product of mass and acceleration due to gravity ($w = mg$). The questions on the worksheet ask students to consider scenarios that direct their attention to different influences on the motion of the falling objects.

Rather than simply going through the questions on the worksheet, my goal for the class was to stimulate as much discussion as possible about free-falling bodies so the students would reveal their own thoughts about the effects of mass, gravity, and air resistance, both verbally and in writing. Whenever the class paused or a student gave a vague response, I tried to push that student (and the class) to further clarify the ideas, hoping they might better understand and explore the logic of their own responses or at least realize their own theoretical inconsistencies.

The Bowling Ball and the Rock

Right from the start, the students expressed some interesting ideas about the motion of free-falling objects. Ron was working on question 1, and he called me over. Here's the question he was thinking about:

> 1. *A bowling ball and a small rock are dropped at the same time from the same height. Which one lands first? Here is a student's answer:*
>
> STUDENT: *"They land at the same time. If there were no air, the bowling ball would land first. But air resistance slows the bowling ball down, so they land together."*

---

1. The question set is included in full in Chapter 7.

Do you agree with the student's reasoning? Disagree? Explain.

Ron: Mr. Hovan.

Dave: Yeah.

Ron: If there wasn't no air the ball would be coming down very slow.

Dave: If there was no air?

Ron: Yeah.

Dave: So you're saying it would come down slower if there was no air?

Ron: Very slow. Like this, very slow, (lowering a book to the ground) steady, because there isn't any air.

Dave: So you're saying air makes things fall faster.

When Ron said, "If there wasn't no air the ball would be coming down very slow," it seems as though he was focusing on the hypothetical student's comment "if there were no air," and arguing that it is the presence of air, as opposed to gravity, that causes things to fall. Since we are surrounded by air in our environment, it might make sense to him that air causes things to fall. This explanation neglects the existence of gravity, but I suspect that if I asked him "What is the thing that causes objects to fall?" he would respond "gravity" instead of "air." It seems that Ron neglected to include gravity in his explanation not because he has never heard of gravity or what it does, but because the hypothetical student's response emphasizes air. This emphasis may have distracted Ron from what he knows about gravity and "tipped" him into trying to make sense of the role of air.

I'm really not quite sure why Ron was confusing air and gravity, but it's also possible he was doing this because of what he had heard about the two outside of the Earth. I've heard students do this a lot. I think they learn both that "there's no air in space" and that "there's no gravity in space" and they conflate the two. He may even have been looking also at the second question (below), and realizing that he would be asked about the Moon, which tipped him into thinking about things "coming down very slow" like the astronauts do when they walk or jump on the Moon.

2. *A bowling ball and a small rock are dropped from the same height at the same time. Which one lands first if this experiment is done:*

(a) on the Earth?

(b) on the Moon (which has no air)?

Be sure to explain your reasoning and to answer both (a) and (b).

Ron didn't respond quickly when I restated what I thought he was saying. But then he wanted more information about the question.

Ron: Yeah … How high is this thing? Like if you dropped it, how high is it?

Dave: For which one?

Ron: For number one.

Dave: Number one, it doesn't matter, any height.

Ron: I mean, if you drop this from a certain height, it wouldn't hit the ground.

Dave: Not at the same time?

Ron: No.

Dave: So are you saying the higher up that you drop something, like, the less likely they are gonna hit the ground at the same time?

Ron: Yup.

Dave: Okay why?

Ron: Because it's heavier. See, I was gonna say if I got—like, if I stand on top of this, right, and I drop this [binder]… along with this [pencil] … the binder's gonna drop first.

Dave: That one's gonna drop first?

Ron: No.

Dave: No this one. Why?

Ron: Because it's a lot heavier.

Dave: So you're saying heavier objects fall faster than lighter objects.

Even with just one student, it was hard to keep up with his ideas. I tried just to listen to him and repeat back what I thought he was saying. It was pretty nonspecific the way he said, "if you drop this from a certain height, it wouldn't hit the ground." What was "it"? In the moment, I assumed he was trying to say that releasing the objects from greater height would make the difference in when they hit the ground more noticeable, but looking back on it now it's really not clear from what he said whether I read into it too much. He confirmed my restatement of his idea, however, and his next idea suggested I had understood him correctly. Ron explained that the heavier object (the binder) would drop first if he stood on top of the table (raised the height). I thought he was saying that heavier objects fall faster than lighter objects, and that this difference would be noticeable if you dropped the two objects from different heights. Khalid jumped in to disagree.

> Khalid: That's not true.
>
> Dave: You don't think that's true? Why not?
>
> Khalid: On Earth it's not true.
>
> Dave: On Earth it's not true?
>
> Khalid: Air resistance.
>
> Dave: So air resistance plays a role in how fast things fall? Like how? How does air resistance affect how things fall?
>
> Khalid: Like if you drop this book and this pencil, they're gonna hit the ground at the same time.

This really caught my attention. First, it was great that Khalid jumped in to argue. My students loved to argue, but it was usually not in the context of the science content. Khalid brought up air resistance, and claimed that it was not true that the heavier objects would fall faster "on Earth." I asked him how air resistance affected how things fall, but instead of explaining *how* air resistance affects falling objects he told me what he thought would happen in the condition Ron described. He may have been arguing that air resistance would "hold back" the heavier object more, causing the objects to fall at the same rate—essentially agreeing with the hypothetical student in question 1. Ron jumped up to try dropping the book and the pencil, and it's obvious even on the video that they landed at the same time.

> Khalid: See, it didn't. That's why I got an A in this class.

Dave: So wait—do you still think that heavier objects fall faster?

Ron: I mean, for real though, if I stand up on top of here and drop both of them, it's gonna land first, before that pen.

Dave: So you're saying that if you were up a lot higher, it would be more clear that this one would fall faster than the pen. Okay why do you think that?

Ron: I don't know, I just know! It's gonna happen.

Khalid was certain that this result proved he was right, and Ron had to consider why the experiment didn't turn out the way he predicted. He insisted that, if he stood on top of the desk, the heavier object would land first. I asked him to explain why but he claimed he didn't know. This is the kind of situation in which I want to really push my students. Their challenge is often in being able to articulate their arguments. Ron had all the pieces to argue that the greater height would show a difference that might be undetectable at the lower height—a difference that would be caused by the different weights—but he just couldn't seem to put it all together. I left him hoping that if he sat and wrote about what he thought, he would have more opportunity to make the argument coherent.

"That's How Space Is"

The second question seemed to bring up the confusion about air and gravity for other students as well. Shortly after my interaction with Ron, Tiera called me over to ask me about it.

Tiera: If you drop a bowling ball and a small rock on the Moon, neither one of them would drop with it because there's no gravity up there.

Dave: So you don't think there's gravity on the Moon?

Tiera: No, because that's how space is.

This was a difficult moment for me—a kind of moment I often encounter in class, where I have to make a quick decision about how to respond to students' incorrect ideas. Tiera was suggesting that neither object would fall, because "there's no gravity up there." Apparently, her idea was that gravity does not exist in space, but only on Earth. Since the Moon is in space, there would be no gravity on the Moon.

As I stated, my intended purpose of the lesson was to have students make sense of the situations themselves without me feeding them too much information. Yet, in the moment, my instinct was to explain to her that *all* massive objects exert gravitational forces on other things that have mass, and that more massive objects exert greater gravitational force.

> Dave: So if you're really far away from massive objects like the Moon or the Earth or the Sun, then gravity is negligible, it's, it's like there's no gravity.
>
> Tiera: So it's…
>
> Dave: So there is gravity on the Moon, yeah. So things do fall on the Moon. Do you think that, do you know if they fall faster or slower on the Moon? They fall slower. Any idea why?
>
> Tiera: Because … there's less gravity.
>
> Dave: Right, so things accelerate slower on the Moon because the moon is less massive than Earth.

I think this instinct reflects my thinking that Newton's universal law of gravitation is something that would not be intuitive to a ninth grader. I think most people learn about this concept by first being told and then seeing its application with celestial bodies. It is not an idea that is immediately obvious. After all, it took over a thousand years for Newton to supersede Aristotle's ideas of physics. Without knowing that there is gravity on the Moon, how could Tiera be expected to reason about question 2? I think this kind of moment happens a lot because many teachers realize that they cannot significantly cover the expected content without providing certain foundational ideas on top of which they can help their students build more knowledge.

The downside of my decision is evident in what happened next in this exchange.

> Tiera: So a bowling ball would drop first, right?
>
> Dave: On where?
>
> Tiera: On the Moon.
>
> Dave: Okay why?
>
> Tiera: Because it's heavier.
>
> Dave: Because it's heavier? So you think that heavier objects fall faster than lighter ones?

Tiera: On the Moon, they drop slower....

Dave: So are you saying that on Earth they would fall and hit the ground at the same time? But on the Moon they wouldn't? Okay so what's the difference between the Earth and the Moon? So why do you think that then?

Tiera: Because it's outer space and there's like, probably less gravity in outer space than it is on Earth.

Dave: Okay so gravity isn't as strong on the Moon as it is on Earth. That's true. But, so if gravity's weaker on the Moon, I mean, things aren't gonna accelerate down as quickly on the Moon, but why would, um, the fact that we're on the Moon like, affect which one hit first? Like wouldn't they both just hit the ground at the same time just at a slower rate, is that possible?

Tiera: So they're gonna hit at the same time?

Dave: That's what I want you to think about, that's what I want you to think about.

Tiera said that the bowling ball would drop first on the moon because it's heavier, but when I checked in with her about how weight affects falling, she switched to talking about objects falling slower on the Moon. I kept trying to listen to what she was saying and flesh out her ideas, but I admit to being frustrated and unclear on what she was trying to say this whole time. It became obvious (especially with "So they're going to hit at the same time?") that she was asking me for the right answer rather than offering the ideas that made sense to her. I think that by offering her "correct" ideas upfront, I made it more difficult for Tiera to express her ideas freely without fear of being wrong. I realized while I was standing there that she was "fishing," trying to get me to give her an answer that I was looking for. I felt awkward and ended up refusing to answer her question one way or the other, hoping that she would reemploy her own ideas in answering the questions. I've taught this lesson and others like it since, and I've worked to be more careful about the messages I send when I really just want students to think. I still struggle when I have interactions like I had with Tiera, however. Sometimes I'm afraid that students latch on to ideas that not only keep them from getting to correct answers, but keep them from reasoning very deeply at all. If Tiera doesn't think there's gravity on the Moon, she can't really pursue the key ideas related to falling bodies in this question

National Science Teachers Association

(i.e., weight and air resistance). If there is no gravity on the Moon, then there is no reason to think about what happens to falling objects on the Moon. They don't fall.

The Class Discussion

It was a lot easier to listen and respond to the students' ideas in these one-on-one interactions than when I had the whole class together later to go over their responses. There were a number of interesting ideas that came up in the class discussion—some that I really didn't expect. One was Tiera's insistence that the baby in question 3 would land first, because "it was dropped first," even though the question clearly states that the father let himself out the window *at the same moment.*

> 3. *To escape a burning building, a father drops his baby out the second-floor window, and at the same moment, the father lets himself fall out the window. They both land in a padded "person catcher" set up underneath the window by firefighters. Who, if either, lands first: the baby or the father? Explain your reasoning.*

I tried to steer the conversation back to what the question was asking, but I was surprised to find out that the students really weren't buying it. Khalid said, in line 170, that the question stated that the father threw the baby out first and then jumped out after the baby, and when I tried to reset the situation again, Ebony questioned whether the situation was really even possible ("How you gonna throw the baby out and jump out at the same time?"). Tiera even insisted (in line 198) that, "You all read the question wrong!" (By which I think she meant *me*!) I found this really strange. Did they just not read the question carefully? I suspect that there was something else going on, and Ebony's question is a clue. The whole situation is so hard to imagine in a real world scenario, that the students didn't even pay attention to the "at the same moment" phrase. That is, rather than read it as it was written, they read it as they could picture it, with the father dropping the child *before* he let himself fall out.

The conversation really got interesting when we started to talk about question 4.

> 4. *Two identical plastic soda bottles, one of them full of soda and the other completely empty, are dropped from the roof of this school at the same time. A student, when asked which object lands first, answers as follows:*

STUDENT: *"We learned from those Galileo experiments that objects of different mass all fall at the same rate. So the full and empty bottle land at the same time."*

Do you agree? Disagree? Explain your reasoning.

Janice was the first to speak up in the class discussion about this question:

Dave: So what do you think? What if we actually did this experiment? We got up on the roof and we dropped an empty soda bottle and a full soda bottle at the same time. Would they both hit the ground at the same time?

Janice: No.

Boy: No.

Dave: Okay. Why not? Janice?

Tiera: Yes they would.

Janice: I think, it's kind, this, uh, feels like, you know, the paper, when, when you had the paper, you drop it like this?

Dave: Uh huh.

Janice: It was like, sailing down slowly. Cuz the bottle doesn't have anything in it but the other bottle does so it would, um, fall fast…

Dave: Okay, so the one, the bottle that's full of soda you're saying is gonna fall faster.

Janice: Uh huh.

Dave: Because it's what?

Janice: It has, uh more mass.

Dave: It has more mass. Okay. Tiera.

Tiera: But when you balled up the paper, and you drop the pen, and uh, the paper down at the same time, they both hit the uh thing at same time, even though the pen had more mass.

I really felt like Janice was using her intuition here. When she said, in line 215, "this, uh, *feels like*, you know, the paper, when, when you had the paper, you drop it like this? ..." she was referring to the demonstration I did with the open and balled-up piece of paper. Her phrase "this ... feels like" is the key to making me think that she was really using her intuition. To Janice, a situation with an empty soda bottle dropped from the roof "feels like" a situation analogous to what she has seen with the paper. Intuitively to Janice, in this situation, the bottle with more mass would fall faster.

Another thing that was great about this conversation was that Tiera jumped in to ask a question that got at the real complexity of this question. We had already seen that objects with different masses would fall at the same rate, so how could this be? I thought this was great. I was planning to push Janice to explain why, in this case, the more massive object would fall first, but Tiera did it for me! Now I had a conversation where students were not only drawing on their intuition to predict outcomes, but they were challenging each other to create explanations that were coherent with what they thought we had figured out.

Seizing on Tiera's statement, I asked the students to explain what was going on that could explain the conflict. Janice suggested that "air resistance" was "pulling up" the lighter object, which she modified to "slowing it down." Here, she claimed she didn't know how air resistance would slow down the lighter object, although later, in line 278, she gave a clear explanation of how she thought air resistance would slow down the bottle with nothing in it.

> Janice: Well, the lighter thing is gonna fall slower because the, um, bottle with, with, uh, the stuff in it, whatever, it has more mass, so it is easier to go through the air resistance. But since the bottle with nothing in it, it has like, this kind of, it takes a longer time to go through the air resistance.

During the discussion about the bottles, Ebony came up with an idea that I really hadn't expected. When I was trying to get Janice and the rest of the class to explain how air resistance slows things down, I asked, "Does it always slow lighter things down?" A number of people said "no," and Ebony drew on something she knew from her experience to make the case.

> Ebony: No, it don't always, uh, do that to light things because if a fat person gets dropped, they fall real slow ... Don't they?
>
> Dave: Okay, if you drop—
>
> Ebony: They don't just go down like a light person just go BOOM. They go like this (floats slowly into her seat).

Even though she was being a little rude, I think Ebony had a reasonable idea here that she thought was relevant. She had this sense that larger (fat) people move more slowly, and she was applying it to the comparison of the bottles. I asked her if it was possible that they might fall at the same rate, and she acknowledged it was possible, but she seemed unconvinced, because, as she said, "I never seen that happen." Using her idea that if she punched a heavy person and a light person at the same time, the light person would fall faster, Ebony claimed that, the "lighter [bottle] gonna fall first, arguing that "Because it is lighter ... it has less stuff to hold while it's falling."

I find this idea really interesting, because while it seems strange for a student to actually think that a lighter object will fall faster, it is consistent with what Ebony thinks she understands about the relative speed with which heavy and light people move. Additionally, it has the seeds of an important idea in it—the idea of inertia. When Ebony said, "it has less stuff to hold while it's falling" I think she was getting at the idea that it takes more force to get a more massive object moving. This is true, and it suggests that Ebony has the basis for understanding inertia.

Reflection

It was refreshing to hear my students engage so actively in exploring these questions. Without hearing their ideas I would have little way of knowing why and how they struggled to understand the physics of free-falling bodies.

Reflecting on the ideas I heard here, I'm struck by how much the context of the particular questions influenced how the students responded by tapping into their intuition. For example, in response to question 3, Khalid, Ebony, and Tiera all seemed convinced that the father threw the baby out first, even though the question clearly says that he let himself fall out of the window *at the same moment*. I think that, imagining the situation, the students relied on their experience of dropping things, rather than accepting the idealized physics situation represented by the phrase "at the same moment." That is, they have lots of experience dropping things, but very little experience dropping things while letting themselves fall down at the same time. In the context of this question, then, it would seem that the baby was dropped first, and they would then assume that the baby would land first.

In question 3, it seems like students' intuition about the physical situation got in the way of them reasoning through the answer, although it's notable to me that both Ebony and Tiera said the father and the baby would land at the same time if they were dropped at the same time. In question 4, it seems like Janice's intuition was really helpful. To this point, students have learned that, in the absence of air resistance, objects fall at the same rate regardless of their mass. In the presence of air resistance, students have seen that objects with different shapes are affected differently by air resistance. However, in this case, it seems that Janice realized that even though the bottles are the same shape, air resistance still has a greater effect on the lighter object than the heavier one (because the full soda bottle has enough "mass" to help it "go through the air resistance"). I think that as she actually pictured the situation, and trusted herself to think about what would actually happen, she could see that the heavier bottle would fall faster.

So what should this mean for my instruction, this realization of how powerful students' prior knowledge and intuition is in influencing how they think about physical situations? I think it suggests that students need more time to talk about questions like this with each other, to make their thinking visible, and to reconcile these different ideas arising from their intuition with the things they learn in physics class. Tiera's response to Janice's idea, in line 223, presented a perfect opportunity for me to practice scaffolding this type of reconciliation. I want students to be able to explain what the particular contingencies are in different situations that are important to consider. There is too much of a tendency to treat physics questions as certain kinds of questions that will always turn out the same way. A question about free-falling objects, for example, will always end with the conclusion that in the absence of air resistance, objects fall at the same rate. Certainly it is important to know this, but to get a full picture of how things work in the real world, it is important for students to struggle with all of the possible ways in which variables such as mass and air resistance interact. This makes physics more real, moving it from a set of equations and received knowledge about the physical world to meaningful principles that can help us make sense about how things happen in the real world.

Facilitators' Notes

Please see the general notes for facilitators in Chapter 3. Here we'll provide specific comments and suggestions for discussing the video and case study. Our purpose isn't to present a thorough analysis of the snippet but to give a sense of possible topics and issues that might arise or that a facilitator might bring up.

Discussing the Question Set

The question set was designed to tap into students' initial conceptions and give them opportunities to reason about free-falling bodies, drawing on their intuition and on what they have learned in physics class. Specifically, the questions were designed to elicit students' thinking about mass, air resistance, gravity, and inertia, and the ways in which these principles apply to real-world situations. The questions are purposely nonstandard, to make it difficult for students to simply repeat rote responses they had heard.

As discussed in Chapter 7, we generally don't have participants work on the questions themselves before examining the students' thinking. If the group has not looked at the student work in Chapter 7, however, working through the questions can give participants a sense of the issues that Dave's students were struggling with. We provide a "key" for facilitators in Chapter 7, with caution about considering the key answers to be the "right" answers in the traditional sense.

If you decide to have participants work through the questions on their own, it's important to keep two things in mind.

1. Since people without a physics background can find it intimidating to share their thinking when they're unsure of their own understanding, it's useful to have participants work in small groups before moving to whole class discussion.

2. Many of the questions have a solution that is consistent with common sense, but participants' attempts to remember and apply what they learned in physics class can distract their attention from simply trying to make sense of the situations. So, it's important to remind participants to think about their common-sense ideas. An appropriate goal for the discussion of these questions, besides exploring the ideas that they may hear from Dave's students, is to help participants practice reconciling their intuitions with other things they know or learned in physics class.

The Discussion to Line 74

Opening the Conversation

We usually stop the recording at line 74, approximately five and a half minutes in, when Tiera says, "So they're going to hit at the same time?" We ask participants how they think it's going, what they notice in students' ideas and reasoning, and what they see in the students' thinking that seems like the beginnings of scientific inquiry.

Emphasizing the Substance of Students' Ideas and Reasoning

We frequently use this case study after participants have used other case studies to gain some experience discussing students' ideas. In particular, we usually precede Dave's case study with Matt's (Chapter 7), in which classroom management and the teacher's behavior are not distractions because the data are students' written work. So, by the time we use this case study, in a preservice teacher education class or in a workshop series for practicing teachers, most participants understand that we want conversations to begin with the student thinking. We have used all of these cases, however, in settings where participants have not seen other cases first.

As in the other cases, participants often want to say something about what the teacher is doing, especially because Dave's interaction with Tiera differs noticeably from his interaction with Ron and Khalid. We try to steer the conversation away from discussion about Dave's moves at this point, assuring participants that we will get back to that discussion. Instead, we try to reorient participants toward focusing on the students' ideas and reasoning. For example, if a participant says, "I like how he's repeating Ron's ideas back to him," we might ask, "What are Ron's ideas that Dave is repeating back? What is Ron thinking?" Likewise, if a participant says, "He's telling Tiera stuff instead of letting her reason," we might ask, "Looking past what Dave is telling her, what can you tell about Tiera's reasoning so far?"

Another common tendency is for participants to comment very generally about what they see and hear. For example, in one session, a participant commented positively on the students' participation, "I mean, they're doing a lot of –they're having a conversation, and they're doing a lot of debating, and they're like, proving their answers."

When we hear these general comments, we use them as starting points for focusing on the specifics of the student thinking. For example, in this case, the teacher was referring to the conversation among Dave, Ron, and Khalid. The facilitator pushed the group to articulate what the students were "debating" about, and how they were "proving their answers."

Interpreting the Substance of the Students' Thinking

Using this case study, we often don't get past this first section (up to line 74), because there are lots of student ideas to consider and significant opportunities to discuss the "menu of possibilities" for instruction based on the students' statements. We see no reason to rush through the case study; this segment alone offers opportunities to cultivate close attention to students' thinking. To that end, we sometimes remind participants of the mental "trick" for listening carefully: Pretend you know the students are gifted, and assume there is some wonderful meaning behind their words that you're trying to figure out.

The first specific ideas that participants mention often follow up upon the general claim that students are arguing or debating: When pressed for examples, participants often point to Khalid's disagreement with Ron's conclusion

that heavier objects fall faster than light objects. In lines 25–29 Khalid says "that's not true … on Earth … [because of] air resistance." Additionally participants note that Khalid suggests a test to support his assertion, that a book and a pen dropped from the same height will land at the same time (line 31), and Ron takes up the challenge by jumping up to conduct the experiment (line 32).

While it's not difficult to point to evidence that Ron and Khalid are arguing and to note that they are arguing about whether objects of different weights land at the same time, it's trickier to interpret *why* each student thinks his position is correct. Khalid states only that "air resistance" is the reason heavier objects fall no faster than lighter objects "on Earth," but participants often point out that he does not explain how air resistance causes objects to land at the same time. If participants do not go further than noting that Khalid's explanation is "air resistance," we push on this: How does Khalid think air resistance has this effect? One interpretation is that Khalid generalizes from the hypothetical student's statement in question 1, that the greater effect of air resistance on heavy objects balances out the presumed greater downward pull due to their greater weight.

Ron's reasoning is even trickier to follow, and participants often note that his reasoning seems to change over the course of his short conversation with Dave. We find it useful to encourage the group to "slow down time" and look at the interaction line by line, to really get a sense of his ideas. Ron's first suggestion (line 3) is that if there were no air, the ball would come down very slowly. Participants who have read Matt's case study often think Ron may be confusing air and gravity, as some of Matt's students seemed to be doing. In one session a participant suggested another possible explanation, that Ron was equating air with wind: "Well that could make sense with him saying that, um, if there was no air the ball would come down slow, if he's thinking about wind when he says air, and he's thinking wind is blowing things down."

Continuing to work through Ron's reasoning line by line, we wonder, why does he agree with Dave's restatement of his idea that "air makes things fall faster" and then immediately ask, "How high is this thing? Like if you dropped it, how high is it?" He apparently thinks that the height makes a difference, but does that connect to his idea about the role of air? If so, how? And what does he mean when he says, "it wouldn't hit the ground." Does he mean to say, as Dave summarized, "They wouldn't hit the ground at the same time"? Or could he be thinking the bowling ball wouldn't hit the ground at all, maybe because he thinks there is no gravity?

Whatever Ron's meaning in line 13, participants usually agree that by line 23 he has decided that heavier objects fall faster than lighter ones, and that this difference can be observed if the objects are dropped from high enough. But why might he think the height makes a difference? Often participants suggest that he might have some intuitive sense that air resistance slows down lighter objects, given enough time.

> Carla: He's thinking the height makes a, um, difference in how fast they're gonna fall. So he thinks that if it's at a higher level, then he would see that the binder would fall first, before the pen.
>
> Facilitator: So, why would he be thinking that? Why might he think that how high you drop it from matters?
>
> Carla: I'm guessing 'cause he's thinking that it'll be more air resistance if it's higher up.

Finally, it's worth having a discussion about Ron's response to the experimental test. It's clear even on the video that the objects drop at the same time, but Ron insists he knows "it's gonna happen" (that the heavier object falls first). Participants note Ron's suggestion that he drop them from higher up ("if I stand up on top of here"), and suggest that perhaps Ron doesn't think it was a "fair test." Still, *why* does he think "it's gonna happen?" What experiences or intuitions make him so certain?

This first section (up to line 74) consists of two conversations, the first among Dave, Ron, and Khalid, and the second between Dave and Tiera. Participants don't always talk about the conversations in order; sometimes they want to talk about Tiera first, possibly because it is the last thing they heard before we stopped the recording, or because her confusion about question 2 is so noticeable.

Most people catch Tiera's idea that neither object would drop at all since the Moon is in space and "there's no gravity up there." Examining Tiera's conversation with Dave, participants usually perceive that she is "fishing" for the right answer. When we press for specifics, participants often point to how she switches her idea that the bowling ball would fall first. When Dave says, "Like wouldn't they both just hit the ground at the same time just at a slower rate, is that possible?" Tiera says, "So they're gonna hit at the same time?"—essentially co-opting Dave's suggestion without an explanation. It's worth having a brief discussion about Tiera's stance toward the assignment. Most people see Tiera, in contrast to Ron, as not trying to make sense of the material, and they identify her behavior as something commonly seen in their classes. Not everyone sees Tiera's behavior as problematic. One participant noted that Tiera was trying to remain engaged in conversation with Dave and trying to understand him, even while others insisted that Tiera was only trying to understand Dave in order to "get the right answer."

> She's like, trying to understand. Cause she's not like, real confident with her words. Like, "There's probably, probably less gravity," like there's like a little

apprehensive[ness]... she's like, wanting to be reassured on it. Like, she wants to, you know, continue the dialogue between the two.

As with Ron, we often suggest "slowing down time" and looking at what Tiera says line by line. Hearing Tiera's idea that neither object would fall on the Moon, Dave corrects her by saying there *is* gravity on the Moon, even though it's weaker, and he tells Tiera that objects fall slower on the Moon. He asks if she knows why, and Janice jumps in to explain that objects fall slower because there's less gravity. When Dave confirms this is correct, Tiera says, "So a bowling ball would drop first, right?" and explains, under Dave's questioning, that it would do so because "it's heavier." Most people interpret Tiera as saying that heavier objects fall more quickly than lighter objects, so people are often perplexed when Tiera responds to Dave's question, "So you think that heavier objects fall faster than lighter ones by saying, "On the Moon, they drop slower...." What does Tiera mean here? Does she mean that on the Moon, heavier objects drop slower than lighter objects? This is unlikely, because she has already said that she thinks the bowling ball would drop first. Or does she mean that on the Moon, *both* objects would fall slower than they do on Earth, an idea she has just heard from Dave and Janice but which does not answer Dave's question about heavier versus lighter objects?

Most participants think Tiera is confusing the two comparisons being made: the difference between falling on the Earth versus on the Moon, and the difference between a heavy and a light object falling under the influence of the *same* gravitational field. Many participants think Tiera is not making this distinction—not "controlling the variables." Furthermore, people note that in line 74 she simply repeats the latest idea she has heard from Dave, which suggests that she is simply grabbing at ideas. In one session, a participant suggested that to Tiera, the idea of doing things on the Moon may be so different that any comparison to falling on Earth might not apply:

> Like, so he told her that there is gravity on the Moon, but for her I think that she says, "Ok, well, there is gravity on the Moon, but there's not enough gravity for being the same, you know for things being the way they are on Earth." So therefore, for her, the concept, it's not—there's no correlation for her.

It's an intriguing suggestion, one we don't often hear. The participant suggested that, to Tiera, being on the Moon means "all bets are off." Unlike the interpretation that Tiera is just trying to grasp at the right answer, this account says she is having trouble *because* she is sense-making, not because she's failing to sense-make.

Moving From Interpretations to Ideas for Instruction

As always, we try to deflect *evaluations* of the teacher toward neutral discussions about possibilities for instruction emerging from the group's interpretations of students' thinking. However, it's difficult for participants to ignore how Dave responds to Tiera differently from how he responds to Ron and Khalid (as Dave himself discusses in his case study). For example, while Dave continuously reflects back Ron and Khalid's ideas, he tells Tiera that there is gravity on the Moon when she says, "there's no gravity up there … because that's how space is." Rather than treating Dave's behavior here as problematic, we ask what Dave *could have done* differently.

Many participants see Dave's move here as appropriate. After all, if he wants Tiera to compare objects falling on the Moon and on Earth, she needs to know that objects fall in both settings. Another frequently suggested option is that Dave could ask Tiera what it looks like when astronauts walk on the moon, to help her figure out for herself that gravity must be present. Some participants suggest that Dave might simply accept Tiera's response and focus instead on what she thinks would happen on Earth. The rationale here is that when the class comes together for whole-class discussion, Dave might bring up the suggestion that both objects will float, and allow the class to discuss what they think.

Based on the interpretation (noted previously) that Tiera does not understand that two falling objects must be compared to each other in each setting (Earth and Moon), some participants suggest that Dave might ask Tiera to draw a description of what the question is asking. This might help her see that she needs to *separately* answer the questions about falling on Earth versus falling on the Moon.

The Discussion to Line 204

We usually don't get past the first snippet. It takes some time to go through Ron and Tiera's reasoning line by line and to discuss options for how Dave could have responded to Tiera.

At this point in the class, Dave had brought the students together for a discussion, and the class talked about each question in sequence. Time permitting, several student ideas warrant discussion. Here we point to some of those ideas and suggest questions we might ask participants to consider.

Questions 1 and 2

In lines 94–102, Khalid restates his argument that the bowling ball and rock land at the same time, due to "air resistance." Here he says a little more than he did in the conversation with Dave and Ron, so we ask participants if they can gain any greater insight into how he thinks air resistance causes both objects to fall at the same rate. Interestingly, when Dave asks if the shape makes a difference, Khalid brings up a sheet of paper, which "can be balled up too" (line 104). Is Khalid saying that this is an exception to his rule? If so, how does he think the shape makes a difference? He says the air resistance affects the flat paper differently "because this one is spreaded out," but what is he thinking in line 111 when he says, "The size ... like ... and the way the air hits it?" Is he thinking of the air as an opposing force that comes into contact with more of the paper when he says "the way the air hits it?" In line 115, Ron says the paper is wide, and so it bumps into air particles. He seems to have a sense that the difference in shape leads to a difference in the number of air particles that the paper can bump into; so why might he have difficulty explaining this, other than to say "the shape," when Dave asks why he doesn't think both the bowling ball and the rock would be slowed by air resistance (line 124)?

The class devotes little time to question 2. Tiera reiterates her claim that "everything floats up there," which can lead to an interesting conversation. Is she continuing to consider the Moon to have no gravity, even though Dave told her that it does? Why might she continue to assert this, even though she has been told otherwise? Ultimately, Dave explains that there is indeed gravity on the Moon, although there's very little air, and Quentin provides an answer that seems to satisfy Dave so that he moves on. What do participants think of Quentin's answer (line 153)?

Question 3

In the discussion of question 3, Tiera insists that the baby is going to land first, because the father "throws the baby out first." This can promote an interesting discussion about how students read these physics questions. Participants can see that Tiera insists that the baby is thrown out of the window first, even though the question clearly says that the father lets himself out *at the same moment*. Ebony even questions the entire premise of the question: "How you gonna throw the baby out and jump out at the same time?"

Moving From Interpretations to Ideas for Instruction

Interpretations of student reasoning lead to possible ideas for instruction. To draw out more of Khalid's reasoning about air resistance in question 1, one possible move would be to ask him how he thinks "the way the air hits it" makes a difference in how the flat piece of paper and the balled-up piece of paper fall. How does the air hit them differently?

With respect to question 3, it might be productive for Dave to lead an explicit discussion with students about what the question says versus what their intuition tells them is happening. There is some of this, but it may not be enough, because Tiera insists that, "You all read the problem wrong." If Dave were to make this clearer, how could he do it? Alternatively, how could Dave change the question itself so that it doesn't violate students' common-sense mental picture of how the father would save the baby and then himself?

The Rest of the Discussion (Line 204 Onward)

Some of the most interesting thinking in the whole-class discussion comes up in this latter portion, especially in the discussion of question 4, so one option is to skip lines 74–204 and go directly to the discussion of question 4. Wherever we stop, we save time at the end for discussing the menu of possibilities for instructional responses.

Question 4

Janice and Tiera disagree on whether the bottles would land at the same time, and it's useful to focus participants on the nature of their disagreement. Janice is emphatic that the bottles would not hit the ground at the same time. What is her reasoning? Do her ideas make sense to people watching the video or reading the transcript? And what about Tiera? Why exactly does she disagree with Janice?

Another interesting idea to focus on, if no one brings it up, is Ebony's argument that light things fall faster than heavy things. This is an unusual idea; most students intuitively think that heavy things fall faster. But Ebony defends her claim. What is her reason? Is it sensible?

Question 5

In the discussion of question 5, some of the student ideas are difficult to understand, and it might be productive to discuss what the students mean. For example, the students say that the ice cubes take the same time to reach the bottom of the ramp. Comparing this question to the previous one, Dave asks why the bigger ice cube wouldn't slide down faster. Tiera replies, "Because it's lighter" (line 308). What is Tiera thinking? Is she simply pointing out that the smaller ice cube is lighter, essentially repeating the idea that the ice cubes have different weights? Is she just not paying attention to or understanding Dave's question, or is there another possible explanation?

Another idea that's a little difficult to understand, partly due to inaudibility, is Ron's response to Dave asking why some students say that the heavier ice cube slides down more quickly. Ron says, "Because it's got more water" (line 316), and when Dave repeats this idea, Ron adds that "you know when it goes down, you know how like it scrapes the ice and (inaudible)." Based on his statement that "it scrapes the ice," it's possible that he's thinking there's more ice to melt into water, thus reducing friction, i.e., keeping the larger ice cube from "scraping the ice" as much. But the question already states that there is no friction. On the one hand, Ron seems not to relate his conception of the ramp scraping the ice to the condition that there is no friction. On the other hand, his possible understanding of friction as something that keeps things from moving on a surface seems to make sense.

What Happened at the End of the Class and the Menu of Possibilities

Regardless of how much of the video we show, participants often want to know what Dave did after this. Since Dave was working hard to just listen to his students' ideas and not tell them anything, people often feel uncomfortable. When are the students going to learn the physical principles that they should learn in physics class? We tell them what Dave did the next day. He discussed the answers that a physicist would probably give to each question, focusing on how the principles of inertia, acceleration, mass, and air resistance fit together in each question. In interviews later, Dave suggested that it might have been a good idea to give similar scenarios later as a quiz, to see how the students reasoned through such questions after greater exposure to the concepts. Upon hearing what Dave did, participants often bring up alternatives. Some have suggested changing up some of the conditions in the question set and seeing how those changes influence students' responses. While considering "the menu of possibilities" for instructional responses is important, we try to keep the conversation grounded in ideas the students brought up.

Discussing Dave's Case Study

We have always shown and talked about the video, at least through line 74, before people read Dave's case study. Showing the video first, we think, helps the case seem more real. It also gives workshop participants the chance to form their own interpretations before they hear what Dave thought.

As we've discussed in earlier chapters, analysis of the written case study can be approached in at least two ways. One is to have participants discuss the case study in a subsequent class or seminar. During this conversation, we prompt participants to first pay attention to the teacher's interpretations—what he saw and heard and thought about it—rather than focusing on the teacher's actions.

Time does not always allow for such a conversation, however. Another option is to have participants, especially if they are students in a science pedagogy class, read the case study and transcript and then write an analysis focusing on either (1) Dave's interpretations and how they fit (or not) with their own, or (2) some of the issues and concerns Dave raises in his case study. We think two issues in particular are worth having participants discuss or write about.

First, Dave describes the great tension he felt in the conversation with Tiera. On the one hand, he wanted to be attentive and responsive to her ideas. On the other hand, he thought that it was difficult for Tiera to reason about the falling-objects question without some background information. He ended up telling her some things, which he was afraid only encouraged her to her wait for him to give out the answers. When we work with practicing teachers, we want to know if they have had similar experiences. How do they manage this kind of tension? In working with preservice teachers, we also have the opportunity to ask about this tension. By the time we reach this case study, our teacher candidates have usually interviewed students about scientific phenomena (see Chapter 9 for details). In these interviews, the teacher candidates often face similar tensions between their desire to guide students toward a certain response and their desire to listen and respond to the substance of students' thinking.

Another issue we might discuss or have participants write about is Dave's claim that the context of the particular questions strongly influenced his students' responses. Do participants agree? After all, as we discuss in Chapter 2, there are different ways that one can understand how students get to "wrong" and "right" answers. Dave's sense that the wording of the particular questions is important might be challenged, if someone thought that the students were expressing fairly stable ideas about free-falling objects. In any written piece, of course, we want participants to ground their interpretations in students' articulated ideas.

CHAPTER 9
Moving Forward

Attending to students' thinking in science can be difficult. Students' thinking can be unclear, and they may express ideas in ways that are different from what we expect to hear. But students *have* ideas about science, and teachers need practice listening for them and to them.

This book has provided materials to support practices of learning to attend to student thinking, in classroom discussions and in student work. It serves to highlight some of the things we might recognize in students' thinking, both in terms of progress toward understanding core conceptual ideas and engaging in practices of inquiry. In this final chapter, we start with a quick reminder of some of the things we noticed in student thinking in these cases. From there, we turn to strategies for instruction. That has not been the main topic of this book, because we have intentionally worked to foreground student thinking as the focus of teachers' inquiry. We hope that now that we have established the focus on student thinking, we can think about how to move from there to a focus on teachers' responsive practices. Finally, we'll discuss how to think about organizing groups to collect videos from their classrooms and to study them for evidence of students' science thinking. We'll also discuss strategies for supervising new teachers to maintain a focus on the substance of students' thinking.

Review

We've been looking for the possible beginnings of science in students' thinking, and we've found plenty, including:

- Students' everyday sense of mechanisms in relationships, such as Robert's sense that the blind snakes may be eating something in the nests that might harm the baby owls in Sarah's class on "The Owls and the Snakes."
- The causes of "shrinking," such as Rachel's description of water evaporating from the skin of a drum during Jenny Tanner's class on "The Rime of the Ancient Mariner."
- Why things fall at different rates, such as Janice's "feeling" that the heavier of two bottles with the same shape would fall faster during Dave Hovan's class about the "Free-Falling Bodies" questions.

And there's a lot more. If we had included other case studies, we would be describing examples of what students think can cause objects to go slower or faster when sliding on ice, or what causes species of organisms to change over time, or about what sorts of materials can provide energy from burning. As we discussed in Chapter 2, students have a lot of useful knowledge about how things happen in the natural world. So we should help students learn to express their understanding through discussions or in writing or drawings, to help them learn to refine it toward precision and consistency.

We've looked for beginnings of science in students' responses, such as when they hear others' ideas and consider them, and how they detect inconsistencies and work to reconcile them. In these case studies, we've seen students

- considering whether their classmates' hypotheses about "The Owls and the Snakes" made sense and judging how well evidence about the owls and the snakes supports various hypotheses proposed by the class;
- questioning whether water could flow from a place there's little of it (the boards of a boat) to a place where there's a lot of it (the ocean), and wondering about how to make that idea consistent with their understanding of diffusion; and
- challenging the consistency of a hypothetical student's claim that a bowling ball and a rock dropped from the same height land at the same time because air resistance holds back the bowling ball.

It's important to help students learn to use and refine their abilities to detect inconsistencies in explanations and to expect that hypotheses are consistent with evidence. We should help students with tools and strategies for expressing their reasoning, for making it more consistent, for hearing and responding to others' reasoning, for keeping track of ideas people have and the evidence they collect in support, refutation, or modification of those ideas. In short, we should help students use and develop their abilities to participate in argumentation.

We have shown that students have lots of valuable knowledge and abilities, and we need to recognize these resources if we're going to help students to develop and refine them. For several reasons, that can be quite a challenge.

Some ideas are hard to explain, and even more so for students if they have had little practice in trying to articulate their ideas. Sometimes, the teacher might understand what the student is saying, but not really understand the reasoning behind the idea—that is, *Why is the student thinking that?* For example, in Dave Hovan's conversations with his student Ron about the Free-Falling Bodies question set, Ron said, "If there wasn't no air the ball would be coming down very slow." Was Ron thinking that since air is all around us, it is air that makes things fall? Or was he confusing air with gravity, as Dave heard other students do?

In some other cases, it might not even be obvious what students are trying to say even if they speak clearly. As we saw in the introductory chapter, Terry wasn't sure what his students meant when they said that matter "has mass" and "takes up space" and when he probed, he got an even greater surprise: Laura said, and Ari agreed, "Air is space." Terry had to probe the girls' thinking to make sure he understood—were they saying that air takes up space, or were they actually saying that it *is* space?

And sometimes it's challenging to listen to students just because it's hard to understand what they're saying, like Brian in "The Rime of the Ancient Mariner" discussion when he was trying to use ideas about water's "universal solvent" properties to explain why salt water would cause the boards on the boat to shrink. Other times it's hard to hear students' ideas simply because of their tone or fluency or volume. In Izzy's "The Owls and the Snakes" class, she had to ask Max twice to repeat his reasoning for why he said "sort of," when she asked him if the table of nestling growth dynamics supported the hypothesis that the snakes were protecting the owls' eggs. Her persistence paid off, as it revealed that Max was still considering the fact that some snakes would be eaten if they did not burrow into the nest quickly enough.

No matter how closely we try to listen to students, it's inevitable that teachers will miss some of what students say; it's inevitable in any conversation that participants don't hear or understand everything that is said. Still, it's always better to miss less and notice more. So we practicing listening, and as teachers, we learn to think of ourselves *first* as *listeners*.

Ideas for Teaching

We've presented these case studies to provide material for teachers, student teachers, and teacher educators to get practice at recognizing and interpreting students' thinking. Ultimately, our goal is to recognize that practice is a critical first step to improve instruction. We have thus chosen these case studies purposefully, using examples mostly from teachers who were just beginning to learn to listen to their students and respond instructionally. This provides a context in which people discussing the case studies can begin to consider the "menu of possibilities" for instructional responses. We turn now to a greater description of how the views of science and science learning that we have discussed suggest approaches to teaching that might inform what goes on that menu.

Objectives of Science Education

To turn to ideas for instruction, we must first ask: What should science instruction accomplish for students?

Established Objectives

Two well-established objectives dominate the conversation about what science teaching should accomplish for students. The first focuses on scientific knowledge: At the end of a lesson, students should be able to answer particular questions correctly or demonstrate an understanding of some fact or information through other means. That view of science education objectives is deeply engrained in the educational system and amplified by a focus on high-stakes tests and standardized curriculum. In most districts, there are significant institutional structures in place to reinforce the focus on producing correct answers that can be measured. The second established objective is about motivation and engagement. We want students to like science, so we also look for our lessons to engage and interest them.

We know that science teaching frequently fails students on both of these objectives. Stop random adults on the street and ask them questions to gauge their understanding or interest in science, and you'll find most of them have little of either. We need new ways to think about science education, and not just about new methods. For years, educators have tried different methods, and the emphasis has shifted back and forth between traditional methods, which tend to emphasize the delivery of the facts and information, and reformed methods, which tend to emphasize students' motivation. Yet over this time, we have seen the same problems again and again. Science education has been failing students for a long time, regardless of the methods. Maybe we need to consider that the methods are not the problem; maybe it's the objectives.

A Different Agenda: Cultivating Resources

We've been suggesting a new way of thinking about what science education should accomplish: cultivating the beginnings of science in students' ideas and reasoning, and helping them to think about science as a refinement of their everyday thinking. That's not directly about motivation, although we find that most students are motivated by the opportunity to express themselves and have their ideas taken seriously. It's really about appreciating the substance of students' ideas and reasoning, and helping them to appreciate that substance.

The new agenda is not directly about facts and information either, although it will support that too. Students who can build from what they know, who question their own and others' ideas and try to resolve inconsistencies, and who insist that new ideas make sense will end up with deeper understanding of the facts and information than students who accept these details on the teacher's or the textbook's authority.

This new agenda we're proposing doesn't conflict with traditional objectives. In particular moments, however, there is tension. Not everything students are motivated to do in science class is productive for learning science,

and not every idea that is correct is sensible, mechanistic, and consistent with students' everyday thinking. If, for example, students are engaged in making up stories about some natural phenomenon—for example that a god has decided to make leaves turn color in the fall so people can enjoy the change in seasons—they might be motivated and engaged, and the teacher might appreciate the students' participation, but that wouldn't make it science. In these moments, a teacher needs to negotiate between cultivating students' resources for thinking scientifically and letting them continue in a discussion they are enjoying. For the example above, it's not quite so difficult, but in other cases it might be trickier. In one of Dan's classes, for example, students were discussing the identity of a "mystery rock" (an owl pellet). Some students were highly engaged in sharing their opinion that the rock was something that Dan had picked out his vacuum cleaner. It would have been a reasonable idea, but other students had already identified bones and teeth in the "rock," and the students arguing for the vacuum cleaner lint weren't even trying to explain that evidence. For Dan, this made a tension between maintaining the students' enthusiasm and guiding them toward more scientific thinking of seeking coherence with evidence.

Another tension occurs when a student is trying to explain her reasoning for an answer the teacher knows doesn't make sense. If the immediate objective is for the student to state the correct answer, the teacher will respond differently than if her objective is to help the student learn to articulate her reasoning. We think the choice in such moments should more often be to focus on cultivating students' resources for reasoning scientifically than to focus on correctness by the canon. If students come up with particular mechanisms that don't lead to the right answer in this instance, their ideas may be part of right answers in other instances, or they may be productive in moving the class toward the right answer, as Rachel's "drum" mechanism did in Jenny's class about osmosis. Rachel was exploring her mental toolbox, learning about what she knew and what was relevant for thinking about the science. That she had the "wrong" mechanism did not turn out to be a problem. Instead it turned out to be a productive idea that the class was able to use. The rest of the class heard Rachel modeling something Jenny hoped to see from all of her students—that they could draw on their everyday reasoning to try to make sense of the situation.

Coordinating With Traditional Objectives

This new agenda of cultivating students' resources for scientific thinking should not replace the others. Naturally, those objectives remain important, but the new focus should be coordinated with them. We expect that cultivating students' resources should be emphasized early in *all* science classes, starting especially in elementary school, so that students may approach their work in science class as primarily being about refining their everyday thinking (rather than arriving at scientists' established ideas), so that they can begin to understand how that is fundamental to science. As students become more established in that approach, the emphasis can shift to the traditional objectives.

This view may be of little help, however, for teachers making short-term choices about what to do with particular students in particular situations. And the challenge of coordinating cultivating resources with traditional objectives becomes greater as students move into high school, when curricula and high-stakes tests make greater demands on content coverage than in earlier grades. Few teachers have the luxury of working with students who are so established in a meaningful approach to science that they can take it for granted, and the challenge of making traditional progress while also achieving and maintaining a meaningful approach is ongoing and difficult.

If students are reasoning about some topic that is already familiar to them, and they can use what they know to understand the particular content that is central to the objectives, then coordinating these two approaches is not that hard. For Sarah, students' everyday knowledge about owls and snakes and about the ways in which organisms interact allowed her to make progress in helping her students to come up with hypothetical explanations for the "mystery relationship," while articulating the main categories of ecological relationships that students were expected to know. It was a relatively simple matter for Sarah to attach the vocabulary to the relationships students had proposed *after* the discussion. Thus, it was not too challenging for Sarah to get students to start thinking about the problem from the basics of their everyday knowledge.

In Chapter 2, we talked about the central importance of students' sense of what is taking place. It's interesting to speculate on how it might have been different if Sarah had introduced the vocabulary first, before introducing the scenario. It's possible the discussion could have gone in a different way—if students' sense of what was taking place was about learning terminology rather than about understanding the natural world. They might have memorized definitions that didn't connect to their everyday knowledge.

In different circumstances, students' sensible ideas might take them in a different direction, one not quite so simple to coordinate with traditional objectives. That's what Dave was trying to manage, as his students thought through the conceptual problems on the free-falling body worksheet. Dave had to consider what to do when Ebony suggested that heavier objects fall slower than lighter objects, based on her experience watching heavy and light people fall down, and he wanted her to have that sense of what was taking place, that she should be thinking in ways that make sense to her. How could Dave both acknowledge the value of Ebony's thinking and send the message that refining ones' ideas is what science is about, while helping Ebony, and all of the students, to understand the relations among mass, gravity, and air resistance as they are described in the canon of physics?

The choices of how to coordinate objectives are particular to the students, the subject matter, the particular objectives that the teacher is trying to coordinate, and even the school context (what high-stakes assessment is on the horizon?). Sarah's and Dave's choices were both specific to the topics in their curriculum and to the ways in which they wanted students to think about the particular problems. It's beyond what we can do here to give advice to how to coordinate multiple objectives in particular topics. It will take many books for that, each a series of case studies tied to a particular curriculum, or at least focused around particular topics.

Having and Valuing Discussions

When we introduced the case studies, we were clear that we didn't choose them to illustrate teaching methods, we chose them because they show student thinking, and thus can serve to support practices of attending to student thinking. If you were to drop in on any of these teachers' classes randomly, you would likely find all sorts of other activities going on, not only discussions, which are the substance of four of the five case studies in this book. We want to be clear that we are not making an argument that all of science teaching should proceed through discussions.

However, we want to also emphasize that discussions should be *part* of science teaching, and they often are not. Our first and main suggestion for science teaching methods is to create space for discussions of students' ideas about science. Teachers must value discussions about students' ideas for what they can help students achieve. They can help students to find, use, and develop their resources for scientific inquiry. We're not thinking only of the discussions seen in this book, like the extended full-class discussions in Sarah's, Izzy's, and Jenny's classes, or the exchanges between the teacher and one or two students, as in Dave's class. We're also thinking of short spontaneous exchanges that may occur in the course of other classroom activities within small groups or between two or more individual students.

Teachers who accept that hearing students' ideas is an important part of science teaching, are probably going to have a lot of discussion in their classes. Focusing attention on students' ideas, however, is likely to be in tension with what typically happens in science class and may conflict with teachers' and students' own expectations of what should be happening. It's useful to say a few things about those expectations, and about how to deal with the tensions that arise.

Keep Track of the Purpose

The greatest tension is over the purpose of discussions: The idea is to hear students' ideas and help them to develop those ideas, rather than guiding them quickly toward scientists' ideas. It's a lot easier to decide that in advance in the abstract, however, than it is to follow through in the moment. When a student says something that sounds *wrong*, it can be hard not to want to fix it, or steer the student away from it. The objective of *correctness* is so engrained that it can sneak its way into where it doesn't belong, nudging out the objective of making sense.

It's useful to look for ways to keep track of the purpose. We recommend teachers think of students as having insights that the teacher really wants to understand—the teacher can set her goal as discovering her students' minds. As experts on what they think, students are the most qualified to help others to understand it. If a student says something that sounds bizarre, that could be the most important nugget. If it's something the teacher doesn't yet understand, it's an opportunity for her to try to understand it.

If teachers can accept that stance—that they learn about students' thinking *from them*—they may find it easier controlling the urge to correct them. Most likely, they'll do a better job of conveying to students that they are interested in students' ideas. Even more, in doing that, the teachers can model what they hope students will do when it's the teacher's turn to explain *her* thinking. It's not easy to really focus attention on someone else's meaning; it's part of what we want students to learn to do, and it's a good idea to model doing that ourselves.

Notice and Arrange Opportunities for Discussions

In some science classes, when students are comfortable and motivated to talk, opportunities for discussions occur frequently—usually when the students have something they want to ask or share about a topic that comes up in class. Unfortunately, for a variety of reasons, students in high school classrooms often aren't motivated or comfortable enough to spontaneously engage in discussions, so teachers may need to think about how to arrange opportunities for discussions. As they do, and as their students gain more experience and confidence, teachers will likely find it easier to start discussions and may find it happening more often spontaneously.

When deciding on a question to launch a discussion, it's useful to think of one for which students might have a variety of reasonable ideas. Often the variety is in conflicting ideas that need to be debated and reconciled, such as in Sarah's "The Owls and the Snakes" class when the students disagreed on the nature of the relationship between the two species, or in Jenny's class, when students disagreed over how salt water causes dehydration.

Questions that lead to a variety of ideas usually make for the most productive discussions, but this is one of those places where objectives of responsive teaching can conflict with traditional objectives. If the purpose were to guide students to a particular idea, the best questions would be ones that pointed to that idea, questions students would be likely to get right as they moved toward the correct answer. That's the Socratic approach of asking questions to guide students in a particular direction, and sometimes that's appropriate. But structuring science discussions through Socratic questioning usually makes for fairly unproductive science talks that give little insight into students' thinking because they don't leave space for a variety of reasonable student ideas.

One useful thing to do when thinking up questions for discussion is to ask oneself, "How might my students respond to this?" and try to anticipate what they will say. If there are a lot of sensible possibilities that a reasonable student might give, that's an indication of a productive question for discussion. If there really aren't many possibilities, another question might be better.

Expect Students to Have Abilities

With some of our case studies, we hear comments from participants such as, "My students would never have a conversation like that." That perspective can serve as a self-fulfilling prophecy. Teachers who think this way may not give their students the opportunities to show how they think nor work very hard to make the opportunities productive. Ultimately, they'll end up proving themselves right: Students never form a sense of what is taking place in science class that would have them engaging in conversation.

We've also heard great surprise—from our preservice teachers and from other teachers we've worked with in seminars—at what students could do in discussions when they really had a chance. Just about any group of students can have these sorts of discussions, as Izzy's "The Owls and the Snakes" case with a self-contained special education class demonstrates. The discussions may take different forms depending on the students involved; the discussion in Jenny's class was certainly more animated than that in Izzy's class. A key part of the challenge of leading these discussions is recognizing what this type of discussion might look like, for any particular group of students. There may be variation in how the discussion is paced, and what kinds of academic language are used, depending on factors such as the students' grade level, cultural and linguistic background, learning disabilities, or even the individual personalities of the students in the classroom or elements of the classroom and school culture.

It's important for teachers to see and experience that students are capable of productive conversations. We find that when teachers we've worked with watch these videos and lead discussions in their own classes, they see positive results and so they work harder and become more imaginative in how

they support student thinking. If teachers find that it's not happening in their classrooms, they should try to figure out why. Maybe students don't know what they're expected to do? Maybe they don't trust that it's really okay to say what they think? A goal for teachers' practice should be to work to create a classroom culture in which students feel comfortable sharing their ideas and understand that is what they're expected to do.

Play a Substantive Role in the Discussions

In a caricature of "student-centered learning" students are treated as natural scientists that simply discover scientific knowledge by themselves, while teachers just step out of the way and let the students do their naturally scientific thinking. In some moments, there are good reasons to adopt such a stance, just as there are also moments when it's a good choice for a teacher to be very directive in a discussion or even give answers and explanations. The hard part for most teachers is recognizing which moments are which and making quick decisions, as Dave did (in Chapter 8) when he realized that Tiera thought there was no gravity on the Moon.

But it's a false dichotomy to say that the choice is either "step out of the way" or "give them the answers." There's a much more substantive role the teacher can play, one that is neither leaving the students to themselves nor guiding them to particular answers. This important role is about guiding students toward using scientific approaches to reasoning, working to articulate ideas clearly, seeking empirical evidence and theoretical coherence, testing ideas for predictive power, and so on, as we discussed in Chapter 2.

We don't expect teachers to stay out of it when students are having these discussions. Certainly students need space to talk, and teachers must encourage them to listen and talk to each other, but it's crucial that teachers also pay close attention to what students are saying and step in to facilitate discussions. Teachers can guide students to use their sense of causes and effects and express tangible ideas about what makes things happen from their everyday thinking. Teachers can help students learn to find confusion *stimulating,* something to address, not something to fear and avoid. They can help them learn to shop through their knowledge of phenomena and look for connections, to try out foothold ideas and see where they lead, or to find new possibilities. They can help students learn, guide them to identify inconsistencies in their own and others' ideas and try to reconcile them, to not simply contradict someone when they don't agree, but to give evidence and reasoning, and to do so respectfully and constructively.

That's what Aaron did in Sarah's "The Owls and the Snakes" case (Chapter 4) when he responded to Michelle's disagreement with his ideas about the snakes protecting the eggs (Michelle said "they were blind, so how could they protect the eggs?") by countering that the blind snakes could "pick up heat around other things" and "detect...prey nearby."

Students *can* do these things, although they don't always show that they can. In some cases they might not even be aware of when they're doing them and when they aren't. Much of the guidance teachers can give is in telling students, through their interest and attention maybe more than with actual words, "That's what you should be doing!" "That's science!"

Keeping Science Sensible

Science lessons should involve many different kinds of activities, from discussions to controlled experiments, to reading about scientific explanations in books, and more. The most important thing is that the whole of what teachers do in science class helps students learn science as a refinement of everyday thinking. That might not happen if the different activities send very different messages, such as if in one activity students debate their ideas about how an acorn grows into a tree, and in the next activity they are asked to copy down the equations for photosynthesis and respiration and memorize the terminology of these reactions.

A useful question to ask of everything students experience in science is whether it promotes or discourages them from treating science as connected to and building from what they know about the world. We talked a little in Chapter 2 about the role of terminology in this view: Students should learn technical vocabulary when and if it helps them to express and understand ideas more precisely. Learning vocabulary for its own sake might do the opposite—get in the way of their expressing their knowledge and experience or even thinking their knowledge is relevant.

To this point, we haven't said anything about science fairs, which has been the main place where schools and teachers expect students have an opportunity for experience in scientific thinking. Teachers want to see students design and conduct their own investigations, and science fairs include rules and strategies designed to guide students in these investigations. The purpose is for students to engage in inquiry, but the typical science-fair image of inquiry doesn't line up easily with the views we've presented here about sense of mechanisms and argumentation. We find the typical practices of science fairs need some adjusting if they are to help students approach science as a refinement of everyday thinking.

Questions

What kinds of questions should students work with? How should they arrive at their topics and questions? Science fair projects emphasize students posing questions that are *testable*, in other words, that can be answered through a

"well-designed," controlled experiment. This encourages questions of a certain type—those that can be easily tested with materials and methods that are accessible to the students: Do plants grow best in red, blue, or white light? Which freezes most quickly: tap water, boiled water, saltwater, or sugar water? What material catches fire most easily: newspaper, white paper, cotton balls, or science-fair poster board? A student can grow plants, varying the color of light; she may prepare samples of water and time how long each takes to freeze, or hold a flame under samples of various materials and time how long it takes them to ignite.

The problem is that the fact that they're testable may be the *only* reason to ask those questions! That's just not a meaningful way to approach science, and it certainly isn't a refinement of everyday thinking, in which we ask questions because we're *interested.*

There are appropriate reasons to ask some of the questions above. Maybe the reason to ask the plant question is that students have heard plants grow better in blue light, but they are suspicious because they don't tend to see people growing plants under blue light, and they can't think of a reason the color of the light should make a difference. They want to know if it's true! Or maybe they've heard that if you boil water and then put it in the freezer when it's still hot it freezes more quickly than water from the faucet. That doesn't seem to make sense, though, because students' experience tells them that the hot water would have to cool down first before it freezes. So they ask the question to find out for themselves what the evidence suggests, and then have the opportunity to think about their understanding of the mechanisms involved if their intuition conflicts with the evidence.

Hypotheses

Science fair projects emphasize that with testable questions come testable hypotheses. Most adults and most secondary students can already tell you what they've learned about a hypothesis: "It's an educated guess!" But an educated guess of what? In most cases we've seen, a hypothesis is treated as no different from an educated guess of what will happen in *this* experiment, a *prediction*, and we have seen materials for guiding science fair projects that have students fit their hypothesis to an "If/then" statement, where the "If" condition is changing the independent variable and the "then" condition is the change in the dependent variable that is predicted to result.

But in a scientific sense, that's not a hypothesis at all! A hypothesis is, as the word itself implies, a "little theory"—a proposed explanation of how something in the natural world works. Thus, at the very least, if a prediction of how the independent variable will affect the dependent variable is offered, it should *at least* include some justification that reflects this little theory. For example, if a student predicts that *if* she grows plants under different colored lights *then* the

plants grown under the white light will grow best, her reasons for thinking this are really *the substance* of her hypothesis. Perhaps she thinks plants will grow best under white light because white light contains all of the light in the visible spectrum, and so the most light is "available" for the plant. In short, when students hypothesize, they should be actively thinking about mechanistic explanations for *why* experiments will turn out the way that they predict. Science fairs rarely push students to think about their "little theories" behind their predictions. When we ask students to hypothesize, we should be asking them to think about how their proposed mechanistic understandings of phenomena shape what they predict will happen in experiments.

Investigations

Most typically, students pursue testable questions through controlled experiments. The controlled experiment is the central focus of the science fair experience, with rubrics organized around designing the pieces of the controlled experiment and labeling those pieces as structural elements of the experiment: the independent variable, the dependent variable, the control (or control group), and the constants. Often a large part of the rubrics for the design are that the students correctly identify these elements and label them in the experiment.

In Chapter 2, we mentioned briefly about how scientific practices of experimental control are essentially forms of argumentation. A scientist controls for a variable because someone else might claim that variable makes a difference, and the scientist can respond by controlling for that variable. Experimental control is most meaningful to students who understand science as argumentation, and see an experiment as an opportunity to confront alternative claims. We want students to learn controlled experiments as a practice in argumentation. But students shouldn't put controls into experiments because the rubrics tell them to—we should help them understand that they should include controls for some sensible reason.

Conclusions

In science fairs, students draw conclusions from their investigations and present their findings to others. Here again, our views of the importance of mechanisms and argumentation might inform what students could be doing when drawing conclusions. They should not simply report what they found—the plants in the blue light grew the tallest, for example, but they should explain *why* the plants in the blue light grew the tallest. What might it be about blue light, or plants, or both, that would cause the plants in the blue light to grow the tallest? If the hypothesis was that the plant in white light would grow the tallest, then this needs to be reconciled with the results. What part of the reasoning in the hypothesis didn't work? This could lead to a new hypothesis and a revised prediction that could be tested with another experiment.

Of course, in many cases, students won't be able to account for their results. That's okay; that's part of authentic science, which is often messy and uncertain. But students should certainly try to explain their results! They might not be able to explain what happened, but they may be able to rule out some possibilities.

In other words, rather than defining the process of investigations in science simply around testable questions and their outcomes, define it as asking interesting questions, formulating ideas about their answers, and finding ways to make progress in figuring them out. The point is that students should see and experience science as about finding ways to answer interesting, meaningful questions.

Science in Big and Small Questions

In professional science, there are big, interesting questions, such as "How old is the universe?" and "How did life begin?" Those would be pretty hard for students to explore in science fair projects, but they're the sorts of questions that capture scientists' interests and drive them throughout their careers. Thinking about them can lead to other smaller questions that might help. Some scientists, because they want to know how old the universe is, have worked on figuring out the processes of how stars form and die, and that in turn has connected to more specific questions they can study in the lab about how particular bits of matter interact. Students should learn in science class that scientists ask such questions—that big questions are definitely asked and valued in science.

Students should also learn, however, that kid-sized questions are appropriate as long as they represent genuine inquiry into understanding natural phenomena. Such kid-size questions might include things like "What causes lightning?" and "Why do eggs get hard when you cook them?" The challenge, as it is in professional science, is to find ways to make progress toward understanding these phenomena. Of course students could look up the answers on the internet, but there's no point to that if the idea is for them to conduct their own investigations.

Julia, a ninth-grade physics student, has heard that lightning is caused by static electricity, and she wants to confirm that. Could lightning really be just a larger version of the small electric shock you can sometimes get when you touch another person? She finds a way to make static electric sparks regularly—maybe by building a device from a design she finds on the internet—to see if they look like lightning. The sparks are very tiny, so she finds a way to magnify them, or maybe make bigger sparks, and she uses a video camera to take pictures. She sees that they do look like little lightning bolts and puts pictures showing that in her project, and uses that to support the idea that lightning is related to static electricity. She hasn't answered her original question yet (What causes lightning?), but she's made good progress: she's decided it might be the same thing that causes little sparks. She's done some nice scientific thinking, and just because she has not done a controlled experiment does not mean she's not doing science. Plenty of science does not involve controlled experimentation.

Ideas for Teacher Education, Professional Development, and Mentoring

This book advances a perspective that emphasizes the resources students bring to science learning and the importance of attending and responding to students' thinking to help them refine, select, and apply those resources. This is only a beginning; we don't know a lot about all of the resources that students may bring to science, but we've made a start. We know to look for students' resources for understanding mechanisms and engaging in coherent argumentation. But we expect the resources that students bring to science to be many and varied, especially as we consider the different ways of knowing that constitute the different physical and biological sciences. It would not be possible for us to provide a catalog of resources and their various manifestations in what students might say and do. We encourage teachers and teacher educators to learn to look for students' productive resources and think of ways to respond to them instructionally.

We have emphasized the importance of learning to notice, appreciate, and elicit the substance of students' knowledge and reasoning. We have found that this collection of case studies, and others we have used, stimulate productive conversations about the substance of students' thinking and potential instructional responses. In addition, we have found the case studies to be very effective in promoting conversations about science. As teachers discuss the students' thinking in our classes and seminars, the conversation often turns to deeper conversations about participants' own science content or even reflections on how the teacher participants themselves view science.

We offer this book as a starting point for teachers and teacher educators who are interested in improving practices of attending and responding to student thinking. In the sections that follow, we describe how you can build on the foundation established by this book to have groups of teachers collect and discuss their own case studies. We then offer some ideas about classroom mentoring and supervision—how we can continue to help new teachers focus on student thinking, even as they are managing the everyday realities of the classroom and of the broader system. But first, it's worth spending some time talking about the broader system in which secondary science teachers work and the ways in which the system can constrain student thinking, but also can offer opportunities for teachers to elicit and attend to students' thinking.

Systemic Constraints on Secondary Science Teaching

As we discussed in Chapter 1, we were surprised that the teachers in our project rarely made instructional modifications in response to students' ideas. In fact, we found it was rare that we had *any* evidence that teachers paid attention or responded to students' ideas, other than for how it aligned with the conceptual outcomes of the lesson. It was also rare to see teachers making efforts to elicit students' ideas and reasoning, except when the elicitation served to draw out wrong ideas and mark them for correction. This experience motivated us to cultivate practices of attending and responding to student thinking among the teachers in our project and ultimately to produce this collection of case studies for cultivating these practices in teacher education.

Perhaps we should not have been so surprised. As we learned more about the context of the teachers' work lives, it became quite clear how little the school system supported practices of attending to student thinking and how much of the system actually drew attention *away* from student thinking. As in most states since the authorization of the No Child Left Behind Act, the students in these classes were required to pass certain high-stakes tests to graduate, and teachers were held accountable for their students' performance on these high-stakes tests. These tests require students to repeat certain discrete bits of knowledge, usually by recognizing the vocabulary associated with certain ideas. Certainly it's not news that teachers and school systems focus on recall of factual knowledge, but the pressure of high-stakes tests made it difficult for the teachers in our project to put aside their concerns about the correctness of students' ideas.

And it's not just high-stakes tests! It's simply not common, in the practices of secondary school science teaching, for students' thinking to be an important consideration. One example is in the way teachers are observed, supervised, and evaluated. Observation rubrics focus on what the *teacher* does, usually without consideration for what the students are doing. A common expectation on such rubrics is that a teacher interacts effectively with students to promote learning. Certainly it's important that a teacher do so, but an understanding of what the students are saying or doing is central to knowing whether the teacher is interacting "effectively" or "promoting learning." The structure of post-observation conversations does not necessarily require that the students' ideas come to bear. What matters is whether the observer thinks that the teacher interacted effectively; the observer can talk about this interaction entirely in terms of the teachers' behavior. Practices such as this draw attention away from student thinking.

Supervising Teachers: Foregrounding Students' Thinking

Considering that so little of the institutional systems of public secondary schools encourages a focus on student thinking, we have made it our mission, as part of our secondary teacher education programs, to amplify a focus on students'

ideas and reasoning. Naturally, a supervisor observing a teacher's classroom, particularly a new teacher's classroom, will need to help the teacher to think about the consequences of her own actions. That is, the observer must help the teacher to think about how she is choosing instructional activities, how she is managing the classroom, and how she is meeting the needs of the various and diverse students in the class. But these considerations are really only meaningful in the context of what is going on in the particular class, and that depends, first and foremost, on what the students are doing and saying in the class.

So we begin our postobservation discussion by asking teachers (or prospective teachers) to consider what ideas they heard during the class and what they thought of those ideas. Sometimes this is challenging for teachers—with so many things to think about in the classroom, they might not be able to recall particular student ideas. We ask them to think about the students' ideas precisely for this reason, because we want them to think that what they should be doing in the classroom is listening for and to students' ideas about the content. As observers to classrooms, we try to keep our own eyes and ears on what the students are saying and doing. If a teacher can't recall particular ideas, we bring them up. We heard this idea—what did the teacher think of it? What did the student mean, and why might the student have been thinking that? And how might it have influenced how the teacher proceeded, or how she might proceed in the future if she heard that idea come up again?

Of course, in some classes, there may be little evidence of student thinking. This is one example of how the initial focus on students' ideas and reasoning can help to structure the postobservation discussion of what the teacher *might do*, or what she *might have done*. There *should* be evidence of the students' thinking during the class; otherwise, how will the teacher know what the students are getting from the instruction? So if we hear very little student thinking in the class, we might encourage the teacher to think about ways she could structure the lesson so that she might hear more. How could the lesson be restructured to make the students' thinking more apparent, to make it a part of the class in such a way that the students can participate and reason mechanistically, or engage in practices of seeking coherence among ideas?

The same idea holds true for classroom management. Typically, supervisors comment on how the teacher has managed the classroom—how she has managed student behavior or structured tasks and materials to manage the flow of the lesson. Again, this should depend on what it is that the students are doing or saying. For example, the class may be very noisy, with students calling out or otherwise seeming poorly behaved. Focusing only on the students' behavior and the teachers' management of that behavior, an observer might offer strategies for managing behavior, changing the seating arrangements, or creating incentives or consequences for certain kinds of behaviors.

But what are they saying or doing? If a teacher has structured an exciting classroom discussion, the class might be noisy because the students are excited to share their ideas. So what are their ideas? Are the students thinking mechanistically and coherently? If so, we might not suggest the teacher make any changes. The point is, again, that choices about how to manage the class depend first and foremost on what the students are saying and doing. If the behavior is off-task and unproductive, then we might want to suggest strategies for managing the discussion to encourage on-task behavior. If, however, the students are loudly and vociferously discussing the topic in a way that connects to their everyday thinking, we might not want to suggest any changes to classroom management strategies at all.

In our experience, more often than not, students misbehave when they are not given opportunities to do interesting thinking. We have found that student behavior is usually not a problem when the teacher has engaged them in interesting and authentic questions and is listening to and honoring their contributions.

Teacher Education: Keeping the Focus on Students' Thinking

The approach to supervising interns in the field should align with the approach in the science pedagogy courses, and we have structured our courses to draw attention to student thinking. Early in the pedagogy courses, we use case studies of student thinking, including the selections in this book, to promote discussion about student learning. Teacher candidates conduct interviews with secondary students, asking them to think about questions like, "What causes the change in seasons?" or "What makes our toes wrinkle in the bathtub?" As teacher candidates begin to plan lessons, we ask them to anticipate what ideas students might bring up, teach the lessons, and then analyze the student thinking that occurred, much like the case studies we've explored here.

Our ultimate goal is for our students to feel comfortable collecting cases of their own students' thinking, to bring them in to share and analyze with their classmates, and for teachers to use this experience to become more attentive and responsive to their students' thinking in their own teaching. We hope this for you as well, whether you're a teacher educator making plans for your pedagogy courses, or a teacher working with a group of colleagues to better your practices. You can collect video or samples of student work and spend some time trying to better understand what your students are thinking, and how they are thinking scientifically.

Collecting Your Own Data

It's important to collect data often. It's useful to have a lot of data to choose from, and we encourage our intern teachers to record their classes as often as they can. It's hard to know beforehand what a class is going to be like, and

whether it's going to be interesting to discuss with others. Collecting class-room video has become a much more common practice, and is required by the Teacher Performance Assessment Consortium and the National Board Certification process.

For the most part, the microphone that comes with the camera will be enough to capture the students' conversation; that's what you heard in most of the video of the case studies in this book. You could try using external micro-phones, which you can place among the students to get better sounds. We've also sometimes used wireless microphones on the teacher's lapel, which is why you hear Jenny's voice so much easier than her students. There are numerous inexpensive options for external and wireless microphones on the market.

Don't worry if there's nobody to stand at the camera. Just place it some-where and point it in a direction that's likely to have some action. If a colleague wants to help and tape you, all the better. Ask him or her to keep it simple: Don't zoom in and out or pan around too much. This isn't cinematography; you're just trying to make a simple record of what happened. If you're not going to make the recordings public—that is, if they're for your personal use only—you can usually skip the hassle of getting permission forms signed by parents and guardians. More recently, we've found that school systems have their own policies for these sorts of things; it's worth contacting your school district about it.

If you can't or don't want to record video of your own class, you could get a lot out of audiotaping. We've used audio sessions in our classes and seminars, and in cases where we don't have equipment, we've even read the transcripts of the case studies in this book out loud, as if we were reading a play. And you don't even need to do that. Teachers could sit down after a class discussion and try to remember some of what the students said, trying to reconstruct dialogue to create something like a transcript that can give a group something to review and consider. People might get some things wrong in remembering, but that's okay. The truth is that any medium you use to keep a record of what happens in class will miss some things, including video. But you'll want to have some way of focusing careful attention on particular things students say, write, and do, and trying to understand their thinking. That's the point of all this, don't forget—don't talk just about the teacher!

So give it a try! You don't have to ask participants to write up formal case studies right away; we've had many wonderful, productive conversations about snippets that teachers have never written about. But as you proceed, we recom-mend that you have teachers begin to write up case studies of student thinking in their classrooms. Maybe they will even choose to make their work public and share what they've learned with colleagues in science classrooms everywhere.

Appendix: Notes

This section contains notes that aren't otherwise included as footnotes in the text and directs the reader to further reading with citations from the literature. Relevant citations are mapped to page numbers and quotes from the text.

Chapter 1

- *Page 1:* Ideas from this chapter are also discussed in an article:

  Levin, D. M., T. Grant, and D. Hammer. 2012. Attending and responding to student thinking in science. *The American Biology Teacher* 74 (3): 158–162.

- *Page 13:* There are other valuable collections of classroom video: for example, video collected for the Third International Mathematics and Science study (*timssvideo.com*). However, this book is the only resource that we know of (aside from an earlier collection for elementary teachers co-authored by the second author—see Hammer and van Zee note below) that is explicitly designed to draw attention to the students' scientific thinking in the videos.

Chapter 2

- *Page 15:* This chapter and chapters 3 and 9 are based significantly on a previous work.

  Hammer, D., and E. van Zee. 2006. *Seeing the science in students' thinking: Case studies of student inquiry in physical science.* Portsmouth, NH: Heinnemann.

- *Page 15:* "The whole of science is nothing more than a refinement of everyday thinking."

  Einstein, A. 1936. Physics and reality. *Journal of the Franklin Institute* 221 (3): 349–382.

- *Page 17:* "It's made up of many different and often inconsistent 'mini-theories,' rather than by a single coherent framework, and that's important for how we think of its 'refinement.'"

  diSessa, A. A. 2000. *Changing Minds: Computers, Learning, and Literacy.* Cambridge, MA: MIT Press.

Appendix

- *Page 18:* "Students were being *rational* in thinking that force causes motion or that, for example, giraffes get longer necks by stretching."

  Clement, J. 1982. Student preconceptions in introductory mechanics. *American Journal of Physics* 50: 66.

  Posner, G., K. Strike, P. Hewson, and W. Gertzog. 1982. Accomodation of a scientific conception: Toward a theory of conceptual change. *Science Education* 66 (2): 211–227.

  Viennot, L. 1979. Spontaneous reasoning in elementary dynamics. *European Journal of Science Education* 1 (2): 205–221.

- *Page 19:* "If conceptual change theory suggests anything about instruction, it is that the handles to effective instruction are to be found in persistent attention to the argument and in less attention to right answers."

  Strike, K. A., and G. J. Posner. 1992. A revisionist theory of conceptual change. In *Philosophy of science, cognitive psychology, and educational theory and practice*, ed. R. A. Duschl and R. J. Hamilton, 147–176. Albany: State University of New York Press.

- *Page 19:* "Answering that was difficult in misconceptions research, mainly because it treated each misconception as the one way someone had to think about the particular topic."

  Part of Strike's and Posner's 1992 revision was to amend this feature of their original theory, to shift toward a view of a "cognitive ecology."

- Page 19: The film *A Private Universe*

  Sadler, P. M., M. H. Schneps, and S. Woll. 1989. *A private universe*. Santa Monica, CA: Pyramid Film and Video.

- *Page 20:* "That's the idea they have firmly engrained in their common sense, closer means stronger, and the misconception we hear is a result of their using that idea to answer this question."

  Hammer, D. 1996. More than misconceptions: Multiple perspectives on student knowledge and reasoning, and an appropriate role for education research. *American Journal of Physics* 64 (10): 1316–1325.

- *Page 20:* "The former interpretation would be part of a program of science instruction to replace everyday knowledge; the latter would be part of a program to refine everyday knowledge."

  Hammer, D. 2000. Student resources for learning introductory physics. *American Journal of Physics, Physics Education Research Supplement* 68 (S1): 52–59.

Smith, J., A. diSessa, and J. Roschelle. 1993/1994. Misconceptions reconceived: A constructivist analysis of knowledge in transition. *Journal of the Learning Sciences* 3 (2): 115–163.

- *Page 23:* "The first thing to appreciate is just how much kids are capable of doing. It may not be obvious, if you haven't spent time watching and listening to them think for themselves."

  Gopnik, A., A. N. Meltzoff, and P. K. Kuhl. 1999. *The scientist in the crib: What early learning tells us about the mind.* New York: HarperCollins.

  Koslowski, B. 1996. *Theory and evidence: The development of scientific reasoning.* Cambridge, MA: MIT Press.

- *Page 23:* "Research on grade-school children shows abilities that surprise adults, maybe especially those used to working with older children"

  Hammer, D. 2004. The variability of student reasoning, lecture 1: Case studies of children's inquiries. In *Proceedings of the Enrico Fermi Summer School, course CLVI*, ed. E. Redish and M. Vicentini, 279–299. Bologna, Italy: Italian Physical Society.

  Duschl, R. A., et al. 2007. *Taking science to school: Learning and teaching science in grades K–8.* Washington, DC: National Academies Press.

- *Bottom of page 23:* The examples here come from our ongoing research project Learning Progressions for Scientific Inquiry (NSF # DRL-0732233)

- *Page 24*: "Earlier we talked about how common sense varies, from one situation to another, and the same applies to reasoning."

  Hammer, D., and A. Elby. 2003. Tapping epistemological resources for learning physics. *Journal of the Learning Sciences* 12 (1): 53–91.

- *Page 26:* "In the study of electricity, for example, key progress came from scientists connecting to their knowledge about liquids, about tension (as in ropes), and even at one point about gears (as in engines)."

  Nersessian, N. J. 2002. Maxwell and "the method of physical analogy": Model-based reasoning, generic abstraction, and conceptual change. In *Essays in the history and philosophy of science and mathematics*, ed. D. Malament, 129–166: Lasalle, IL: Open Court.

- *Page 26:* "When, for example, a student ventures an analogy to some other phenomenon (e.g., the topic is metamorphosis and the student thinks of an analogy to human growth)…"

  Warren, B., C. Ballenger, M. Ogonowski, A. S. Rosebery, and J. Hudicourt-Barnes. 2001. Rethinking diversity in learning science: The logic of everyday sense-making. *Journal of Research in Science Teaching* 38 (5): 529–552.

Appendix

- *Page 27:* "Even younger kids, research on learning has shown, notice and care about establishing consistent patterns of causality."

  Schulz, L. E., and E. B. Bonawitz. 2007. Serious fun: Preschoolers engage in more exploratory play when evidence is confounded. *Developmental Psychology* 43 (4): 1045.

- *Page 30:* "Research on learning has revealed diverse forms of everyday reasoning in students' experience that could be valuable for science."

  Bang, M., and D. Medin. 2010. Cultural processes in science education: Supporting the navigation of multiple epistemologies. Science Education 94 (6): 1008–1026.

  Rosebery, A. S., M. Ogonowski, M. DiSchino, and B. Warren. 2010. "The coat traps all your body heat": Heterogeneity as fundamental to learning. *Journal of the Learning Sciences* 19 (3): 322–357.

  Seiler, G. 2001. Reversing the "standard" direction: Science emerging from the lives of African American students. *Journal of Research in Science Teaching* 38 (9): 1000–1014.

- *Page 31:* "How do students, or teachers, experience the situation?"

  Berland, L. K., and D. Hammer. 2012. Framing for scientific argumentation. Journal of Research in Science Teaching 49 (1): 68–94.

  Ford, M. J. 2005. The game, the pieces, and the players: Generative resources from two instructional portrayals of experimentation. *Journal of the Learning Sciences* 14 (4): 449–487.

  Tang, X. W., J. E. Coffey, A. Elby, and D. M. Levin. 2010. The scientific method and scientific inquiry: Tensions in teaching and learning. *Science Education* 94 (1): 29–47.

- *Page 31:* "These levels of thought and knowledge, of metacognition and epistemology, come into play all the time in everyday thinking, and they're of central importance in the development of scientific reasoning, so we should spend some time on them."

  Hammer, D. 1995. Epistemological considerations in teaching introductory physics. *Science Education* 79 (4): 393–413.

- *Page 33:* "For many students, mathematics is another subject they experience as divorced from everyday thinking, rather than building from it."

  Schoenfeld, A. 1991. On mathematics as sense-making: An informal attack on the unfortunate divorce of formal and informal mathematics. In *Informal reasoning and education*, ed. J. F. Voss, D. N. Perkins, and J. W. Segal, Hillsdale, NJ: Erlbaum.

- *Page 34:* "For students, the situation could be that they're following the instructions they were given, or it could be that they're trying to keep track and make sense of their data."

  Lehrer, R., and L. Schauble. 2002. *Investigating real data in the classroom: Expanding children's understanding of math and science.* New York: Teachers College Press.

Chapter 3

- *Page 47:* "Evaluating the teacher draws attention away from the students."

Research in both mathematics and science education has shown how both novice and experienced teachers transition from focusing on the teachers' actions to focusing first on students' thinking as they gain experience watching classroom video. Examples include:

Levin, D. M., and J. Richards. 2011 Learning to attend to the substance of student thinking in science. *Science Educator* 20 (2): 1–11.

Sherin, M. G., and S. Y. Han. 2004. Teacher learning in the context of a video club. *Teacher and Teacher Education* 20: 163–183.

Star, J. R., and S. K. Strickland. 2008. Learning to observe: Using video to improve mathematics teachers' ability to notice. *Journal of Mathematics Teacher Education* 11: 107–125.

Chapter 4

- *Page 53:* "The Owls and the Snakes" activities in this chapter and the next are based on the following article:

Gehlbach, F. R., and R. S. Baldridge. 1987. Live blind snakes (*Leptotyphlops dulcis*) in eastern screech owl (Otus asio) nests: A novel commensalism. *Oecologia* 71 (4): 560–563.

Chapter 6

- *Page 103:* "The Rime of the Ancient Mariner"

The full poem can be found easily on the internet. A good hard copy version, with commentary and illustrations is cited here.

Coleridge, S. T. 2008. *The rime of the ancient mariner.* Edison, New Jersey: Chartwell Books.

Chapter 9

- *Page 192:* "In other words, rather than defining the process of investigations in science simply around testable questions and their outcomes, define it as asking interesting questions..."

Some districts and schools have changed their traditional science fair into a "science inquiry conference," in which students discuss their questions with each other.

Index

*Page numbers in **boldface** type refer to figures.*

Index

National Science Teachers Association

Index

Index

Index

what happened next and menu of possibilities, 128–129

S

Science
  definition of, 8
    Einstein, 15, 16, 17, 199
  learning how to learn, 8
  meaning of truth in, 40
  in students' everyday thinking, 15
Science education
  inquiry-based, 9, 13
  keeping science sensible, 189
  objectives of, 5, 7–8, 181–185
    coordinating with traditional objectives, 183–185
    different agenda: cultivating resources, 182–183
    established objectives, 182
  role of classroom discussions in, 185–189
  standards-based, 13
  teacher education, professional development, and mentoring, 11–12, 193–197
    collecting your own data, 196–197
    keeping focus on students' thinking, 196
    supervising teachers, 194–196
    systemic constraints on secondary science teaching, 194
  understanding of sense of situation in science class, 31–34
Science fair projects, 189–192
  hypotheses for, 190–191
  investigations for, 191
    conclusions of, 192–193
  testable questions for, 189–190, 191, 192–193, 203
Scientific argumentation, 24, 38, 53, 55–56, 180, 189, 191, 193
Scientific knowledge, 22, 30
Scientific principles, 40
Scientific terms, 29–30. *See also* Vocabulary
Scientific thinking, 31–42
  compared with everyday thinking, 34–35
  refinement toward, 34–42
  understanding of sense of situation in science class, 31–34
Scientists, as professional learners, 8, 22
Shopping for ideas, 25–26, 37
Standards-based science education, 13
Strike, Ken, 19, 200
Students' reasoning, 2, 3, 22–30
  attending to precision and clarity, 28–30
  beginnings of science in, 25–30
  capabilities for, 23–24, 187–188, 201
  in different situations, 24–25
  everyday, 22–30
  monitoring of, 4

National Science Teachers Association

Index